FRENCH SOCIETY 1589–1715

Sharon Kettering

Longman

An imprint of **Pearson Education**

Harlow, England · London · New York · Reading, Massachusetts · San Francisco · Toronto · Don Mills, Ontario · Sydney
Tokyo · Singapore · Hong Kong · Seoul · Taipei · Cape Town · Madrid · Mexico City · Amsterdam · Munich · Paris · Milan

Pearson Education Limited

Edinburgh Gate
Harlow
Essex CM20 2JE
United Kingdom

and Associated Companies throughout the world

Visit us on the World Wide Web at
www.pearsoneduc.com

First published in 2001

ISBN 0 582 30706 6 PPR

British Library Cataloguing in Publication Data
A CIP catalogue record for this book can be obtained from the British Library.

10 9 8 7 6 5 4 3 2 1
05 04 03 02 01

Typeset by 35 in 10/13pt Bembo
Produced by Pearson Education Asia Pte Ltd
Printed in Singapore

For J.H.M. Salmon
and Orest Ranum

CONTENTS

GENERAL EDITOR'S PREFACE

For far too long 'social history' was regularly, even routinely defined dismissively and negatively along the lines of 'history with the high politics, economics and diplomacy left out'. Over the latter decades of the twentieth century, however, a virtual revolution in the sub-discipline of 'social history' has gathered momentum, fuelled not only by historians but specialists from such established academic disciplines as anthropology, economics, politics and especially sociology, and enriched by contributors from burgeoning cultural, demographic, media and women's studies. At the cusp of the twenty-first century, the prime rationale of the recently launched 'Social History of Europe' series is to reflect the cumulative achievement and reinforce the ripening respectability of what may be positively yet succinctly defined as nothing less than the 'history of society'.

Initiated by the late Professor Harry Hearder of the University of Wales, the 'Social History of Europe' series is conceived as an ambitious and open-ended collection of wide-ranging general surveys charting the history of the peoples of the major European nations, states and regions through key phases in their societal development from the late Middle Ages to the present. The series is not designed to become necessarily either chronologically or geographically all-embracing, although certain pre-eminent areas and periods will demand a systematic sequence of coverage. Typically, a volume covers a period of about one century, but longer (and occasionally shorter) time-spans are proving appropriate. A degree of modest chronological overlap between volumes covering a particular nation, state or region is acceptable where justified by the historical experience.

Each volume in the series is written by a commissioned European or American expert and, while synthesizing the latest scholarship in the field, is invigorated by the findings and preoccupations of the author's original research. As works of authority and originality, all contributory volumes are of genuine interest and value to the individual author's academic peers.

Even so, the contributory volumes are not intended to be scholarly monographs addressed to the committed social historian but broader synoptic overviews which serve a non-specialist general readership. All the volumes are therefore intended to take the 'textbook dimension' with due seriousness, with authors recognizing that the long-term success of the series will depend on its usefulness to, and popularity with, an international undergraduate and postgraduate student readership. In the interests of accessibility, the provision of notes and references to accompany the text is suitably restrained and all volumes contain a select bibliography, a chronology of principal events, a glossary of foreign and technical terms and a comprehensive index.

Inspired by the millennial watershed but building upon the phenomenal specialist progress recorded over the last quarter-century, the eventually multi-volume 'Social History of Europe' is dedicated to the advancement of an intellectually authoritative and academically cosmopolitan perspective on the multi-faceted historical development of the European continent.

Raymond Pearson
Professor of Modern European History
University of Ulster

PREFACE

This book is a survey of the social history of seventeenth-century France intended for classroom use. It covers 'the long seventeenth century' from 1589 to 1715, that is, the reigns of the first three Bourbon kings, Henri IV, Louis XIII and Louis XIV. Emphasizing books in English, it gives the English translations of books in French whenever possible, and surveys the work of the Annalistes in particular. Chapter by chapter endnotes (at the end of the book), using abbreviated short titles, are meant to serve as an annotated bibliography, and an up-to-date introduction to the scholarly literature for advanced students and specialists in other fields. Curiosity about briefly discussed topics in the text may be satisfied by exploring the endnotes. There is a suggested reading list of books in English at the end of each chapter, and an essay on recent trends in social history at the end of the book.

Archival examples have been used to add a flavour of reality and, since I know the Provençal archives best, there are more examples from this sunny southern province than from any other. Much of early modern French social history has, in fact, been the work of historians specializing in the Midi. The south of France is fortunate in having extensive archives in contrast to the north where archives were often damaged by war. Books published since 1970 have been emphasized, and there are brief analyses of some current arguments over historical interpretation. Chapter 6, in particular, presents both sides in a recent controversy over the power of the early modern state. It is hoped that these analyses may provide the reader with some insight into how generally accepted historical interpretations are reached.

I would like to thank Thomas Adams, Joseph Bergin, Gayle Brunelle, Barbara Diefendorf, Jonathan Dewald, T.J.A. Le Goff, Joseph Klaits, J.H.M. Salmon, Robert Schneider and Donald Sutherland for reading parts or all of the manuscript. Whatever mistakes remain are my own. I would also like to thank Bonita Favin of the Montgomery College Interlibrary Loan department for helping me to obtain books, the university libraries that so generously lent them and the staffs of the Library of Congress and the Folger Library in Washington DC, who have so graciously helped me over the years. Finally, as always, my gratitude to John for his support.

INTRODUCTION

SOCIAL SOLIDARITIES

The opening of the Estates General in Paris in 1614 illustrates the importance of rank and position in early modern French society. The Estates General was a national meeting of provincial deputies to ratify royal tax demands. The three Estates held a preliminary general meeting on 14 October, and then met separately to establish rules of procedure. After much argument, the first estate or clergy agreed to a seating order based on rank, but they could not agree on a marching order, so in desperation they decided that clerics below the office of bishop should line up without distinction in the opening procession. Because the debate became so noisy, they decided that in future deputies could bring with them only one servant or page, who had to be left outside in the coach or with the horses. Nobles of the second estate drew their swords during the discussion. The third estate, representing everyone else, calmly discussed what robes they should wear in the opening procession, and decided on plain serge. The clergy, however, afraid that they would ruin the procession, sent a bishop to tell them curtly to wear something decent, and follow the orders of the master of ceremonies.

At eleven o'clock on Sunday morning, 26 October, the opening procession began to wind its way slowly along the left bank of the Seine and across the bridge to hear mass at Notre Dame. Two arguments broke out, the first when the nobility wanted the procession to start earlier because it looked like rain, which would have spoiled their finery, and the second when the cardinals wanted a place nearer the king. The Estates General officially opened the next day in the great hall of the Hôtel de Bourbon. Important nobles and cardinals were seated at the front of the hall on a large platform raised three steps above the floor and, behind them, elevated two more steps, was a second platform where the royal family sat. In the centre was a raised royal throne covered with purple velvet for the king. The deputies sat below on the hall floor on benches behind government officials. When the doors opened, the Third Estate deputies all rushed in together, noisily pushing and shoving! The clerical and noble deputies considered their behaviour disgraceful, and were furious at being seated with them. They complained so loudly that they were allowed to move their benches forward a little so that they sat apart.[1] Disputes over precedence had made everyone forget why they were there.

Public events were often marred by disputes over who went first or where they sat. Nobles had to assert their right to precedence or have their rank questioned, and officials had to do so or risk losing their authority. Precedence indicated privilege and power. Public appearances of nobles and officials assumed great importance for this reason, so meticulous attention was paid to marching and seating order, dress, number of attendants and deferential behaviour by inferiors. Churches often became the scenes of precedence disputes.

A *Parlement* councillor was sitting in the first chair of the choir in the Augustine church of Aix-en-Provence in 1628 when a *Cour des Comptes* president entered to hear vespers. Although the Parlement was the more prestigious judicial court, the president held the higher office, so his servant spread a kneeling rug before the first chair, and the other worshipers moved back to leave a place. The councillor refused to move. After an unsuccessful appeal, the angry president seized the councillor's sash and pulled hard. The councillor in return slapped him, doffed his hat with a flourish, and strode out of the church! A Cour des Comptes president had torn off the sash and ripped the robe of a Parlement councillor during a seating dispute in the same church in 1615. The archbishop of Aix insisted on seating his nephew and coadjutant in the first chair of the cathedral choir in 1622, although the Parlement first president declared that the chair was his by right of office. At the next celebration of mass, the first president seized the chair and would not relinquish it. The archbishop refused to say mass with the first president sitting there and huffed out of the church. Using Christmas as an excuse, he had a platform built that covered the first chair and put his nephew on it! It took a decree of the royal council to get it torn down.[2]

Precedence disputes quickly escalated into duels and brawls.[3] The duc de La Rochefoucauld reported in his memoirs that he and the duc de Brissac had decided to duel immediately, without seconds, after a disagreement in 1651 that began as a precedence dispute over who went first through a door.[4] The prince de Condé and the comte de Soissons quarrelled in 1620 over who would have the honour of handing the king a towel. The duc de Guise, who had been feuding with Soissons, quickly rallied to Condé's support and, when a mob of their noble friends and clients gathered at Condé's Paris mansion, a brawl seemed likely. Fortunately, the affair was settled without bloodshed.[5] If rank and place were that important, how were they determined?

Individuals identified themselves and their position in society in many ways, including whether the duties and obligations of their personal relationships had been fulfilled or not. Fulfilment was necessary to an individual's honour. Honourable behaviour was the observance of a code of ethics that helped to determine an individual's social and self-identity. Honour was the inner feeling of self-worth that resulted from being known as someone who observed a code of ethics. The most widely accepted ethical code was that in Christianity. Both Catholicism and Protestantism were quite explicit about what constituted ethical behaviour toward others, and how parents, spouses, children, servants, neighbours, the poor, the sick and churchmen should be treated. An individual's treatment of those around him reflected upon his rank because honour was his understanding of who he was and where he belonged within the ranks of society. This explains why honour was so important to nobles as members of a hereditary elite, and why its defence was a motive for so much of their behaviour. An individual lost his honour when public opinion judged him negatively and, when he lost his honour, he lost an important element of his social identity and self-worth. Cowardice, disloyalty, dishonesty and a failure to fulfil one's duties and obligations were all considered dishonourable behaviour.[6]

Public expressions of disrespect damaged an individual's reputation, and had to be challenged or honour was lost. Such discourtesies included bad language, insulting remarks, derisive laughter, obscene gestures, a failure to salute, remove one's hat or bow, a refusal to receive someone or offer him refreshment. *Ingrat*, *insolent* and *impertinent* were frequently heard insults, and were a strong response to the failure to show gratitude or the proper respect and courtesy. Deliberate public discourtesies easily escalated into violence, as Henri d'Escoubleau de Sourdis, archbishop of Bordeaux, learned to his dismay.

The governor of Guyenne, the duc d'Epernon, detested the archbishop and, from their first public meeting in 1628, sought to insult and humiliate him. On that occasion, he withheld the keys to the cemetery of the Carthusian monastery where the archbishop was intending to bury his brother. The funeral procession came to a sudden, unexpected halt when he could not open the gate! It took Richelieu's intervention to get the governor to relinquish the keys. Returning to Bordeaux a few years later, Sourdis made a formal entry only to discover that there would be no reception because the governor had summoned all members of the municipal government to a meeting at that very hour. When the cook went to buy fresh fish for the archbishop's dinner, he discovered that the governor had closed the fish market. Sourdis complained, and the governor in response sent twenty of his guards under the command of a lieutenant Naugas, who met Sourdis in his carriage in front of the cathedral and asked to speak to him. Sourdis refused and told his coachman to drive on. Naugas's guards seized the horses' reins, and the lieutenant, hat in hand, told Sourdis that he had a message for him. Sourdis replied that he would hear it only in the cathedral or at his official residence. The lieutenant insisted, saying that he had orders to speak with him wherever he found him. Sourdis, furious, left his carriage and stormed through the streets

3

of Bordeaux, robes flapping, with Naugas running after him, vainly trying to make him listen.

Several days later Sourdis accidentally met the governor in the square in front of the cathedral. The governor shouted that he was disturbing the peace and threatening public order. The archbishop shouted back that he had been doing his duty. 'Troublemaker, rabble rouser, insolent,' screamed the red-faced, apoplectic governor. Losing his temper completely, he knocked off Sourdis's hat with his walking stick, pushed the stick into his stomach, and waved it in his face. Two of the governor's guards had to spring between them to pull him off before he did worse. Sourdis fled into the cathedral, and excommunicated the governor on the spot, placing the city of Bordeaux under interdict and closing all of its churches. The governor had to do public penance on his knees before the archbishop in the cathedral square to have his own excommunication and the city's interdict lifted, and his office restored.[7]

Honour and duty were synonymous in early modern society.[8] Duty was the conduct due superiors and kin, the loyalty, obedience, courtesy and respect owed rank, office and kinship. An individual had to defend, not only his own honour, but also that of his family. He was dishonoured when he failed to do so, or when others failed to do their duty to him. Some personal relationships demanded exclusive loyalty, that is, their obligations were expected to take priority over other duties and loyalties. Although primary loyalty may have been expected, it was not always forthcoming. Early modern society, in fact, was preoccupied by what duty and loyalty meant, and to whom they were owed, which was not always easy to determine. Contemporaries were enmeshed in complex webs of overlapping relationships that created competing, conflicting duties and loyalties. There was no easy solution to the problem of which had priority, a problem compounded by warfare. The honour of individuals and the longevity of relationships were at stake.

During the War of the League in the 1590s, for example, all of the French parlements except Bordeaux split into rival judicial courts. The parlements divided into royalist courts loyal to the Protestant king, Henri IV, and opposing Leaguer courts loyal to the Holy Catholic League. Many judges retreated to their country houses and refused to sit in either court. Families were split when fathers, sons, and brothers-in-law chose to sit in different courts. An internal juggling act was necessary to reconcile personal religious and political beliefs with the duty and loyalty owed kin and in-laws who had different beliefs. Catholic royal judges and nobles agonized over the duty and loyalty owed a Protestant king, while Protestant judges and nobles did the same when Henri IV converted to Catholicism.[9] What was honourable behaviour in such cases, and how was it determined?

Honour was a social solidarity. Solidarities were the basic forces for continuity, conformity, and constraint that helped to create and maintain a general community. There was a genuine need for social cohesion and unity in seventeenth-century France, and solidarities were forces for interdependence that helped to counteract the widespread instability, fragmentation and insecurity. Robert Mandrou has described five major groups of social solidarities: faith, church and parish; nuclear family and extended kin; state and monarchy; social hierarchy and rank; village, youth groups and feast days.[10] These are all discussed in the following pages, plus others.

Using the case study method of exposition, this book examines significant changes in social solidarities during the seventeenth century. These changes included the weakening of some solidarities, the strengthening of others, and the emergence of new ones. Solidarities are defined here as the personal bonds and loyalties that acted as adhesive forces in holding society together, and determining social and self-identity. Yves Durand has defined social solidarities as personal relationships and the loyalties they generated.[11] This book looks at changes in personal relationships affecting identity, that is, an individual's understanding of who he was and where he belonged within the ranks of society. Solidarities discussed include rank, honour, and reputation; family, household and kinship; faith and church; state and obedience to the king; seigneurial and patron–client ties; sociability; work-related ties; and regional ties, including village and neighbourhood loyalties.

Changes in social solidarities during the seventeenth century included the proliferation of nuclear family ties at the expense of gradually weakening extended kinship ties. Labour mobility and absentee landlordism undermined traditional rural ties of family, village and seigneury. Urban ties of neighbourhood, sociability and work proliferated with rapid urbanization. There was a significant transformation in the traditional role of the nobility, while a new emphasis upon loyal obedience to the king and an emerging national consciousness changed how the French saw themselves. A resurgent Catholicism sought to reform the church by imposing Tridentine orthodoxy, and by eliminating Protestant heresy and Jansenist heterodoxy. Individuals on the margins of society such as beggars, vagrants and criminals, who lacked many of the ties and solidarities characterizing the rest of society, are discussed in the last chapter. France by 1715 had become a more peaceful, civilized place in which to live, and this book discusses some of the reasons why. What follows is a bird's eye view of social change in France during the 'long seventeenth century' from 1589 to 1715.

CHAPTER 1

FAMILIES AND HOUSEHOLDS

Some of the funniest scenes in Molière's dark, bitter comedy, *The Miser*, involve the matchmaker Frosine, who tries to arrange a marriage for Harpagon, an old miser, with Mariane, a pretty young woman, in return for as much money as she can get. In this play, Molière is satirizing human greed and hypocrisy, ambitious and wealthy urban elites, and his own fear of growing old and dying.

Frosine compliments Harpagon on his youthful appearance, telling him that he is slender, not skinny, a good-looking man who even coughs gracefully. Evidently, he coughs a lot. She tells him that she has shown his portrait to Mariane, who is delighted at the proposed match. She says that Mariane dislikes young men, preferring those who are at least sixty years old with long, white beards, skinny legs and spectacles, and will be charmed by Harpagon's old-fashioned, out-of-date clothes. A flattered Harpagon agrees that young men are silly, rude, overdressed, mincing fops with squeaky voices. As an enticement, Frosine tells Harpagon that Mariane will bring him a dowry of 1,200 *livres* a year.

Mariane, however, is in love with Harpagon's handsome young son Cléante, and appalled at the prospect of having to marry his old, ugly father. Frosine tells her that young men may be pleasing to look at, but tend to be poor as church mice, and that happiness in such a marriage will not last. Mariane would be wiser to marry an old man with money who could give her what she wants while alive, and then leave her a wealthy widow. That is lasting happiness. Mariane declares that Frosine has an odd notion of marital happiness if her husband has to die to make her happy. Frosine replies that it is a really good match if he dies within three months of the wedding! She tries to discourage the young lovers but, relenting, she suggests a way that Cléante can dissuade his father from marrying Mariane. He must tell his father that a provincial, titled lady with 100,000 *écus* in cash, plus property, wants to marry him. The prospect of such a match should make Harpagon forget all about Mariane, and of course, it does.[1]

What does Molière tell us about marriage in seventeenth-century France? Matchmakers, usually family or friends, scoured the marriage market for potential spouses in an age when marriages were arranged. A father asked his brothers, uncles, brothers-in-law and friends to find suitable candidates for his children to marry because a neutral third party could make the initial approach discreetly, sparing the families any unseemly haggling. The situation was delicate because a rude rejection could damage a family's honour. The matchmaker's role stopped short of the actual proposal by the family. The families then negotiated the marriage contract, which was drawn up by a notary and signed in their presence.

Jacques-Auguste de Thou's marriage to Marie de Barbançon was arranged by mutual friends, Pierre du Val, who was the doctor of both Jacques's widowed mother and his future mother-in-law, and Charles Turcant, who was the brother-in-law of the bride. Du Val's praise of the widowed Madame Barbançon de Cany and her daughter to Jacques's mother persuaded her to make the match, which Turcant strongly encouraged, although the actual marriage proposal was made by Jacques's brother-in-law, the comte de Cheverny.[2] Marguerite Thomas wrote to her brother, a judge in the financial high court of the *Chambre des Comptes* of Rouen, that a certain sieur Croule, a secretary of the late chancellor, Pomponne de Bellièvre, was seeking a marriage with her daughter through a niece who was married to one of his friends. She asked her brother to find out what he could about the man, adding that she was delighted by the news of the marriage that her brother had arranged for his own daughter.[3] Philippe Hurault, comte de Cheverny and Jean de Selve arranged their children's marriages, as did Etienne Pasquier and Jean Morin. The duc de Saint-Aignan supposedly arranged his daughter's marriage in fifteen minutes, although lengthier negotiations were more common.[4] Mothers and grandmothers arranged marriages, as did brothers, sisters, uncles and aunts.[5]

Matchmaking was a form of kin assistance, a duty demanded by family honour, loyalty and affection, and professional matchmakers were used only when family and friends could not help. The duc de Saint-Simon's marriage to a daughter of the maréchal de Lorges was negotiated by a Madame Damont, who was the lowborn sister-in-law of Madame Frémont; the maréchale de Lorges had been a Frémont before her marriage. Undoubtedly, Madame Damont received something for her trouble.[6] The comtesse de Gramont negotiated the marriage of the son of a wealthy clerk in the high court of the Parlement of Paris for a percentage of the bride's dowry.[7] Living in the Low Countries during the late 1660s, Jean Hérauld de Gourville developed a close relationship with the house of Brunswick, thereby attracting the attention of Hugues de Lionne, secretary of state for foreign affairs, who asked Gourville to broker a marriage between John Frederick of Hanover and Bénédicte of Bavaria, a French princess who was the sister-in-law of the prince de Condé's eldest son. In exchange, Gourville asked that Lionne secure an interview for him with Colbert.[8] Professional matchmakers offered their services in exchange for a fee, which was usually cash but could be something else, a favour, the use of influence or connections, the acquisition of good will or credit for future use.

Families arranged marriages carefully because their social standing and material welfare were involved, as well as the perpetuation of their name. Marriages were usually endogamous, that is, within a group sharing the same religion, rank, geography and occupation; exogamous marriages occurred outside these groups. Marriages were made to secure wealth, property, titles, offices and consolidate adjoining lands; to climb the social ladder through the reflected prestige of in-laws; to acquire political power, influence and connections; and to strengthen a family's position, secure allies, reconcile enemies, stop feuds and make peace. Church and state favoured marriage because it put an end to immoral practices, produced legitimate heirs and created new families.[9] Romantic love was not usually a consideration, although historians disagree on the extent to which love characterized seventeenth-century marriages. It was presumed that conjugal love would follow after marriage, but that it did not always is clear from contemporary representations of marriage as joyless, loveless bondage. Love was supposed to reinforce marital duty, making it joyful rather than grudging, but duty, not love, was the glue holding many marriages together. The hidden resentment and anger in such marriages must have contributed to domestic strife.[10]

The lower down the social scale, the less frequently matchmakers were used because there were fewer assets at stake. As a result, there was more freedom to choose spouses. Poor peasants without dowries often chose whom they married, as did those who went to the cities to find work. There were many opportunities for young peasants to make the acquaintance of potential spouses, for instance, during winter work evenings in barns and stables. The women would spin and knit; the men would husk, sort, strip hemp and play cards. There would be gossiping, singing and dancing, and the boys would walk the girls home. Other opportunities included church attendance; working in the fields; domestic service; market days; assemblies of young people to sell their labour as hired hands or domestic servants; fairs; pilgrimages; dances and other social events organized by youth groups and bachelor associations; and Mardi Gras, feast days, celebrations of Saints' Days and other traditional holidays.[11]

Marriages among the nobility and wealthy urban elites were usually arranged by parents with only token consultation because of the assets involved. Dowries, which increased steadily in size, were important in these matches; personal appearance, less so. Marriages occurred at an earlier age among nobles, usually at twenty-three or twenty-four for men, and at a somewhat younger age for women, although nobles often married at much younger ages than this.[12]

The marriage rate was high. The greatest number of weddings occurred in winter when the fields were empty, and the fewest took place in December and March because of the church prohibition against marriages during Advent and Lent. The illegitimacy rate was low, about 2 per cent in the country-side and 5 per cent in the towns. The parish registers of Aix-en-Provence record thirteen illegitimate children born to parents in 1695, and sixty-three abandoned children, presumably illegitimate, or 4.9 per cent of that year's births; this percentage increased after the mid-eighteenth century, especially in towns. Pre-nuptial conceptions were common enough in the seventeenth century, however, occurring in 10 to 15 per cent of marriages. Until the middle of the century, betrothals often began a trial period in which couples lived together before marriage, but the church put a stop to this practice as immoral.[13]

THE INSTABILITY OF FAMILIES

Family, kin and household were universal social solidarities, but who were family and kin? The word family had two meanings in seventeenth-century France. It meant, first, everyone living under the same roof in a household, including the nuclear family of father, mother and children, as well as kin who were often widowed, orphaned, unmarried or separated from their spouses, and non-kin who were apprentices, hired hands, paying boarders or domestic servants. Household size, particularly the number of servants, was related to rank; the higher the rank, the larger the household. Second, family also meant everyone of the same blood line extended over several generations and to several degrees of cousinage. A household was everyone living and working together under the same roof, although not necessarily related by blood or marriage. Family and kin were related by blood and marriage, but did not necessarily live under the same roof. It is unclear at exactly what degree extended kinship ended. Kin relationships on the fringes of an extended family are obscure because the word cousin was used loosely for non-kin as a com-pliment, an indication of friendship and a form of boasting. In general, the French vocabulary of kinship has comparatively few terms.[14]

France can be divided geographically and climatically by a line running from Nantes to Geneva. There is a striking difference between the overcast skies and green, well-watered fields of the north and the clear, sunny skies and hot, dry landscape of the south. In the seventeenth century, there were significant socio-economic differences as well. In northern France, three-quarters of the families were nuclear, and the age gap between spouses was small. The age at first marriage was late; men were generally 28 to 30 years old, and women 25 to 27. The reasons were economic. A husband was ex-pected to be self-supporting and to provide a separate home, while a wife was expected to bring a dowry to help in its establishment. Marriages were post-poned until these conditions could be met.

In the south, complex families were more numerous, and only half of the families were nuclear. In the stem family, the oldest son and his family lived with his parents, so there were three generations under one roof. In the lineage family, collateral branches were added to the stem family, that is, other married siblings of both sexes and their children lived with their parents and the oldest son's family, so there were several families as well as several generations under one roof. In the *frèreche* family, all the brothers in the family lived together with their families and their parents or widowed mother. A son wanting to establish himself independently had to wait until his father died for his share of the inheritance, although he might try to obtain a cash gift from his parents, kin or godparents in order to set up on his own, or find work on his own. Daughters needed dowries to marry. As a result, in complex families, younger sons and daughters without dowries often remained at home, unmarried.[15]

The comparatively late age at marriage, their mid-twenties for women, determined the fertility rate because it acted as a form of birth control by reducing the number of a woman's reproductive years. Mothers were usually in their early forties at the birth of their last child. The average number of children in families with both parents was seven or eight, one born every two years, but this number dropped to four or five when families were truncated prematurely by the death of a parent, which often happened. Breast-feeding for long periods of time, which was practised in the countryside, reduced a woman's fertility and also acted as a form of birth control. Noblewomen and wealthy urban women, who sent their newborns to be wet-nursed, did not have this protection, and so they tended to have a higher birth rate. Malnutrition and illness caused by famine and disease also reduced fertility and lowered the birth rate. Induced abortion and infanticide were not infre-quent, but the abandonment of children was probably more common. Contra-ception was increasingly practised by the end of the seventeenth century.[16]

The most effective form of population control was a high infant mortality rate. The neonatal death rate during the first month of life was one child in every five or six, usually from birth defects or accidents at birth caused by ignorance and dirt. One child in four died before its first birthday; the rate was especially high at weaning, and only one child in two lived until its fifteenth birthday. Death was less frequent after adolescence. The late seventeenth-century neonatal death rate has been estimated at 178 per 1,000 live births, the infantile rate at 352 per 1,000 live births, and the juvenile rate at 532 per 1,000 live births. Of the four or five children born to an average family, only two or three survived to replace their parents, a number barely sufficient to ensure generation renewal, although more children survived in wealthier families. At Aix-en-Provence in 1695, there was an average of two to three children per family, while at Paris in the same period, there was an average of a little more than two children per family.[17]

Philippe Ariès has argued that there were significant changes in family life during the late seventeenth century, although his argument has been criticized. These changes included the proliferation of the nuclear family, and a new perception of childhood as a separate life stage. Children had previously been treated as small adults, and their high death rate had kept parents at an emotional distance until they could be expected to live. But this changed with the decline in the death rate during the late seventeenth century. Families were now regarded as safe havens where the emotional needs of adults could be met and children reared. Increasingly, families became nuclear, that is, limited to parents and their children and, as families withdrew into themselves, the modern family emerged – small, private, domestic and emotional. Critics, however, insist that Ariès has overemphasized the early modern failure to recognize childhood as a separate life stage, and exaggerated the lack of parental affection and indifference to the fate of young children who were likely to die. Other critics insist that he made sweeping generalizations about medieval parenting and European families based on early modern French evidence, and failed to distinguish sufficiently between the attitudes of men, women, nobles and peasants.[18] Recently, the focus of research in family history has been on family interaction with the community, state, church and school.[19]

The adult death rate was high throughout the seventeenth century and, because at times it exceeded the birth rate, it acted as a form of population control. Half of first marriages occurred after one or more of the spouses' parents had died, and only the better off and well nourished lived much past the age of sixty. French bishops lived on the average to fifty-eight in the early seventeenth century, and sixty-six in the late seventeenth century. Between thirty and forty per cent of adults in the Beauvaisis died around age sixty in the seventeenth century, and twenty per cent around seventy, while half the adult population of the Beauvaisis, the poorer half, died before age sixty. Two-thirds of Parisians in the eighteenth century died between the ages of forty and fifty; the mortality rate was always higher in cities.

Adults died from chest infections (influenza, pleurisy, pneumonia) in winter, and gastro-intestinal disorders in summer. They died from tuberculosis, cancer and syphilis at any time of the year, as well as from childbirth, war and accidents in an age when hard physical labour was the lot of most men. There were periodically devastating epidemics of infectious diseases, including bubonic plague, measles, scarlet fever, typhus, smallpox, typhoid and dysentery, which were always worse in summer. The working-class diet of bread and soup was barely enough to sustain life, and the chronic malnutrition increased susceptibility to infection. Among the economically more fortunate classes, an overly rich, unbalanced diet led to a high incidence of heart attacks and strokes. Medicine was in its infancy, and did more harm than good. The practice of bleeding for the high fever accompanying most serious ailments, for example, only weakened the victim, and the lack of public santitation and personal hygiene compounded these problems.[20]

The grim reality was that most marriages were cut short by death after fifteen or twenty years, and marriages of thirty to forty years were unusual. Besides the loss of parents, the blows dealt by death included the loss of infants, young children and grandparents, and the sudden appearance of step-parents, their children and the birth of new step-siblings. Remarriages, step-families and stepchildren were common; one marriage in four in the seventeenth century was a remarriage. Fifty per cent of widowers, and twenty per cent of widows remarried within a year. Widowers with dependent children were more likely to remarry quickly, sometimes within weeks, while young widows were more likely to remarry than older widows with property who cherished their independence.[21]

The high death rate made seventeenth-century families unstable and prone to a process known as the family life-cycle. Nuclear families became two families biologically when a second family of step-parent and step-siblings joined the original nuclear family, which had been truncated by the death of a parent, and might be so again. Death periodically made stem or multi-generational families nuclear when grandparents died. A newly married couple would live with the husband's parents, whose death would make the couple and their children a nuclear family for a while, until their oldest son would marry, recreating the stem family.[22]

Stepmothers did not always like the children of their husband's previous marriage, preferring their own children to his, and it was the same for step-fathers. The wicked stepmother was a stock character in the early modern literary imagination for good reason, and the story of Cinderella, or *Cendrillon*, written by Charles Perrault in 1697, is the classic example; violence and abuse may have been more frequent in step-families. Kin and servants living with a family enlarged the household, and familiarity intensified the inevitable bickering. Large noble households were notorious for their jealousies, in-trigues and quarrels. The households of great nobles at Henri III's court in the late sixteenth century were described as turbulent, and their members as foul-mouthed, quarrelsome and violent. Cramped, squalid living conditions intensified domestic strife, so most people spent as little time indoors as possible, preferring the open fields and city streets.[23]

FAMILY TENSION AND STRIFE

Martin Guerre was a wealthy peasant from the mountainous village of Artigat on the Languedoc side of the Spanish border. Suddenly, he abandoned his home, wife and family, and was not seen again for years. Then he came back, or so everyone thought, but after several years he was unmasked as an imposter, who was subsequently brought to trial. The man, Arnaud du Tilh, had almost persuaded the court that he was Martin Guerre when at the last moment the real Martin Guerre appeared, and the imposter was found guilty and hanged. This mid-sixteenth-century trial inspired two contemporary accounts, one by a judge of the court, and over the centuries it has been retold many times in books about well-known imposters and famous trials, inspiring a play, two novels, an operetta, two films and a scholarly study. Why did Martin Guerre leave home? Where did he go, what did he do and what does this indicate about early modern families?

The supposed reason for his departure was that he had stolen a small quantity of grain from his father, and was forced to leave because theft within a family was unpardonable; it destroyed family honour. Martin was an only son who would have inherited everything, and he may have regarded the grain as an advance on his inheritance, not as stealing. Almost certainly, the theft reflected a disagreement between a strong-willed father and a rebellious son living under the same roof. The other strong personality in the family was Pierre Guerre, Martin's uncle, who managed his inheritance while he was away after his father had died. The longer Martin was gone, the more Pierre may have hoped that he would never return so that he could inherit the property. Pierre Guerre was the one who denounced Arnaud du Tilh as an imposter, motivated by their quarrels over his management of the property. Pierre may have been disappointed when the fake Martin returned home, and was almost certainly pleased to discover that he was an imposter.

Martin had been unhappy at home. Married at a young age, he had been impotent for a while, the object of village ridicule, and he had dreamed of a life beyond its walls and fields. The possibilities included going to sea on a whaling expedition, joining the army, going to school to pursue a professional career or joining a great household as a domestic servant. He chose the last, and became a lackey in the bishop's palace at Burgos in Spain. Later he joined the entourage of the bishop's brother, Pierre de Mendoza, whom he accompanied into the Spanish army, probably as his valet or batman, and then to Flanders, serving in the army that Philip II used against the French at Saint-Quentin. Martin was wounded in the leg, which had to be amputated, and was replaced by a wooden peg. This disaster ended his soldiering days, although it took several more years for him to make his way back home to Artigat. He had been gone for twelve years.[24] His story illustrates both the cohesive forces holding families together, and the tensions and conflicts pulling them apart.

One cause of the conflict, as in the case of Martin Guerre, was the division of property after the family head had died. There were three types of inheritance in early modern France. In the north where nuclear families predominated, every child received a share of the family inheritance. There was a tendency for sons, especially first-born sons, to receive more than daughters, and for children favoured by their fathers to receive more in this egalitarian system deferring to a father's wishes, but everyone received something. In the west, where there were both nuclear and complex families, there was strict egalitarianism, and the family property was divided equally among all the children without regard for a father's wishes. In the north and the west, therefore, there was a tendency for family holdings to be subdivided by inheritance, although this tendency was counteracted by endogamous marriages made for economic reasons, and by dowering only one or two daughters; the rest entered a convent or remained unmarried. In the south where complex families were more numerous, the tendency toward subdivision was counteracted by a preferential system of inheritance, that is, a majority of the family property went to one child, always a son and usually the first-born. The heir lived with his parents, even after he married and had children of his own, and younger, unmarried siblings also lived with them. These differences in inheritance were responsible for regional differences in marriage ceremonies. Noble inheritance, however, did not always follow these rules, and rental property was not divided at death, allowing tenant farmers to keep their lands together despite the death of a family head.[25]

In complex families, therefore, younger children tended to remain at home unmarried until their father died, and the quarrelling often became intense, even violent. There was conflict between generations, and among women: mothers-in-law fought with daughters-in-law, and stepmothers with step-daughters; there could only be one mistress in a household. Authoritarian fathers kept control of the purse strings into old age, demanding obedience from dependent sons who became more impatient and rebellious as they grew older. Conflict between the generations was a serious problem among nobles. There was also sibling rivalry between older and younger children, and children of first and second marriages.[26]

Sending younger children out of the house tended to reduce domestic strife, and the number of mouths to feed. Children in nuclear families were expected to leave home after they married or even before. Poverty sent younger children, who would not inherit, to other farms to work as hired hands or domestic servants, and to the city to find work or learn a trade. There tended to be less strife in nuclear families because there were fewer children at home, and this reduction in domestic strife probably contributed to the proliferation of nuclear families. Their proliferation caused a gradual erosion in extended kinship loyalties and obligations. Increasingly, ties to third and fourth cousins were ignored, and less was expected or demanded of second and first cousins. Households began to shrink in size because fewer extended kin were living with families that were increasingly nuclear in composition. Rural labour mobility and immigration to cities also contributed to the growing prevalence of nuclear families. Other reasons for the decline in household size during the late seventeenth century included a new desire for privacy, a new civility, greater piety and changing attitudes toward child-rearing. Apprentices and hired hands began to live elsewhere, and by the late eighteenth century extended kin had disappeared from most households.[27]

Families often needed help in finding ways for younger children to become independent. Nobles had a greater problem because they married at a younger age, and employed wet-nurses, so they produced more children, who survived in greater numbers because they were better fed. A family turned first to kin for assistance because honour demanded their help. Kin assistance was sought during sickness, childbirth, death and harvest, or when celebrating family occasions, searching for potential spouses or seeking employment for younger children. A family helped its sons before its daughters in a patriarchal society, so paternal relatives were often asked first. Other considerations included the closeness of the blood tie, the affectionate nature of the relationship, whether a debt would be cancelled, if a quid pro quo was involved, and the status and resources of the respective families. When kin could or would not help, non-kin were asked. A father turned to his own relatives for help in arranging marriages, then to his wife's relatives, his friends and finally to a professional matchmaker. Family honour was tarnished when help was refused, and could also be tarnished by a father's failure to provide; a mother's neglect of her children; a husband who was cuckolded, hen-pecked or beaten by his wife; daughters and wives who were known to be unchaste or unfaithful; incest; life-threatening beatings; alcoholism; and whatever made a family look ridiculous in the eyes of the world, causing gossip and laughter.[28]

The most common solution to the problem of surplus children was to send them to live, board and work in the household of someone else, usually kin, godparents, neighbours or friends with few or no children of their own who were willing to help. Orphans were taken in by relatives, however reluctantly, as a family duty. During the sixteenth century, nobles had sent their sons to serve as pages and gentlemen-attendants in the large households of kin and acquaintances but, during the seventeenth century, they began to send their sons to colleges and academies. Large households began to fill with non-noble domestic servants, whose numbers proliferated and, by the end of the century, most households had one or two domestic servants. They entered service as adolescents, saved their wages, learned a skill and left service for good when they married in their late twenties. Domestic service was the fate of many younger children.[29]

Surplus younger children also joined the army as Martin Guerre had done, or went to sea. Kin, friends, neighbours and business acquaintances were canvassed for jobs, and a place might be found for a child as a hired hand, woodcutter, shepherd, day labourer in a trade or domestic servant. The alternative was to emigrate to the city to seek work as an apprentice, shop assistant or servant, so there was a steady stream of rural emigrants to the cities. Some returned home after they had learned a trade; some remained. If the child had a vocation, he or she might be encouraged to enter the church as a member of the lower clergy. The younger children of nobles became members of the higher clergy, although not always voluntarily.

Pretty young girls from families of some means might be married off with a small dowry, or even without a dowry, to wealthy men who were undesirable as husbands because of their age, ill health, physical deformities, bad reputations or general unattractiveness. In November 1651, the twenty-five-year-old daughter of a Parisian engraver was 'sold' in marriage to the son of a wealthy fish-merchant, probably because her dowry was small or non-existent. The groom was lame, hump-backed, scrofulous and a drunkard, and the spectacle on their wedding night of the four men needed to undress him and unscrew his iron leg so horrified the reluctant bride that a week later she sprinkled poison on an egg, ate it and died in less than an hour, saying only, 'I must die because my father's greed demands it.'[30]

Françoise d'Aubigné was the granddaughter of Agrippa d'Aubigné, a celebrated man of letters and a friend of Henri IV. Unfortunately, her father was also a spendthrift and a wastrel, and she became a penniless orphan shunted among aunts. She was beautiful and clever, but she lacked a dowry, and the convent seemed her only option until a well-known Parisian literary figure, Paul Scarron, proposed marriage. He was forty-two, more than twice her age, paralysed with rheumatoid arthritis, shaped like a Z, poor and in debt, but she accepted him because she did not want to enter a convent.[31] The fate of these unfortunate young women suggests that Molière's Harpagon was truer to life than might be expected. Younger children in poverty-stricken families suffered fates just as tragic. They either remained at home, a burden to their family, or they joined the vast underbelly of society as vagrants, beggars, pickpockets, thieves and prostitutes.

Godparents sometimes took surplus godchildren into their homes, even adopting them if they had no children of their own. Adoption was an unpopular alternative because children put up for adoption were presumed to be illegitimate, and both the Catholic and Protestant churches disapproved of adoption because it disguised immorality. There were also legal prohibitions against non-biological children inheriting property, while nobles seldom adopted because they thought it threatened their lineage and rank. Adoptions occurred anyway, however, because there was a genuine need for them in a society with a high rate of child mortality; approximately twenty per cent of Parisian couples were childless in the late seventeenth century. Childlessness was always attributed to the wife, and provoked amusement as did impotence; both damaged family honour. Most adoptive parents were childless, and their motives included the desire to rear a child; affection for a child already known through kinship, godparentage or wet-nursing; a desire to help friends or relatives unable to bring up the child; a need for the labour from an extra pair of hands; and a desire for help and support in old age.[32]

Parents asked kin and close friends to act as godparents to their children, and being asked implied the obligation to accept; refusal was an insult. The church considered godparentage a serious spiritual responsibility, and godparents brought their godchildren to the baptismal font to give them a Christian name, thus becoming responsible for their religious and moral education. As pseudo-parents, they were prohibited from marrying or having carnal relations with their godchildren, and were held responsible for their physical and material well-being. To symbolize this responsibility, godparents distributed candied almonds and hazelnuts at the church door after the baptism, and offered them to guests at the baptismal party, and to neighbours. These sweetmeats symbolized their willingness to protect godchildren from physical abuse, incest, wicked stepmothers, tyrannical fathers and unwanted marriages, to help them find a place in the world, and to find them an acceptable spouse when of the right age.[33]

Charles de Grimaldi, marquis de Régusse, a presiding judge in the high court of the Parlement of Aix-en-Provence, married Marguerite de Napollon on 23 December 1631. She gave birth to thirteen children over the next twenty years. Her last child, born in 1652, died immediately; another daughter died at birth; a one-year-old son and a three-year-old daughter also died; and nine children survived. Régusse's daily account book gives the names of twenty-four godparents of whom twenty-two were relatives; only two were friends. Evidently, kin served as godparents more often than friends. Of the twenty-two, nineteen were his relatives, and only three were his wife's kin. Godparents from her family included her mother, who served twice, and the widow of a cousin. Of his nineteen relatives, his father served as a godfather eight times, and three of his aunts were godmothers, one twice, while a great-aunt served, as did two of his maternal uncles, the widow of the nephew of one of his uncles, his sister and her husband, and the elderly widow of an unspecified paternal relative. Grimaldi-Régusse chose paternal kin as godparents more often because his family had greater social prestige and better connections than that of his wife. A more common pattern is illustrated by the Lacger, a robe noble family from Castres in Languedoc. Sixty-nine godparents of thirty-five Lacger children can be identified, and they were mostly the parents' own siblings, especially the father's brothers and the mother's sisters, who were usually the first choice to act as godparents.[34]

17

Godparents were expected to give substantial gifts on the important occasions in their godchildren's lives, perhaps a silver cup or a spoon at baptism, a missal and rosary, or a chain with a cross, at their first communion. Poorer godparents gave chickens, a piglet to fatten or a lamb. Godparents were also expected to give substantial gifts on New Year's day, on birthdays, and for weddings. Catherine de Bourbon, the sister of Henri IV, gave her goddaughters jewellery as well as unset precious stones, buttons of gold, rubies and pearls, and cash gifts. The duc de Lesdiguières's son received a pair of intricately engraved guns and a small horse, richly harnessed, from his godparents.[35] Godparentage ceased at marriage when children were considered to have become adults.

Duty, affection, loyalty and honour created family cohesiveness, while the stress of daily life within multi-generational, multi-parent and step-families, and the competitiveness of delayed or selective inheritance, created conflict. As nuclear families became more prevalent, extended kinship ties became weaker, that is, the obligations to extended kin became more narrowly defined, while households became smaller. This change should not be exaggerated, however. Seventeenth-century society was kinship-dominated, and kinship contributed significantly to social cohesion and unity. Extended kin were spouses and godparents; they shared living and working arrangements; and they were the most reliable source of help in emergencies. The community in which an individual was born, lived and died, whether a village or an urban neighbourhood, contained a multitude of his extended kin, and children who left home to live independently usually moved only a few houses away or into the next street or village. Families were embedded within communities of their extended kin. Kinship mattered more to nobles, whose rank was based on birth and lineage, while nuclear families became more prevalent among non-nobles, who increasingly identified themselves in terms of smaller families. The proliferation of nuclear families was the result of endemic strife within complex families, although there were also other reasons such as rural labour mobility and immigration to the city. By 1715, many families were limited to parents and their children. Although elderly, ailing, widowed, orphaned or unmarried kin might be included, married children lived independently, which was a significant social change.

Suggested reading

Philippe Ariès, *Centuries of Childhood: A Social History of Family Life*, tr. Robert Baldrick (New York, 1962).

André Burguière *et al.*, eds, *A History of the Family*, 2 vols, vol. II, *The Impact of Modernity*, tr. Sarah Tenison (Cambridge, Mass., 1996).

Roger Chartier, ed., *Passions in the Renaissance*, tr. Arthur Goldhammer, vol. 3 in *A History of Private Life*, eds Philippe Ariès and Georges Duby (Cambridge, Mass., 1989).

Natalie Davis, *The Return of Martin Guerre* (Cambridge, Mass., 1989).

Cissie Fairchilds, *Domestic Enemies: Servants and Their Masters in Old Regime France* (Baltimore, 1984).

Jean-Louis Flandrin, *Families in Former Times, Kinship, Household and Sexuality*, tr. Richard Southern (Cambridge, 1979).

Robert Forster and Orest Ranum, eds, *Family and Society: Selections from the Annales*, tr. Elborg Forster and Patricia Ranum (Baltimore, 1976).

Kristen Gager, *Blood Ties and Fictive Ties: Adoption and Family Life in Early Modern France* (Princeton, 1996).

Tamara K. Hareven, 'The History of the Family and the Complexity of Social Change', *American Historical Review*, 96 (1991), 95–124.

Annik Pardailhé-Galabrun, *The Birth of Intimacy. Privacy and Domestic Life in Early Modern Paris*, tr. Jocelyn Phelps (Philadelphia, 1991).

Martine Segalen, *Love and Power in the Peasant Family*, tr. Sarah Matthews (Chicago, 1983); idem, *Historical Anthropology of the Family*, tr. J.C. Whitehouse and Sarah Matthews (Cambridge, 1986).

Robert Wheaton and Tamara K. Hareven, eds, *Family and Sexuality in French History* (Philadelphia, 1980).

CHAPTER 2

WOMEN AND MEN

The plot of Molière's play, *The Learned Ladies*, is role reversal, the problems that occur when women command and men obey, a popular literary plot of the period. In this play, Philaminte, a strong-willed, ambitious woman, becomes head of the family and household because Chrysale, her husband, refuses to assert himself. She is a social climber, who holds a weekly salon with the help of her older daughter, Armande. A pretentious bluestocking, Armande has rejected a longtime suitor, Clitandre, because he does not share her intellectual interests. She declares that she will never marry.[1]

Then Clitandre falls in love with her younger sister, Henriette, a witty, intelligent young woman who agrees to marry him. She gives him blunt, practical advice on how to win her father's permission for their marriage, fakes obedience to her mother's wishes, and jokingly teases and cajoles her grumpy sister. Her father gives his permission for the marriage, but her mother insists that Henriette should marry the star of her salon, Trissotin, whose name means 'triple fool', a pedantic bore and a fortune-hunter interested only in her dowry.

Armande does not like losing a suitor and, with jealous spite, she tells her mother that Henriette intends to marry a man who finds her poetry comic and her salon boring. Philaminte angrily replies that Henriette will wed Trissotin that very evening! Ariste, who is Philaminte's brother, tells Chrysale that he must stop the wedding, or he will have a pompous fool for a son-in-law. But Chrysale cannot convince his bullying wife that the marriage is a mistake. A tragedy seems inevitable, when Ariste intervenes and sends a letter announcing that Chrysale has gone bankrupt, so Henriette will not have a dowry. Trissotin promptly disappears, and Clitandre declares that he will marry her without a dowry because he loves her. When Ariste admits the letter was a fake, Philaminte agrees to the marriage, and a notary is summoned to draw up the contract.[2]

The Learned Ladies illustrates the contemporary assumption that women must obey men as the natural order of things. Molière is ridiculing domineering wives and hen-pecked husbands as a reversal of this order. A woman's natural role is marriage and motherhood, and her refusal to marry and have children is unnatural unless institutionalized within a convent. Trouble ensues when women reject their natural role. By making themselves ridiculous and their families a laughingstock, domineering women such as Philaminte, and unmarried bluestockings such as Armande, tarnish family honour and cause turmoil.

Women in seventeenth-century France must have arranged family marriages, however, for Molière's play to be regarded by contemporaries as funny. Widows, in fact, often arranged the marriages of their children. Madame de Sévigné tried unsuccessfully for years to find her son a wife. Her letters to her daughter contain at least half a hundred references to her matchmaking efforts on his behalf, all futile. On 12 August 1675, she wrote that she had seen the comtesse de Meslay, and added, 'I would like her daughter to marry my son, but the daughter has other ideas.' Madame de Sévigné was still pursuing this match two years later. Her thirty-five year old son finally married in 1684, to her great joy and relief.[3]

The widowed Marie de Nicolay, whose husband had died in 1627, arranged the marriage of her daughter with the help of a brother-in-law, and Jacques de Lacger, a Protestant royal secretary, was considering marrying a Catholic in 1613 until his widowed mother gently but firmly intervened. Antoine de Noailles indicated in his will that his children's marriages were to be arranged by their mother, Jeanne de Gontault, with the help of his two brothers and a cousin. It took Jeanne three years to find a suitable match for her oldest son. Discussing the marriage market with friends, she sent her son descriptions of potential wives, and he finally agreed to her selection of a wealthy heiress, whose father had died and who had no brothers. The marriage contract, signed in 1578, was negotiated by three women, Jeanne, the bride's mother and her grandmother.[4]

Wives also arranged marriages. Marguerite de Lacger, from a seventeenth-century robe noble family of Castres in Languedoc, was able to marry Guillaume de Clausel because of the help of her mother's relatives, while Madame de Venel in 1650 arranged the marriage of her sister-in-law, and Catherine Maignart in 1597 that of her granddaughter. Marguerite de Selve, the first lady-in-waiting of Jeanne d'Albret, had married the baron de Tignonville, a widower, after Jeanne had provided the dowry and arranged the marriage, and Jeanne's daughter arranged the marriage of Marguerite's daughter.[5] We have already seen that professional matchmakers tended to be women. Despite Molière's mockery, women often adeptly arranged marriages in seventeenth-century France.

The Learned Ladies illustrates the discrepancy between the prescriptive role of women, that is, their culturally determined role in a patriarchal society, and the reality of their daily lives. Not all women were willing or able to conform to every aspect of their socially prescribed role. As a result, they concealed intentions and actions that deviated from their prescriptive role, and routinely disguised their independence. Henriette is a good example. Seemingly submissive and docile, she was, in fact, a woman with a mind of her own seeking to control her destiny, although she discreetly hid her true intentions. Women such as Philaminte and Armande, who refused to disguise or hide their independence and nonconformity, were considered dangerous troublemakers by their society.

Catherine Meudrac masked her intentions and used guile to achieve her goals. Going with her mother to pay a call on the duchesse d'Angoulême, she encountered a good-looking man who stared at her boldly. Her sister discovered that he was the sieur de La Guette, a household gentleman of the duc d'Angoulême. La Guette cultivated a friendship with Catherine's brother-in-law in order to be invited to the house, and they fell in love. He asked for her hand in marriage, but her father refused. La Guette had recently been made captain of a company of light cavalry, and was leaving soon to fight in Louis XIII's wars. Her father said that he would make a bad husband because he would be gone all the time and would die young. Catherine insisted that she wanted to marry him, anyway. Her father was adamant, so they ran away to be married without his consent.[6]

DEPENDENCY AND MANIPULATION

To what extent did a patriarchal society shape women's lives? To what extent did women control their own lives and influence events? A central issue in women's history has been the nature and extent of their power and independence. Historians agree that women lost power and autonomy during the sixteenth and seventeenth centuries, but they disagree on the extent of this loss. In fact, the powerlessness of women has probably been exaggerated. Women may have had more power and independence than historians have realized.

Although Molière's comedy was not a wholly accurate portrayal of women's lives, historians have often accepted prescriptive evidence such as this as an indication of the restrictions on women's activities without knowing much about the reality of their daily lives, that is, whether these limits were observed or not. Because most women were illiterate, they did not leave memoirs or letters. A few upper-class women such as Madame de Sévigné did leave written accounts of their lives, and their numbers were growing.[7] But little is known about the lives of most ordinary women. Evidence about women can be hard to find, demonstrated by the case of Madame de Venel, the governess of Mazarin's nieces. When the young Louis XIV became enamored of Marie Mancini, a match which neither Cardinal Mazarin nor the Queen Mother favoured, the two young people were separated. In June 1659, Mazarin's niece was sent from court with her sisters and their governess to the château of Brouage, where they stayed until Louis XIV married Marie-Thérèse of Spain in June 1660. During this year, Mazarin wrote at least twenty-eight letters to Madame de Venel, about two a month.[8] There are internal references in his letters to her weekly reports on his nieces, which he must have saved because he answered them carefully, but none of her fifty or more letters has survived. Mazarin died in March 1661. Did his heirs discard her letters, or did an archivist do so later, considering them unimportant?

The permanent legal status of women as minors has tended to mask the reality of their daily lives. In law, seventeenth-century French women were always under the guardianship of men, first as daughters and sisters, then as wives and mothers. A woman only reached her majority when she became a widow heading a family and household, thus assuming male authority.[9] Widows such as Madame de Sévigné, who had numerous opportunities to remarry, often did not choose to do so because they preferred their freedom. Unmarried women with property, whether widows or spinsters, had more independence than married women. When unmarried women lacked an income of their own and were forced to live with a male relative, they lost their freedom and independence.

A husband formally administered his own property and that of his wife, who might often, in fact, actually manage their property. She could not act for him, however, without his written consent, which was needed for all her legal actions, such as signing a contract or appearing in court. If she was unmarried, she often needed a male agent to act for her. A husband could not sell or transfer his wife's dowry without her consent, but he enjoyed its use and profits. He could not dispose of her dower or widow's rights to his property without her consent, but he determined their use. His authority and control even extended to her person. He chose their place of residence, and could compel her to look after his household, even to engage in gainful employment for which he received the reward. He had the right to chastise her, including corporal punishment. In short, women had no political and few civil rights in seventeenth-century France.[10]

The legal restrictions on women's activities increased as the early modern state extended its control over family formation by regulating marriage, separation, divorce, legitimacy and inheritance, usually in favour of male family heads. Sarah Hanley has argued that a 'family–state compact' developed, which subjected the interests of women and children to the patriarchal family and state, thus weakening the church's authority.[11] Her argument has been criticized, however. Fathers were not always in control, especially if they sought to placate wives and children whom they loved and who were skilful at manipulation. Family relationships were often more complex and overlapping than a simplistic opposition of men versus women, children versus parents, while a dichotomy of family and state versus church is dubious. The church, a teacher and model of patriarchy, is not easily opposed to the patri-archal authority of family and state.[12]

Interpreting the legal evidence on which arguments such as this rest can be tricky. For example, clandestine marriages in which couples married without parental consent occurred frequently during the sixteenth century until the state began to prohibit them. The ordinance of Blois in 1579 declared that the banns announcing a marriage had to be said in the parish church three times before the ceremony, which to be valid had to be solemnized in public before four witnesses, and a royal ordinance in 1639 made parental consent necessary for marriages of men under thirty and women under twenty-five. An ordin-ance in 1697 further decreed that priests could marry newcomers to the parish only with the written authorization of their former parish priest. These ordin-ances were meant to prohibit clandestine marriages, although they never did so explicitly in order to avoid conflict with the church.[13] But how often were such ordinances actually enforced? Were they enforced for all women, or only for upper-class women with property?

Legal evidence, although a widely used source, does not always reflect the reality of women's lives. Notoriously deceptive and difficult to use, it tends to emphasize restrictions. But what did the growing legal restrictions on marriage actually mean? Were they evidence of the increasing powerlessness of women to control the most important event in their lives?[14] Were they evidence of the greater frequency of love matches and more control by women over whom they married?[15] Were they evidence instead of something com-pletely different, the development of the early modern state?[16] To what extent is law a mirror of society? Does law shape society, or does society make law?

In early modern society, only unusual cases were settled at law because of the expense and delay, so there is always the question of how representative legal evidence is. Moreover, the facts in a case often had to be manipulated to fit statutory requirements. Divorce is a good example. It ordinarily took the form of a permanent judicial separation of property or persons. Although separations of persons were difficult to obtain, separations of property were common. Both types, however, were granted only if specific legal require-ments could be met, and the successful plaintiff had to manipulate the facts in his case, the reality, to fit the legal requirements of a judicial separation.[17]

There was also the problem of enforcement. The existence of a statute, or the issuance of a court decree, did not mean that either would be enforced, especially in the jurisdictional chaos of early modern society, and many were never enforced. Legal evidence does not always accurately reflect the actual facts of a case. Many legally intact marriages, for example, were in reality fiction because the spouses lived apart permanently, one in a Paris town house, the other in a country château. Other possibilities included long visits to family and friends, residence at the royal court, frequent travel or business trips, military, colonial and household service, or monastic retreat.

The dependence of women was not only legal but social. Women were defined socially by their relationship to men. Marriage determined not only a woman's personal happiness, but also her social identity, status and lifestyle. The governor of Lyon, for example, met the new intendant's wife for the first time when they entered a room to find the archbishop waiting. There were only two armchairs, and after the governor took one and the archbishop the other, Madame the Intendante had to sit on a hard wooden chair. Precedence emphasizing differences in rank and authority had pushed aside gallantry in this instance because the intendant was third in the power structure, so his wife got the third chair.[18] The lifestyle of Jeanne-Marie Bouvier de La Motte was determined by her marriage. She was sixteen in 1664 when she married a much older man of great wealth but lower rank. Her parents had agreed to the match without telling her, and she had signed the marriage contract without knowing what it was. She noted that she was the only sad person at her wedding. Her married lifestyle was spartan despite her husband's great wealth because her disapproving, penny-pinching mother-in-law lived with them and ran the household. Her husband became a semi-invalid four months after their wedding. She described her married life as slavery.[19]

It is widely recognized that powerlessness tends to produce submissive behaviour. Dominance requires deferential behaviour from subordinates, so those who are subservient are expected to show deference to those who are dominant. Women, therefore, were expected to show respect, obedience and deference to men. They were expected to be docile and submissive and, internalizing exhortations to obey, most women were submissive. Madame de Motteville observed that Anne of Austria contributed to her own unhappiness by defying Louis XIII, and wrote that 'she [Anne] showed she did not sufficiently understand that for a good wife the wishes of a husband, when supported by reason, must be a law to receive and follow with submission'.[20]

Women tended to disguise their noncompliance for this reason, and to conform, at least outwardly, to the role demanded by a patriarchal society. They dissembled; they manipulated by flattery and nagging; they shirked and malingered; they played dumb, acted innocent, pleaded physical or emotional fraility, procrastinated, insisted upon the priority of other duties and dumbly refused to do as they were told. They laughed, joked and criticized men behind their backs, even sometimes to their faces. They camouflaged their noncompliance, and female kin and friends conspired to help them. Their covert disobedience was tempered, however, by the fact that they were involved in intimate and family relationships with the men in question, so their futures were intertwined. The duchesse d'Orléans wrote about her husband, Louis XIV's homosexual brother, '. . . even if there were a way [to take revenge], I would not want to do it, since whenever a bad thing happens to him, my husband, I myself am necessarily affected as well. For if he is aggrieved, I have to bear the brunt of his bad humour, and if some other misfortune befalls him, it is bound to fall on me as well.'[21] Women's covert disobedience was another reason why a patriarchal society considered them sly and deceitful.[22]

Françoise d'Aubigné, marquise de Maintenon, became Louis XIV's second wife. He enjoyed working with a few ministers in her private apartments at Versailles while she sat quietly reading or sewing. He received returning ambassadors and generals there, held war councils, and a full council of state in 1710, and often interrupted the discussion to ask for her opinion. Saint-Simon observed that she was able to control much of the distribution of royal patronage in this way. She did not always get her own way, however, because she had too many enemies, and the king had a horror of being controlled by anyone, especially a woman. So, she had to work out ways of circumventing him. According to Saint-Simon, she would discuss in advance with the appropriate minister the course of action best suited to her interests, leave it to him to present a doctored list of options to the king, feign ignorance when a perplexed Louis asked for her advice, and then support the minister's view, which was her own. With the connivance of the ministers, whom she was able to play off against each other, she ensured that news was carefully filtered before reaching the king. She wrote to the archbishop of Paris in 1696 that she was obliged to 'hide many things' from Louis because of the difficulty of eradicating first impressions from his mind. Sudden assertions of authority on his part, however, ruined the best-laid plans, and Madame de Maintenon's ill-concealed tears occasionally reminded the court of who was master.[23]

The duchesse d'Orléans disliked Madame de Maintenon, whom she called 'the old trollop'. She wrote:

Two days ago I heard of another piece of dreadful spite wrought by the old trollop. Monsieur le Dauphin was willing to marry my daughter and said so to the old crone; she did not contradict him, lest he speak of it to the king earlier than he meant to do. Instead, she called in the Princesse de Conti and her friend, Mademoiselle Choin, and ordered them to keep after Monsieur le Dauphin until he agreed to put this marriage out of his mind. Those two kept after the good Monsieur le Dauphin day and night for two months until he promised them, and he kept his promise, too.[24]

Not only does this letter demonstrate Madame de Maintenon's skill at manoeuvring; it also shows how other women helped her to do so. We have already seen that Catherine Meudrac had the support of her sister in seeking to marry La Guette.

Natalie Davis has observed that women used many strategies to get around the constraints in their lives, including 'sneaky manipulation that made their husbands fancy themselves the sole decision-makers'.[25] Davis believes, for example, that Bertrande de Rols, the wife of Martin Guerre, was playing a double game. Bertrande was actually the accomplice of Arnaud du Tilh, whom she had always known was an imposter. She had fallen in love with him, and conspired to convince everyone that he was genuine. When their duplicity was discovered, she pleaded the stereotypical fraility of women, insisting that she had been duped as thoroughly as the other villagers. Her conduct is an example of the calculated machinations of women, who had to manoeuvre within a male-dominated society to achieve their goals. Davis elsewhere has described how women accused of homicide sought royal pardons by using and manipulating contemporary stereotypes to excuse their actions.[26] Dependency produced manipulation.

THE BATTLE OF THE SEXES

The attempt by women to circumvent the authority of men has been called 'the battle of the sexes'. In fact, the relationship between women and men was a constantly shifting power balance determined by emotional closeness, age, health, family and public reputation. A woman's exercise of power tended to be informal, indirect and dependent upon her relationship to men. The exceptions were widows and spinsters with their own incomes, and women in religious orders. The convent was largely a woman's world, and membership in convents soared during the seventeenth century.[27]

Women tended to be more influential in affectionate relationships with husbands, sons and other male relatives, while husbands tended to listen more to wives who were nearer their own age. The older a woman was at marriage, and the more life experience she had had, the more likely her husband was to value her opinions. Charles Perrault, for example, at age forty-four arranged a marriage with Marie Guichon, who was nineteen. Because he was Colbert's financial agent, Perrault requested the minister's consent to the marriage. Inquiring if it was a love match, Colbert said he could arrange a marriage for a much larger dowry. Perrault replied that he had only seen the girl once since she had left the convent where she had lived since age four, but that he had known her mother and father for years. He liked them, which was why he had arranged the marriage: he and his father-in-law were compatible. Colbert agreed that this was an important consideration, and gave his consent.[28] How much influence, at least initially, did the new Madame Perrault, whose life experience had been the convent, have in a marriage in which the groom, twenty-five years older than she, had married her because he liked her parents?

Women who were constantly pregnant, worn out by numerous pregnancies, chronically ill, physically exhausted from hard work or weakened by malnutrition had little energy to put into relationships, and less influence as a result. Peasant women had more freedom in choosing their husbands, and they married at an older age, producing fewer children, but they suffered more from hard work and a poor diet. Noblewomen and urban elite women had less freedom in choosing husbands, and married at a younger age, giving birth to more children, but they were better fed and had more servants.

There were few ways, besides silent endurance, for most women to cope with abusive, drunken, philandering, profligate or otherwise intemperate husbands. They could complain to the magistrates and the courts, or they could appeal to their own or their husband's families, especially if their kin were numerous, influential and lived nearby, or if the erring husband had a bad reputation. Formal complaints were infrequent, but informal interventions by kin and community were common. Cardinal Richelieu married his favourite sister, Nicole, when she was nearly thirty, to a younger man, Urbain de Maillé, marquis de Brézé, who was known as a womanizer. The marquis abandoned his wife for months at a time, making her miserable and she was frequently ill, becoming mentally unstable. His treatment of her might have been worse if she had not had a powerful brother, or if his own reputation had been better. If a husband beat his wife severely, or worse if she beat him, if a wife failed to become pregnant after a year or if lovers let their adultery become known, a community charivari might be held. Paraded around sitting backwards on donkeys, the culprits would have their houses pelted with rotten vegetables, and endure nightly serenades of tambourines, bells, rattles, horns and pot-beating. Second marriages in which there was a big age difference between the spouses were the most frequent reasons for charivaris.[29]

The adultery of a woman was considered more serious than that of a man because of the double standard, neatly described by the duchesse d'Orléans: 'Does the young duchess not know that a woman's honour consists of having commerce with no one but her husband, and that for a man it is not shameful to have mistresses but shameful to be cuckolded?'[30] A woman's honour was sexual and the responsibility of her kin in a way that a man's was not. She was expected to be chaste and faithful, and lost her honour when she was not, which meant that her male kin were dishonoured because they had failed in their duty of supervising her behaviour. A higher standard of family loyalty was expected of women, a mother's self-sacrificing love and duty, which was not expected of men.[31]

WOMEN, WORK AND HOME

An important determinant of a woman's power and independence was what she contributed to her family's welfare and prosperity. The more essential her contribution, the more powerful she was, both inside and outside the family. An obvious contribution was the transmission of lineage, rank and property through bearing and raising children, but there were other contributions women could make. Men sought marriages with higher-ranked women because of their influential family connections and greater social prestige, and hypergamy, that is, marrying into a higher social group, was the most common form of social advancement. Jeanne-Marie Bouvier de La Motte's husband had married her for this reason, and Jérome de Phélypeaux de Pontchartrain married Eléonore de La Rochefoucauld-Roye for only a modest dowry because he would thus be allied by marriage to the ducal families of La Rochefoucauld, Durfort de Duras, Saint-Simon, and La Tour d'Auvergne de Bouillon. Seeking to marry any daughter of the well-connected duc de Beauvilliers for the same reason, the duc de Saint-Simon had chosen a father-in-law and a family, not a wife.[32]

A mésalliance was marriage to someone of a lower rank. Noblemen could marry non-noble women because rank was transmitted through the male line in a patrilineal society, and the bride would thus be ennobled by the marriage. Such marriages were usually made for a substantial dowry. After her stepson had married a wealthy tax-farmer's daughter for her large dowry needed to pay the family's debts, the daughter of Madame de Sévigné remarked in a letter, 'It is sometimes necessary to put manure on one's lands', an observation not original to her. When noblewomen married non-nobles, their husbands and children did not acquire their rank. The existence of Cardinal Richelieu's sister Isabelle was long unknown to historians because when she was thirty, having no hope of a family-arranged marriage, she had eloped with the non-noble son of a medical family from Poitiers, and her children became non-noble, thus disappearing from view. Her action was regarded as dishonourable by her offended family, a blemish on their social standing, and their consent to this mésalliance was refused, making her a forgotten outcast.[33]

Women could hope to marry up socially. Men shared this hope, but in addition, they could make their own way up the social ladder through successful military, political, business or financial careers, and the accumulation of wealth. Women were excluded from direct participation in the first two careers, and there were serious obstacles in the way of their pursuit of the others. None the less, maternal relatives and in-laws, especially those who were influential and wealthy, could be as important as paternal relatives in launching and advancing male careers. Upper-class wives and mothers worked hard to secure patronage and to promote male family members by cultivating and entertaining individuals who could provide advancement opportunities, using their own charm to compensate for charmless husbands and sons. In so doing, they left the private sphere of family and home, and entered the public sphere of the royal court, Parisian salons, provincial and urban high society. Women also contributed to family advancement by arranging marriages; securing and paying off dowries, loans and mortgages; dealing with creditors; collecting debts; and increasing family revenues.[34]

In a pre-industrial society, the home was also the workplace. Because women's activities were centred in the home, they moved easily from producing for household use to craft production and small-scale commerce. Nominally, there was a division of labour and space by gender, but this division was not clear cut. A woman's place was inside the home and a man's outside, but these distinctions overlapped. Many men, especially in cities, worked in their homes and in connected shops, while women worked outside, selling goods in the streets and markets or running small shops while their husbands worked elsewhere.

The household was a woman's responsibility. On a farm, the house included the kitchen, bakehouse, vegetable garden, smokehouse, wash-house, dovecote and farmyard with its chickens and geese. Women lit the fire, cooked and made bread; they drew water, did the laundry and cleaned the house; they spun, wove, sewed and knitted; they took care of the children and the garden. To supplement the family income, they made and sold butter, milk, cheese, eggs, soap, candles, lace and so forth, and marketed their own labour as wet-nurses, midwives and laundresses.

A man's work was outside the household. He worked the land, planting and harvesting; saw to the orchards, vineyards and wine cellar; chopped wood; took care of the stables, barns and animals; carted and carried heavy loads. He supplemented the family income by craft production. His world included hunting and fishing, the village square and town hall, social gatherings and taverns. Women and men shared much labour on a farm, however. Women helped men in the fields during planting, harvest and haymaking. They fed animals in barns and sheds as an extension of the farmyard, and helped in tying up vines, harvesting grapes and picking fruit. Men wove cloth for sale, made baskets, heated the oven for making bread and helped in drawing water.[35]

Women managed the family lands when men were absent, incompetent or incapacitated. Madeleine-Ursule des Porcellets, comtesse de Rochefort, began to keep a daily journal in May 1689, when her heavily indebted husband left for army service, taking with him their remaining cash as well as their estate manager. She was left alone with two small sons and only the servants to help. Harassed by creditors and tradesmen, whom she put off with promises to pay at harvest time, she tried to squeeze more money from her tenant farmers, and to borrow from whomever would lend to her. She rose at dawn every day to inspect their estates, seeking to increase crop yields, planting more vines, postponing needed repairs and payment of her servants, even considering a sale of assets to raise money. She made a number of household savings, including using her own petticoats to make linen for her children. Somehow, she managed to hold everything together until her husband came home and even to save a little money. This was not the first time that she had staved off financial disaster by taking over the management of the family estates from a disinterested, spendthrift husband.[36] Her success must have increased her power and independence within the marriage. Power struggles between spouses produced tension and strife, but the knowledge that spousal fortunes were entwined for life encouraged cooperation.

Elite women added capital assets to their husband's fortunes. Their dowries grew in size as time went on, and besides property and cash included the bride's jewellery and sometimes her table silver or plate. A source of ready cash in emergencies, jewellery and plate could be pawned, exchanged, sold or melted down. Some women retained control of their own fortunes after marriage, either through express provisions in their marriage contracts or because there was no contract, and others inherited fortunes while married. Women with access to capital made money by buying and selling real estate, lending money at interest, investing in municipal bonds and consortiums to collect taxes. Of forty-eight houses damaged during a fire in the Nantes parish of Saint-Nicolas in 1680, ten were owned by women; one was three-quarters owned, and five were half-owned by women; and two were shared by the owner's sons and daughters. Noblewomen, especially widows, invested in tax-farming, and Madame Duplessis-Bellière, the Séguier daughters, the duchesse de Guise and her daughter, and the duchesses de Chevreuse and d'Aiguillon were professionals who pursued their investments in tax collection treaties with as much success, skill and perseverance as any financier or tax farmer.[37]

Ladies at the royal court made money by brokering information and gambling at cards. Madame Pochon de Rosemain proposed ways of increasing royal tax revenues to influential people at court and, when her money-making schemes were adopted, she split a finder's fee with them. Forty years old and the wife of a naval engineer working in Majorca when she was arrested for influence peddling in December 1702, Madame Pochon de Rosemain was the mistress of a marquis who had an apartment at Versailles. She had spent fifteen years at court as an information broker, employing her contacts in the royal household and naval ministry to get schemes adopted. Sent to the Bastille, she protested that the similarly employed princesse d'Harcourt and duchesse de Guise had not been arrested. She confessed to getting thirty-three proposals adopted, and the names of many important court personages, mostly women, were found among her papers.[38]

Urban wives worked as saleswomen and cashiers in the family business, and they dealt with customers, shop assistants, apprentices, journeymen and neighbouring shopkeepers. They kept the accounts, took over management of the business whenever necessary and sometimes ran it alone as widows, although they needed guild permission to do so. Ordinarily excluded from membership in male-dominated guilds, women tended to be active in whole-sale and retail trade and, if they ran their own business, it was usually con-nected in some way with their household work or their husbands' occupation.[39]

Women participated in the cloth trade at Rouen from 1570 to 1620 as producers, wholesale and retail merchants, bleachers and dyers, makers and sellers of silk, lace, ribbons, braid, stockings, hats, dyestuffs, linen cloth, knitted and sewn garments. Rural women were spinners, and their husbands weavers in textile manufacturing. Some urban women became wholesalers, usually as wine merchants or grain brokers, but most were small retailers selling bread, butter, fruit, vegetables, fish, meat, wood, leather and so forth in the city's streets and markets. The largest number were street vendors selling second-hand goods for meagre profits. Women also ran wine shops, taverns and inns, and sold their labour as domestic servants, which was the most common occupation for lower-class urban women outside the home. Urban women who ran their own businesses suffered from a lack of skills and capital, male competition and exclusion by male-controlled licensing laws and guilds.[40]

There were many husband-and-wife taverns in Nantes. The husbands worked in a trade, and their wives ran taverns catering to workers in that trade or to neighbourhood residents, thereby giving the family two incomes. The wife of carpenter François Desvignes harvested their grapes, made the wine and sold it in their tavern. The provost's agents found twenty people illegally eating and drinking on Sunday morning in Jan Maurat's tavern; taverns had to be closed during high mass. Jan was a shoemaker, and his wife, who ran the tavern, told the agents, 'You should be in church, not visiting taverns!' The provost's agents found forty people drinking in the illegal establishment of Claude Macan, a cooper, who admitted that his wife sold the wine.[41] The overlapping daily labour of men and women in town and country makes it impossible to insist upon a strict division of work by gender.

Some historians have argued that a division between the public and private spheres of life accompanied the development of capitalism and the early mod-ern state. As a result, women were excluded from the public sphere, and restricted to the private sphere of family and household, which increased their powerlessness.[42] But the realities of daily life make the division between a public male sphere and a female private sphere meaningless.[43] Women's power-lessness and lack of autonomy have been exaggerated. Men and women had to work together to survive, and this reality increased women's power within the family, and by extension within society, although their power was often indirect and hidden. Contemporaries recognized that French women were more independent than their Spanish or Italian counterparts.[44] Their autonomy was due to their participation in income-producing activities essential to their families' prosperity and well-being. The solidarities in women's lives included not only the bonds of family, kin and household, but also the bonds of work created by managing the family business or lands, and participating in farm work, craft production and small-scale commerce.

The independence of French women should not be exaggerated. Their life in a patriarchal society was restricted by prohibitions on all sides, and their lives were narrower, more isolated and more limited than those of men. Ordinarily, women could not independently choose whom they were to marry, and they had a child every other year, half of whom died. Most working-class women were underfed, overworked and exhausted, as were their husbands. Women had a higher illiteracy rate than men, and were legally minors with no political and few civil rights. They faced growing barriers to their control of wealth, whether they had earned or inherited it. Excluded from male-dominated craft guilds, they were relegated to small-scale retail trade and poorly paid marginal occupations. In short, women's lives were defined, determined and constrained by men, and this did not change much during the seventeenth century.[45]

Suggested reading

Gayle Brunelle, 'Dangerous Liaisons: Mésalliance and Early Modern French Noble-women', *French Historical Studies*, 19 (1995), 75–103.

James Collins, 'The Economic Role of Women in Seventeenth-Century France', *French Historical Studies*, 16 (1989), 436–70.

Natalie Davis, *Women on the Margins* (Cambridge, Mass., 1995); idem, *Society and Culture in Early Modern France* (Stanford, 1975).

Georges Duby and Michelle Perrot, eds, *A History of Women*, 5 vols, *Renaissance and Enlightenment Paradoxes*, vol. 3, eds Natalie Davis and Arlette Farge (Cambridge, Mass., 1993).

James Farr, *Authority and Sexuality in Early Modern Burgundy (1550–1730)* (Oxford, 1996).

Wendy Gibson, *Women in Seventeenth-Century France* (New York, 1989).

Sarah Hanley, 'Engendering the State: Family Formation and State Building in Early Modern France', *French Historical Studies*, 16 (1989), 4–27.

Julie Hardwicke, *The Practice of Patriarchy. Gender and the Politics of Household Authority in Early Modern France* (University Park, Pa., 1998).

Olwen Hufton, *The Prospect Before Her. A History of Women in Western Europe, 1500–1800* (New York, 1996).

Carolyn Lougee, *Le Paradis des Femmes. Women, Salons, and Social Stratification in Seventeenth-Century France* (Princeton, 1976).

Elizabeth Rapley, *The Dévotes. Women and Church in Seventeenth-Century France* (Montreal, 1990).

Martine Segalen, *Love and Power in the Peasant Family*, tr. Sarah Matthews (Chicago, 1983).

Merry Wiesner, *Women and Gender in Early Modern Europe* (Cambridge, 1993).

CHAPTER 3

PLAGUE AND PEASANTS

Pierre Prion spent most of his life in the service of the marquis d'Aubais, who inhabited a château and village of the same name on the Languedoc side of the Rhône river. Pierre has left a fascinating account of daily life in the Midi, and his descriptions of the famine of 1709, and the reaction at Aubais to the outbreak of plague at Marseille in 1720, are of particular interest. At the age of nineteen, Pierre entered the service of the abbé Vernet at Coupiac near Rodez as a valet. He served the abbé at mass, kept his books, filled his woodshed, took care of his horse, bought his food and made his bed. Pierre wrote that, during the winter of 1709, there was a heavy rain for several days, followed by a ten-day freeze. The ice became so thick that the trunks of big trees snapped and split wide open. Wine froze in the cellars and frozen bread had to be cut with an axe. All plant life was destroyed, and wild animals such as wolves and rabbits were found dead in the fields.[1]

A curé in Lyon noted that the winter of 1709 began on the sixth of January when the Rhône froze solid. The ice was so thick that it could support the weight of a loaded wagon. Claude Bernard wrote that the ground, drenched by several days of continual rain, froze to a depth of three feet, and that the Saône river froze nearly to the bottom. Everywhere there were reports of people found frozen to death. A cleric at Beaune observed that travellers died in the countryside, livestock in the stables, wild animals in the woods, and that nearly all the birds had been killed. Passage on the Rhône was blocked by large chunks of ice, and there was ice floating in the Mediterranean. The cold lasted until March. The winter wheat crop was destroyed, and so were all the olive, fruit and chestnut trees. Vines either died or were barren the next year, and agriculture was paralysed.[2]

Famine followed the ruined harvest. There were shortages everywhere, and large numbers of people took to the roads in late March searching for food. Pierre wrote that starving peasants roamed in hordes through the fields and woods looking for grass, weeds, berries, roots, anything to eat. The roads and fields were full of corpses of all ages dressed in rags with their sacks and mouths full of grass, or with green stains around their mouths, and whole families could be found lying dead together. Pierre helped to carry the bodies to the cemetery to be buried three to a grave, and the abbé for months kept a cauldron of oatmeal boiling on the fire to give to starving peasants who came to his door. They flooded into the cities in search of food, and the cities in desperation closed their gates, trying unsuccessfully to keep them out. Because of the demand, the price of wheat in Lyon rose 25 per cent in March, and continued to soar because, as always, the distribution of grain from unaffected regions was inadequate. The severity of a famine was measured by how high the grain prices went. There were a number of serious famines during Louis XIV's reign, the last occurring in 1720.[3]

Pierre wrote that the 1709–10 famine brought with it an epidemic of 'malignant fevers'. The chronic malnutrition, worsened by the food shortages, more than doubled the normally high summer death rate from infectious diseases. The city of Lyon, for instance, had more deaths than conceptions from August 1709 through January 1710.[4] This crisis was particularly severe, but similar high death rates occurred in other bad years. Periodically, there were years of demographic crisis when the death rate was higher than the birth rate, although normally the birth rate was higher. In crisis years, the death rate was twice the average, and famine, disease and war were the causes. Each was a cause in itself, and each aggravated the other two. Bad weather ruined the harvest, and food shortages tripled or even quadrupled prices, intensifying the effects of chronic malnutrition and causing death from starvation. An epidemic of infectious disease, carried by soldiers in transit, would worsen the death rate, and a general rural exodus followed, spreading the disease. The resulting turmoil in the countryside prolonged the crisis.[5] The Four Horsemen of the Apocalypse, death, famine, disease and war, rode across France in crisis years, trampling all before them.

Bad weather occurred frequently because a 'little ice age' had begun in the mid-sixteenth century, lasting for two centuries. After 1560, winters were cold, while springs and summers were cool and wet. Wheat was particularly susceptible to cold, wet weather, and the effect on the wheat harvest was disastrous. The weather was cold and wet in 1618–21, 1625–33, 1635–6, 1646–52, 1660–2, 1682–1703 and 1711–13, and there was famine in 1618, 1630–1, 1649, 1661–2, 1682, 1693–4, 1709–10 and 1712–13.[6]

Having spent most of their day outside, peasants at night slept in poorly roofed, badly lit cottages, which were malodorous and dirty, with everyone sleeping together in the same room with the animals. Hard physical labour, inadequate food, vitamin deficiencies and chronic diseases such as tuberculosis and rheumatism weakened their health, and the constant cold and hunger made their lives a misery. Epidemics of contagious disease often accompanied famine because undernourishment and a filthy environment made everyone susceptible to infection. Epidemics were so disruptive they caused famine by interfering with planting and harvesting, and epidemics among farm animals were just as devastating as those among people.[7] The most feared human disease was plague. The speed with which it struck and victims died was terrifying because causes and cures were unknown.

Pierre Prion was living at Aubais in June 1720, when bubonic plague appeared in Marseille. On 25 May, a ship had returned from a ten-month voyage to the eastern Mediterranean. A Turkish passenger had died of plague on the return trip, followed by eight sailors and the ship's doctor. When the ship docked, three sailors who were still alive were taken to a city hospital, thus spreading the disease. By early August, 50 people were dying every day in Marseille, with 300 a day by mid-August and 500 by late August. After September, the number of deaths began to decline and, before it was over, half the city's population of 100,000 had died in the last great outbreak of bubonic plague in France.[8]

The bacillus causing bubonic plague, which is endemic in central Asia, was only discovered a century ago. It is transmitted by the fleas of black or ship's rats, which are particularly susceptible to the bacillus. Fleas which left dying rats carried the disease, and fleas on unwashed people spread it quickly. The outbreaks in cities were always much worse because of the dense human habitation. Symptoms include headache, high fever, vomiting, intense thirst, swollen tongue, and then the dreaded, unmistakable signs of the disease, one or two reddish-purple buboes the size of an almond or an egg, bloody swellings of the lymph glands. The mortality rate was 60 to 80 per cent; some died within hours, some within a day and most within 2 or 3 days. Outbreaks caused mass panic, and Marseillais fleeing the city in August had caused huge traffic jams at the gates. Commerce and industry halted; corpses piled up in the streets; soldiers and galley prisoners had to be brought in to bury the dead in mass graves.[9]

Plague usually arrived in ships from the Levant to spread inland, and Mediterranean ports such as Marseille and Toulon were always hard hit. Provence suffered greatly. There were outbreaks of plague in France about every fifteen years from 1536 to 1679, but Provence had twenty-nine outbreaks in this period. Ordinarily, outbreaks were local but, occasionally, they were more widespread as in 1585–6, 1596–7, 1627–31, 1636–7, 1652, 1665–8, 1676, 1701 and 1719–21. Between 1600 and 1670, plague caused more deaths than any other disease in France. The overall death rate from plague during the seventeenth century was about 35 per cent of the population, or between 2 and 4 million people. Outbreaks often followed hot, humid springs and summers during which fleas multiplied rapidly, but disappeared in winter because cold killed the fleas; plague abated in Marseille after October. Years that did not have serious outbreaks of plague were often colder than usual.[10]

The contagion was spread by travellers, including refugees from plague-stricken areas, merchants, peddlers, muledrivers, vagabonds, beggars, prostitutes, sailors and soldiers. Plague outbreaks in the north were often the result of troop movements between Picardy and the Low Countries. France participated in six foreign wars during this century, and the army increased in size from about 30,000 in 1615 to about 400,000 in 1690. The fighting was mostly outside the borders of France, but there were regular troop movements to and from the frontiers. Sporadic domestic unrest also required pacification by royal troops. It is not an exaggeration to say that soldiers were everywhere in France during this century.[11]

Troops on the march were billeted on towns and villages for a few days or weeks, and for months during the dormant winter season. They were lodged in private homes, and their behaviour was often destructive. Unpaid, drunken soldiers pillaged, extorted money by threats, kidnapped for ransom, raped and murdered. They provoked violent protests. The village of Les Mées in Provence rioted in July 1637 because of the misbehaviour of the Boissac light horse company billeted there. In May 1640, the towns of Fréjus and Draguignan rioted for the same reason, killing two cavalrymen of the La Chapelle regiment. In December 1656, the village of Avignonet in Languedoc rioted because of the misconduct of the d'Estrade regiment, although this time the soldiers fought back, burning houses and killing three villagers. The Auvergnat parish of Mandailles chased away a marauding cavalry company in 1652. Soldiers also spread infectious diseases. In July 1629, infantry regiments returning from the Italian wars brought plague to Provence, and there were rumours in May 1640 and August 1657 that troops in passage through the province were again carrying plague. Venereal disease was always a problem. The construction of military barracks after 1670 was insufficient, and most of the army was still not in barracks in the mid-eighteenth century.[12]

Infantry regiments sometimes filled their depleted ranks by impressing local inhabitants, which nearly happened to Pierre Prion. Bored with country life, he had set out in the autumn of 1710 to find work in Montpellier. On the way, he had met an infantry captain who tied his hands behind him, and forced him to march along with him to Toulon in order to join his regiment. Pierre was only able to free himself at about three o'clock in the morning, and hid at the top of the church tower in the village where they had stopped for the night. The captain spent the next day noisily searching for him, then gave up and went on his way. Pierre climbed down shortly after midnight. It took him an hour to open the church door, and then he crept silently away, keeping his head below the village walls.[13]

Pierre was living in the village of Aubais in the summer of 1720 when plague spread rapidly up the Rhône river valley from Marseille. The village awaited its arrival in terror. Wild chicory, garlic and onions were eaten as a preventive measure, and white wine, muscat and brandy were drunk in large quantities for the same reason. Charlatans sold charms and quack medicines containing antimony, arsenic and ammonia to ward off the disease. Sulphur, myrrh, resin, camphor, old leather, cow horns and chicken feathers were burned to purify the air, while vinegar, absinthe, camphor and snake venom were used as disinfectants. Braziers burned continually before the doors of village houses and the streets were swept constantly. Pierre joined the newly established health bureau, which ordered a dry stone wall (without mortar) to be built around the village. Guards were posted at the gates to inspect everyone entering, and turn away those from infected areas. Royal troops stopped all traffic on the roads to and from the stricken areas to halt the spread of the disease, which fortunately never reached Aubais.[14]

The most effective measure against the spread of plague was a *cordon sanitaire*, a strictly enforced quarantine by royal troops. No one was allowed in or out of a stricken area until the contagion had abated, which usually took 60 to 80 days, or until the ground froze. Marseille was placed under quarantine in August 1720.[15] Life inside a closed, plague-stricken city was nightmarish. All those who could flee had done so, abandoning children, aged relatives and servants in their haste to get away. The air was filled with sulphur fumes and the sickeningly sweet smell of rotting corpses. Streets were empty and silent; shops were boarded up; and vacant houses had been looted. Because of delirium from the high fever, there was bizarre behaviour among the sick and dying, wild laughter, singing, dancing, mad running through the streets and climbing across the roofs. Plague was regarded as a punishment by God, so there were public rituals of contrition including processions by robed, hooded penitents to appease divine wrath.

Outbreaks of plague became fewer during the late seventeenth century, and disappeared entirely during the eighteenth century, because of cordons sanitaires, better sanitation and hygiene, the black rat's disappearance and its replacement by the more plague-resistant gray or house rat.[16] The disruptiveness of plague outbreaks had far-reaching consequences for agriculture.

WHY WAS AGRICULTURE STAGNANT?

Annalistes historians have proposed a neo-Malthusian explanation for what they regard as a lack of agricultural growth during the seventeenth century.[17] A population explosion in the previous century had caused a disintegration in the size of peasant landholdings, and the widespread system of egalitarian inheritance had worsened the fragmentation. The result was that most peasants, who were 85 per cent of the population, became small-scale farmers using family labour to work their own tiny plots as well as scraps of land rented from others. Overall, peasants did not own much land. Subsistence-oriented, they grew enough to feed themselves and their families, with a little left over for necessities, taxes, dues and rent. Their goal was self-sufficiency, not a surplus to sell. They were not interested in increasing their profits by maximizing their landholdings or their productivity for commercial markets, and the disruption caused by the plague did not encourage them to change either these attitudes or their goals.

As the demographic crisis ended, however, a period of land concentration began. More land was now available from death or abandonment, and better-off peasants were able to increase the size of their farms by buying land from less fortunate neighbours. These well-to-do peasants became large-scale tenant farmers, who rented and worked blocks of land belonging to others as well as their own landholdings. They were market-oriented, that is, they produced for regional and urban markets, and they were entrepreneurial, that is, innovative, well-equipped and willing to invest capital in order to maximize their productivity and profits. As the only capitalists in the countryside, they thrived, but they were in the minority.[18]

In contrast, most seventeenth-century peasants were deeply resistant to change. Pierre Goubert has described the French peasantry as 'a rooted, sedentary, stable population', and rural society has been called a *société immobile*, or unchanging, for this reason. Most peasants used traditional farming methods, and were hostile to technical innovations and enclosures to create larger farms. They lacked capital and were poorly equipped. They lived in isolated villages with other subsistence farmers, who were as unprogressive and illiterate as themselves. Most spent their lives within a twenty or so mile radius of where they had been born. Barely self-sufficient, they were easily wiped out by famine, disease and war. Small-scale subsistence farming, and the conservative mentality behind it, were responsible for the agricultural stagnation of the seventeenth century.[19]

The conservatism and pessimism of most peasants, and their fear of change, was a psychological effect of the demographic crisis. In their world, no one lived for very long. Death or disaster could occur at any moment, a view that changed slowly only after the demographic crisis had ended.[20] Peasants were averse to taking risks because they believed that change could only be for the worse, so they clung tenaciously to the present. Their motto was 'safety first', and their goal was an unchanging self-sufficiency that has been called the 'subsistence ethic'.[21] Theirs was a world of fear dominated by a search for security based on personal relationships that included family, extended kin, household, village, *seigneur* (big landowner) and parish priest.[22] These were the solidarities of the peasant world.

The Annalistes' view of seventeenth-century agriculture, however, has been challenged in recent years. The Annalistes have been accused of overemphasizing the effect of population size on property-owning and agricultural productivity, and of exaggerating the psychological effects of the demographic crisis.[23] Critics have noted that the crisis was more devastating at some times and in some places than in others; its effects were not uniform. The famine of 1628, caused by an outbreak of plague in the Midi, spared the Paris area, Normandy,

Brittany and the northeast. The famine caused by the Fronde did not extend to Brittany, Normandy, Provence or Languedoc. The famine of 1661 hit the Paris area hard, but not the east or the southeast.[24] Provence and Brittany mostly escaped the high death rates. Provence was moderately prosperous for much of the century, and its birth rate was high enough to compensate for plague deaths, while Brittany experienced a population increase because it was subjected to fewer troop movements than elsewhere. In general, eastern France suffered more devastation from troop movements and warfare than western France.[25] Plague outbreaks tended to occur more frequently in port areas and along troop routes. Some historians insist upon the importance of famine in causing the crisis, while others emphasize the impact of epidemics.[26] The high death rates of crisis years were variable and unpredictable.

Pierre Goubert has acknowledged that his model for the demographic crisis was northern, eastern and central France, where the population was dense; wheat was the primary crop; and the weather was cold and wet. Crops in the south were more diverse, and the weather was hotter and drier. Emmanuel Le Roy Ladurie has acknowledged that, at least through the mid-seventeenth century, the north suffered more demographic catastrophes than the south, although he notes that droughts were frequent in the south. He argues, none the less, that the pressures of population growth were increasingly felt in the Midi after 1560, and especially after 1690. His study of the peasantry of Languedoc is the classic exposition of the neo-Malthusian argument.[27] Significant regional variations call into question the universal applicability of the Annalistes' thesis, and suggest that other factors in addition to the demographic crisis were responsible for agricultural stagnation.

The Marxists have argued that the root cause of stagnation was an exploitative property and class structure that retarded economic development.[28] Roland Mousnier and his students have insisted that overtaxation was at fault. Heavy taxes, collected inefficiently, were levied to support the constant warfare and a rapidly growing army. These taxes were so burdensome that they provoked peasant revolts and retarded economic development.[29] Other historians have argued that the basic cause was structural, including inadequate markets, an unintegrated economy, poor transportation and communication, insufficient money in circulation, limited capital and credit, excessive legal and administrative restrictions, political and institutional weaknesses, such as the tangle of property rights, lack of famine relief and high taxation. Maximizing production only lowered prices in an economy handicapped by bad roads and fragmented markets. In such an economy, peasants made a rational choice when they engaged in subsistence farming because increasing productivity would have gained them nothing. They were motivated by pragmatism, not by fear. They made efficient use of their resources and, if they did not innovate, it was for good reason, not because they were afraid of change.[30]

41

Rural society was characterized by ease for a few at the top; most of the rest suffered poverty and degradation. At the top were farmers, leaseholders and ploughmen. Farmers worked their own land; leaseholders worked land they rented; and each did both. The amount of peasant-owned land varied from province to province, but there was never enough to go around. Ploughmen owned their equipment and animals, which they could hire out, and they might own, rent or sharecrop some land. Next in the hierarchy came farm workers, who had only their labour to offer; they worked for others. Most were day labourers or hired hands, who were paid by the day, and might also sharecrop. They usually owned the house in which they lived and their tools, as did rural craftsmen, vineyard workers, woodcutters and herdsmen, who raised and sold livestock. At harvest time, farm workers became seasonal labour migrants, moving from farm to farm because there was an overabundant labour supply. Near the bottom of the hierarchy were domestic servants, who were usually young, owned nothing and worked for their food, lodging and clothes. At the very bottom were the poor and destitute, who had nothing and did not work. Peasants increasingly supplemented their income by craft production at home, especially textile manufacturing. Middle men from nearby towns brought raw wool to rural spinners and weavers, then marketed the finished cloth. This cottage industry has been called protoindustrialization, or the industry before industrialization, a controversial and probably now outdated concept.[31]

The Annalistes have recognized the diversity of peasant income-producing activities but not the implications, insisting that there was little peasant participation in the commercial economy.[32] A growing number of historians, however, disagree and point out that peasant commercial and industrial activities have been overlooked. Increasingly, peasants sold to regional and urban markets, diversifying what they produced in order to meet market demand and satisfy urban consumers. They increased the size of their landholdings whenever possible, and they engaged in credit transactions, accumulated capital and invested it in agriculture. Peasants participated in cottage industry, not only as spinners and weavers, but also as middle men, and they acted as brokers in the grain and wine trades. They were entrepreneurial, market-oriented and innovative, and not as psychologically devastated by the demographic crisis as the Annalistes have claimed.[33] Some historians even argue that a slow growth in agricultural productivity began after 1680, particularly in the north.[34]

HOW UNCHANGING WAS RURAL LIFE?

The high incidence of labour mobility in the countryside, and its implications, have also been overlooked. In searching for work, Pierre Prion displayed considerable geographic mobility. His father was a notary at Réquista near Rodez, and Pierre was sent at age seven to the local school. When he was twelve, his father found him a place as a copyist with a lawyer, and then with a judge in the seigneurial court at Rodez. When he was fourteen, he was sent to work as a copyist for a lawyer in Toulouse, but city life and the hubbub of the law courts frightened him. Homesick, he gave up his position and returned to Réquista. For several years, he supported himself as a shepherd and a fruit picker; his father had evidently washed his hands of him.

Then in 1710 his father and mother both died. His father's will left all his property to his sister, Pierre's paternal aunt, with instructions to distribute it among his five children as she thought best. She gave it all to her namesake and niece, Pierre's sister. The four boys received nothing. Turned out of the family house, they were left to fend for themselves. One brother joined the army, where he died in 1712. Another went to Nîmes to learn the trade of a shoemaker, and then returned home. The third married a very short woman, 'big and round like a barrel of wine', probably because she had an income, and Pierre, the oldest, went into service with the abbé at Coupiac.

Pierre was young and restless, and he soon left to find work in Montpellier. His encounter with the infantry captain so scared him, however, that he entered a marquis's service as a copyist in the spring of 1711. After three safe but boring months spent copying all day in a room in Arles, he set out again for Montpellier. This time he arrived safely, worked as a copyist over the winter, saw the city's sights and then returned home. In the spring of 1712, he entered the service of the marquis d'Aubais as a secretary and jack of all trades, and there he remained, unmarried, for the next fifty years until his death.[35] He travelled widely with the marquis, and most of his memoirs are devoted to his travel experiences while in domestic service.

At about the same time that Pierre was learning to be a copyist in the Midi, Edmond Restif was training to be a law clerk in Burgundy. He had gone to the local school and, in 1710 at the age of seventeen, he was sent to the nearby town of Noyers to clerk in a lawyer's office. He came home for the harvest, stayed to plant winter wheat and then went back to the lawyer's office. The following spring he came home to help with the sowing and stayed for the harvest. In November 1712, he set off to work as a clerk in the office of a royal attorney in the Parlement of Paris. It took him five days to walk there, carrying a change of clothes wrapped in a goat skin. As he approached the city gates, he was stopped by an old man who asked for his help in carrying a package, which he obligingly rolled up in his goat skin. They agreed to meet later, and he went on alone to the city gates. The guard searched the goatskin, but found only his clothes. When they met later, the old man insisted that he accept a gold coin. Bewildered, he asked why, and the old man, cackling with laughter, told him that he had brought 100,000 livres worth of tax-free goods into the city for him! The old man was a well-known smuggler and Edmond had unwittingly carried precious stones for him. Edmond clerked in the law office for three more years until his father died. Then he went home to inherit, marry and start a family. He never returned to Paris.[36]

Pierre and Edmond belonged to the upper ranks of the peasantry because they were literate. Their fathers could afford to send them to the village school and do without their labour in the fields. The literacy rate of the peasantry had begun to rise in the late seventeenth century, but always lagged behind that of the towns, and increased faster in the Midi.[37] Both boys left their village to seek employment in a nearby city and then returned home as Pierre's brother did. The temporary migration of peasants to a nearby town or city to work for a time was common. Employment in the Marseille soap and textile industries attracted peasants from all over Basse-Provence. Peasant weavers of the Rouergue flooded into the industrial town of Lodève in large numbers. Urban domestic servants were usually poor peasants. Women entered service because it offered the opportunity to save money for a dowry, while it allowed men to save enough to set themselves up in another occupation. When they had saved enough, they returned home, married someone from their village or parish and began a new life.[38] Cities were dependent upon the surrounding countryside for manpower, but there was also a flow of skills and money in the other direction.

If the Annalistes' view of seventeenth-century agriculture is open to question, so is their view of rural life, which may not have been as sedentary as they suggest. The isolated, timeless nature of rural society may have been exaggerated. The rural solidarities of family, village, seigneur and the relationships on which they were based, changed during the seventeenth century. The causes included absences due to labour migration, increasing landlord absenteeism, greater rural exposure to urban life and new attitudes from the spread of commercial agriculture and cottage industry. There was mobility and change in rural life.

The demographic crisis was responsible for a countryside in motion until the late seventeenth century, as the Annalistes have noted. Refugees from famine, epidemics and war were driven by destitution to abandon their villages in large numbers. Usually, they returned home when the crisis had ended; sometimes they did not.[39] Labour migration became widespread. Prompted by economic necessity, migration was a response to land shortages and the need to find employment for surplus children. Young peasants left home to work on someone else's farm, enter domestic service, become an apprentice or seek urban employment, and there was a steady stream of rural immigrants to the cities from the surrounding countryside. Most were young, single males who became day labourers and domestic servants. Some stayed in the city permanently; others returned home after a while. Peasants also left home for long periods of time to serve in the army, as Pierre Prion's brother had done.[40]

Seasonal migrants who left home for less than a year were mostly agricultural day labourers. They were gone for a few weeks or months during the planting, harvesting, threshing and haymaking seasons. Peddlers, handymen, porters, woodcutters and itinerant craftsmen, such as masons, plasterers and roofers, also had to move around to ply their trade. Some seasonal migrants were gone for five or more months a year, and in some villages half or more of the adult males were seasonal migrants.

Temporary migrants were gone for more than a year. Poor peasants from the mountainous centre and southwest of France had for centuries made the trek to the Mediterranean littoral and Spain in search of work. Martin Guerre was one of these. They were usually gone for more than a year, as were those who went to Canada, the West Indies or elsewhere overseas to work. The harder it was to find a job, the farther a migrant had to go, the longer his absence. Permanent migrants never returned home.[41] Those who took to the roads for other reasons included travel-adventurers such as Pierre Prion, students, journeymen, soldiers, highwaymen, plague refugees, beggars, vagrants, criminals and those who were bored, unhappy at home, or seeking to escape a disreputable past.[42]

Frequent or prolonged absences tended to weaken family, seigneurial and village ties, although close family ties were the least affected by absence. The obligations and expectations of relationships became less important, and participants relied less upon them. After an individual had been gone for more than a year, not as much was expected or demanded of the relationships he had left behind.

Seigneurial ties were weakened by landlord absenteeism. Nobles became absentee landlords because they lived increasingly in town. Great court nobles spent much of their time at Paris or Versailles, while provincial nobles kept a house in the nearest town or the provincial capital and spent the winter there. The rest of the year they lived on their estates in the country, but they tended to spend less and less time on their lands and more in town.[43] Noble landowners thus became strangers to their tenantry, and their absence weakened the seigneurial and patron–client loyalties of peasants whom they no longer saw or knew.[44] The tendency of wealthy urban elites to invest in land in the surrounding countryside reinforced this trend because their principal residence was urban, so they, too, were absentee landlords unknown to their tenant farmers.[45]

Seigneurial and village solidarities were a multiplex of overlapping relationships based on property, production and exchange as well as kinship, friendship, neighbourhood and clientage.[46] The spread of commercial agriculture

45

and cottage industry introduced new attitudes and behaviour that changed some of the values and assumptions on which these relationships were based. Notions of duty and honour, for example, acquired an economic dimension. It was increasingly necessary to have a reputation for being honest, trust-worthy, reliable and hard-working in order to find employment. Employers, on the other hand, needed to have reputations for paying good wages in full on time, meeting debts, fulfilling obligations and treating employees fairly in order to attract workers. Reputation determined the ease with which indi-viduals found jobs, hired or kept labour, borrowed money, secured credit, negotiated deals and made temporary relationships permanent. Farmers de-veloped relationships with middlemen, brokers, wholesalers and customers, as did farm workers engaged in cottage industry, and the longevity of these relationships depended upon honesty, hard work and reliability.[47] Most of these relationships were non-familial, non-seigneurial and non-village in origin, but when they overlapped with existing relationships, they added a new eco-nomic dimension that helped to undermine existing rural solidarities.

Rural exposure to city life increased during crisis years from the need for jobs and charitable assistance. After the plague had subsided, a continuing rural fascination with city life prompted visits, which may have stimulated rural change and innovation. During Pierre Prion's first visit to Paris in 1714, he spent hours on the Pont-Neuf watching the people and the carriages. The bridge had a carnival-like atmosphere with peddlers and vendors crying their wares, and toothpullers, beggars, pickpockets and prostitutes at work. Charlatans sold quack medicines and cures, while acrobats, tumblers, magi-cians, marionettists, mimes, singers and musicians entertained the crowds of strollers, who included dandies, young girls, law clerks, attorneys, nuns, young lovers, idlers, children, servants and porters. There were cafés at both ends of the bridge where passersby could drink coffee, play dominoes and watch the crowds, while neighbouring shops sold books, trinkets, fabrics, jewellery, toys, engravings, pistols, cutlery and canes. One could buy dogs, face powder, wooden legs, glass eyes, false teeth, food, flowers and fruit on the bridge itself. No wonder Pierre lingered! There are traces of this atmo-sphere today on the Pont-des-Arts and at neighbouring booksellers' stalls along the banks of the Seine.

About five o'clock in the afternoon, Pierre went to his Paris lodgings where he was given a glass of beer. Never having tasted beer before, he thought it was lye and spat it out, furiously accusing his host of trying to poison him. He drank beer with gusto on his next trip to Paris, however! Pierre stayed eight months on his first trip, visiting Versailles on Sunday when it was open to the public. He was impressed by the king's grandeur, the well-dressed court women, water gardens, menagerie, aviary and observatory.[48] His travels were unusual in their variety and extent, but visiting a nearby city to marvel at its wonders was common enough. The growing exposure to city life may have helped to bring an end to rural isolation and to increase peasant openness to change.[49]

Pierre Prion left Réquista permanently and kept in touch only with his brothers. Edmond Restif returned to his native village and spent the rest of his life there. Pierre and Edmond represent the two rural societies, the stable village core of married couples who owned land or rented it, and the massive floating population that swirled around them, the labour migrants, often single males, without land or means of support except their own labour.[50] Pierre was one of these, although migrants could settle down and join the stable village core as Edmond did. These two societies, the stable and unstable, existed side-by-side, and both must be taken into account when discussing rural life.

Suggested reading

Marc Bloch, *French Rural History*, tr. Janet Sondheimer (Berkeley, 1966).

Thomas Brennan, *Burgundy to Champagne. The Wine Trade in Early Modern France* (Baltimore, 1997).

Laurence Brockliss and Colin Jones, *The Medical World of Early Modern France* (Oxford, 1997).

James Goldsmith, 'The Agrarian History of Preindustrial France', *Journal of European Economic History*, 13 (1984), 175–99.

Pierre Goubert, *The French Peasantry in the Seventeenth Century*, tr. Ian Patterson (Cambridge, 1986); idem, *The Ancien Regime: French Society, 1600–1750*, tr. Steve Cox (New York, 1973).

George Grantham, 'Jean Meuvret and the Subsistence Problem in Early Modern France', *Journal of Economic History*, 49 (1989), 184–200.

Daniel Hickey, 'Innovation and Obstacles to Growth', *French Historical Studies*, 15 (1984), 208–40.

Philip Hoffman, *Growth in a Traditional Society. The French Countryside, 1450–1815* (Princeton, 1996); idem, 'Land Rents and Agricultural Productivity: The Paris Basin, 1450–1789', *Journal of Economic History*, 51 (1991), 771–805.

Emmanuel Le Roy Ladurie, *The Peasants of Languedoc*, tr. John Day (Urbana, 1976); idem, *The French Peasantry, 1450–1660*, tr. Alan Sheridan (Berkeley, 1987); idem, 'French Peasants in the Sixteenth Century', *The Mind and Method of the Historian*, tr. Siân and Ben Reynolds (Chicago, 1981), pp. 97–122.

W. Gregory Monahan, *Year of Sorrows. The Great Famine of 1709 in Lyon* (Columbus, 1993).

Liana Vardi, *The Land and the Loom. Peasants and Profits in Northern France, 1680–1800* (Durham, 1993).

CHAPTER 4

CITIES AND CHANGE

Thomas Platter visited Marseille for the first time in February 1597. His ship dropped anchor outside the harbour at midnight, but he had to wait until the next morning for the iron chain across the entrance to be loosened, so his ship could berth at the foot of some stairs. The harbour of Marseille was a long, natural rectangle with a narrow, rocky entrance.[1] Jean-Baptiste Bertrand, a doctor during the 1720 plague, described the city as standing on the Mediterranean side of a range of low hills, and added that the harbour was nearly a mile in length but less than a half mile in width. In Bertrand's day, Marseille sprawled in a half-circle around the port but, a century earlier, it had lain huddled along the western edge of the port. This area became known as the old city after the enlargement of 1666.[2]

Thomas Platter wrote in his journal:

> The harbour is especially convenient because it extends into the centre of town. Houses surround it on three sides, and merchandise can be brought ashore in front of the shops where it will be sold. Because the garbage and sewers are emptied into the water, it has to be cleaned out by a curious machine worked by convicts from the galleys. In summer, they say it stinks so much that you cannot come near it on an empty stomach. Indeed, I felt ill myself when the weather was warm, but you get used to it in time. The odours are counterbalanced by the scent of all kinds of spices, and by the smell of tar that is used every day on the ships, which are so many and crowded together that the water cannot be seen.[3]

Bertrand loved Marseille, where he had been born, but even he remarked that 'strangers complain with some justification of the dirtiness of the streets where they throw the rubbish and excrement from the houses'. The old city was notorious for its narrow, winding, dirty streets, and its small, dark, crowded houses. A colleague of Colbert remarked, 'I am not surprised that plague ravages the city; its houses are without water, badly built, crammed full of people from the cellars to the attics and filthy.' Bertrand noted that water flowed through channels in the streets to carry the filth into the port, where the current and 'a number of pontoons constantly employed in cleaning' carried it away into the open sea. Refuse from the fishing boats and fish markets, waste from the tanneries and garbage from the berthed ships also

48

went into the harbour. The streets of the old city were badly paved, their rubbish-choked staircases crumbling, and there were few boulevards or squares. The quaysides, the biggest open space, were filled with people walking, talking and taking the air on summer evenings.[4]

Going around the harbour to look at the ships, Platter thought that the great lateen-rigged galleys with their banks of oars at rest, and the small fishing boats without sails known as caïques, were typically Mediterranean. The numerous Spanish tartanes, with two lateen-rigged sails and eight benches for rowers, were coastal traders; so were the small two-sailed skiffs. Big merchant ships, which sailed to Alexandria and Africa, were sixty feet long and twenty feet wide with a raised cabin on deck, and warships were similar, but filled with soldiers and cannon. Platter wrote, 'Vessels that had just berthed were unloading merchandise of all kinds on the quays, spices in incredible quantities, rhubarb and medicines, monkeys, strange animals, oranges, lemons and a thousand other things.'[5] The quays of earthen brick were busy at all hours, and the nearby streets were full of shops selling what the ships had brought.

Platter wrote, 'After a meal I went for a walk beside the Royal Gate, where there are many beautiful gardens with walls or fences around them. This is the biggest of the [five] gates of Marseille, and the best guarded.' It was also the busiest. Located in the city wall behind the harbour, it opened on to the heavily travelled coast road running east to Toulon. Marseille in 1597 was encircled by thick walls; most French cities at that time were walled. Within a century, the walls had been torn down, and replaced by less substantial fortifications which, in turn, were soon removed entirely because the city was growing so rapidly.

Platter continued, 'The morning of the 18th [of February] I went up to the hills overlooking the city to view the countryside. . . . I have never seen any town more surrounded by farms and country houses. The reason is that when there is an outbreak of plague, which happens frequently because of all the people who come here from everywhere, the inhabitants take refuge in the country.' The Marseillais owned 2,000 properties beyond the walls in 1597, and the surrounding countryside, known as the *terroir*, fanned out behind the city for miles. Bertrand remarked, 'An immense number of country houses . . . called *bastides*, are scattered all over . . . and give the appearance of a second city.'[6] A few days later Platter left Marseille by the Aix gate to ride north across the hills toward Avignon. It would have been cool and wet in February, the air pungent with the smell of pine.

Travellers entering Marseille by the Aix and Royal gates knew immediately that they were in a different world, a crowded, filthy place of masonry and stone where all sorts of people lived and worked cheek by jowl. The old city was an anthill; there were people everywhere. The narrow, airless streets, partly in shadow during the day, were pitch-black at night because there were no street lights. The sunlit quays of the big, open port must have blinded people emerging from the gloomy streets around them. There was constant noise and activity during the day, but silence at night because few ventured out if they could avoid it; the streets were neither safe nor clean. Entering Marseille for the first time must have been an overpowering experience for someone used to the fresh air, sunlight and space of the countryside. But it must also have been exhilarating. The city's streets had a vitality and energy that was electrifying. Fernand Braudel described early modern towns as electrical transformers that recharged human life by stimulating growth and change. He wrote, 'Towns generate expansion and are themselves generated by it . . . growth can be perceived in towns and cities more clearly than anywhere else.'[7]

Change within early modern cities had an impact on the larger society, and many of the forces transforming early modern life first appeared in cities. By 1720, the medieval walls of Marseille had been torn down and the city had been substantially enlarged. What caused this expansion, and what were the accompanying social changes? The following account of change in Marseille is both a case study and an overview of trends in urban growth and development during the seventeenth century.

URBAN GROWTH

The population of Marseille doubled during the seventeenth century, increasing from about 45,000 inhabitants in 1600, to about 75,000 in 1700, and 90,000 including the surrounding terroir or suburbs, which contained 20 per cent of the city's population. The surface area more than doubled at the same time. By 1700, Marseille was the third largest city in France after Paris and Lyon, and soon surpassed Lyon to become the second largest city, which it remains today.[8] Because of its size and importance, Marseille was not a typical city, but many of the changes it experienced also occurred in other French cities during the seventeenth century.

The most enduring change was the steady growth in the size of urban populations. A high urban death rate from unhealthy living conditions was balanced by a high urban birth rate, except in crisis years.[9] The real reason that city populations doubled, however, was the steady flow of rural immigrants. From 1600 to 1660, Marseille had an annual growth rate of 0.6 per cent, which dropped to 0.4 per cent during Louis XIV's reign. In rapidly growing cities such as Marseille, Rouen, Bordeaux, Caen and Lyon, half of the population were recent immigrants. In 1721, slightly less than half (1,141) of all marriages in Marseille (2,471) were between native-born Marseillais. In slightly more of these marriages (1,330), either one or both spouses had not been born in the city. The great majority of these spouses (916) came from Provence, a minority (340) from other provinces and only a few (74) from outside France. The recent plague outbreak may be thought responsible, but, in fact, this pattern was typical. In the early eighteenth century, 48 and 40 per cent of the newly-weds in Lyon and Bordeaux, respectively, were not native-born, and 80 per cent of them came from the surrounding region.[10]

Most French towns and cities doubled in size from 1500 to 1700, both in surface and population. By 1700, the population of cities was between 15 and 20 per cent of the total population of France.[11] What happened after 1700 is less clear. The assertion that urban population growth continued at a fairly constant rate during the eighteenth century has been challenged, and a counter argument made that the rate of urbanization slowed after 1700. Marseille grew less rapidly in the eighteenth century; its population was only 120,000 by 1789. Whether this was the case for all French cities remains to be seen. The population of most cities and towns, however, grew at a faster rate than the total population during the seventeenth century.[12]

To accommodate this increase in population, the walls of Marseille were torn down and the city expanded to the north, east and southeast in an enlargement known as the new city. Wide boulevards, large squares and handsome, well-built houses characterized the new city, which had half the density of the old. Many cities expanded outward during the seventeenth century to accommodate population growth. The walls of nearby Aix-en-Provence, the provincial capital, were razed and rebuilt to incorporate a large, new district of broad streets and aristocratic mansions to the south. In contrast to medieval cities, which had grown haphazardly, seventeenth-century enlargements were planned with careful attention to spaciousness, sanitation and appearance. Colbert himself directed the modernization of Paris and Marseille.[13]

As part of this modernization, the royal galleys were separated in 1665 from the sailing fleet at Toulon, and transferred to Marseille where they were housed near the refurbished Arsenal at the eastern end of the harbour. New galleys were built and, by 1690, there was a fleet of fifty galleys manned by 15,000 men. Their officers welcomed the move to a larger city offering more diversions, and the merchants of Marseille gladly supplied what the galleys needed. The city's economy absorbed their crews as casual labour, which was important because the galleys, floating prisons, were often in port with idle crews, especially during the winter. Warehouses and shipyards sprang up beyond the Arsenal along the southeastern side of the harbour, which was dredged and enlarged. Colbert authorized these improvements by letters patent in June 1666, and the city paid for them.[14]

The painted, gilded galleys and their rows of *forçats*, or convict oarsmen, fascinated visitors. Madeleine de Scudéry, who accompanied her brother when he became governor of the fortress of Notre-Dame-de-la-Garde in November

1644, wrote to a friend, 'I can still say that the most beautiful thing I have seen are the galleys on Christmas Day with their tents, pavillons and pennants in a hundred different colours'. She noted that aboard the 22 galleys were 3,000 or 4,000 convicts in iron chains with blue shirts, red caps and shaven heads. When she visited Notre-Dame-de-la-Garde, which had a panoramic view of the city, she would sit gazing at the white limestone fortress of the Château d'If, shimmering on an island in a haze on the horizon, and listen to the sound of oboes from the galleys.[15]

Thomas Platter wrote about his visit to a galley,

> There was such a noise of chains on board, and of shouting, that it seemed like . . . an immense forge. I counted thirty-one benches of oarsmen on each side. Four, and sometimes five, men of every nationality were chained to each oar. . . . Once or twice a week the men are given meat, but their other food is appalling. They are dressed all the same, cropped and shaven to avoid vermin, and are confined to the galleys day and night, winter and summer. . . . Some knit, sew and carve wood; others chat, sweep, wash, cook, do the dishes, etc. Every one works because, when they are at anchor and not employed cleaning the streets, squares and port, each one works for himself in order to gain a few sous to buy wine or linen.'

Later, the younger, healthier convicts lived ashore working in the city, and 77 Marseille merchants, manufacturers and artisans were employing more than 1,000 convicts by 1702.[16]

Contemporaries thought differently than we do about what distinguished a city from a town. What was the difference between rural and urban? How was an early modern town distinguished from a village?[17] Government officials considered the smallest town to have about 2,000 inhabitants, a standard that historians have adopted. But many places with fewer than 2,000 inhabitants were still considered towns. An additional distinction, which took this discrepancy into account, was the presence or absence of walls, a clear line of demarcation between town and country. This definition did not apply to the suburbs, the outlying areas just beyond the walls, because of their symbiotic relationship with the city. The suburbs, illustrated here by the terroir of Marseille, were neither rural nor urban. The Annalistes have been interested in the nature of this rural–urban relationship.[18]

The terroir of Marseille was composed of 16 districts in 1597, and was considered part of the city for census, tax and judicial purposes.[19] Well-off Marseillais owned country houses and farms in the terroir, which they used as a retreat from city life. They escaped to their bastides from the plague, the summer's heat and stench, and the overcrowding. At harvest time, everyone went out to work or watch; in the mid-seventeenth century, the city council was unable to meet because all of its members had gone out to their bastides. By 1700, there were 1,800 bastides around Aix-en-Provence and more than

5,000 around Marseille. Working-class Marseillais went out to the terroir in search of jobs as seasonal farm labour and wage labour in manufacturing, construction and transportation. Rich and poor alike went out to hunt, fish, gather wild herbs and buy meat, vegetables, fruit and wine. Those who wanted to play *pétanque* (bowls), practise archery or just enjoy the country air also went out to the terroir, which was full of people on Sundays and holidays.

The terroir was able to supply Marseille with only enough food for three or four months of the year because most of its land was dry and stony. The best land was enclosed in gardens near the city walls, and produced vegetables, fruit and flowers for urban consumption; market-gardening was profitable for terroir residents. Madeleine de Scudéry rhapsodized over the oranges, lemons, figs and almonds, the anemones, narcissi, pinks and jasmine, but remarked that the hot Provençal sun killed roses. Only about half of the terroir was planted, mostly in olive trees and vineyards. Platter observed, 'The land is not suitable for the cultivation of wheat, but produces large quantities of olives and wine. It is forbidden under penalty of a fine to buy foreign wines before all the local wine has been sold.' This monopoly allowed local wine to be sold at high prices, and was profitable for the city because its sales tax on wine brought it 40,000 livres a year, two-fifths of its revenues in the mid-seventeenth century. Wine smuggling was widespread.

The other half of the terroir was used for grazing herds of sheep and goats sold in the city's markets, and providing wood for fuel. There were not enough trees by the seventeenth century to supply the city's domestic needs, so wood had to be imported from the Var and Corsica. Terroir residents worked in Marseille as day labourers and domestic servants. They ran small workshops manufacturing goods for urban consumption, quarried for limestone and other types of building stone, and made roof tiles and earthen bricks. There were numerous inns and taverns outside the walls for muleteers, wagon drivers and others who transported what the city imported or produced, while fishermen lived along the coast. Most French cities and their suburbs were as interdependent as Marseille and its terroir.[20]

The Annalistes believe that early modern cities exploited the countryside, consuming what it produced and draining off its resources and labour force. The country thus supplied the raw materials and workers that a town needed, and provided the markets for what it produced or imported. Marseille in the mid-seventeenth century exported tobacco grown in Guyenne to Italy, and textiles produced in lower Languedoc to the Levant and Italy. Noble landowners lived in towns for part of the year where they spent their agricultural rents. Officials lived in administrative cities where they decided how to spend the agricultural taxes they collected, and a wealthy urban elite bought up the surrounding countryside.[21]

A revisionist interpretation, however, suggests that town and country were interdependent, with labour and resources flowing in both directions. Rural immigrants did not always remain in the city; many returned home. From 1640 to 1790, for instance, 26 of every 100 couples left Rouen after having resided there for a time. There was considerable mobility among the Rouennais during the seventeenth century because of the demographic crisis. When couples left the city, they took with them the skills they had acquired and the capital they had accumulated. In weakly urbanized provinces such as Dauphiné, city walls meant less, and there was a close relationship between town and country. The extent of urbanization varied by province. The so-called 'embourgeoisement' of the countryside may be regarded as a flow of urban capital in the opposite direction, that is, an investment of urban commercial and industrial capital in the rural economy through the purchase of land and its improvement. The growing prevalence of rural textile manufacturing, in which raw materials and markets were supplied by merchant capitalists and their agents, was an urban investment in the rural economy that took jobs away from city workers. The rural–urban relationship was interdependent.[22]

CAUSES AND EFFECTS OF URBAN GROWTH

When Henri de Séguiran visited the Provençal coast in 1633 to report on its trade and defences, he began with Marseille, noting that it traded with the eastern Mediterranean or Levant cities of Alexandria, Cairo, Sidon, Acre, Aleppo, Smyrna and Constantinople; the North African or Barbary coast cities of Tripoli, Tunis and Algiers; and the coastal cities of Italy and Spain. Marseille's monopoly on the Levant trade filled its warehouses with wheat; cooking oil; silk; cotton; Egyptian and Turkish carpets; pepper, cinnamon, ginger and spices; opium, gum and other drugs; musk, myrrh, aloe, sandalwood and perfumes. From the Barbary coast, its merchants brought Moroccan leather, horses, animal skins, sponges, coral, mother-of-pearl, ostrich plumes and dates. From Spain and Italy, they imported capers, anchovies, citrus fruits and, from the New World, sugar, tobacco, rice, indigo, Brazilian wood and the red dye cochineal. From northern Europe, they brought pickled herring, salted codfish and sardines in oil. In exchange, they exported French textiles, in particular high quality woollens from the north and a lesser quality from Languedoc, as well as hats, bonnets, paper, wine, cognac, soap, honey, olive oil, nuts, figs, cheese and saffron. Goods were trans-shipped between Mediterranean and North African ports, Europe and the New World colonies. Marseille was a big entrepôt or warehouse port, and would soon become the most important Mediterranean port. The city's economic life centred around its port area.[23]

Marseille's foreign trade stagnated from 1610 to 1670 because of war, piracy, plague and taxation, although local trade thrived.[24] The French war with the Barbary states, lasting from 1604 to 1628, damaged Mediterranean trade, and covert hostilities lasted for three more decades. Piracy increased, and the Levant and North African coastal trades, which were based in Marseille, suffered a decline. The Turks and their client Barbary states had been seizing French ships and cargoes in the Mediterranean for years, but now Barbary pirates began to raid the French coast, and soon approximately 100 ships and 8,000 Frenchmen were taken.[25]

War with Spain began unofficially in 1624, officially in 1635 and lasted for twenty-five years, disrupting the city's trade with Spain and Italy. Marseille, as a result, had a total of 650 ships in port in 1635, but only 310 in 1636. The city's trade suffered during plague outbreaks because merchants preferred to use the smaller, nearby coastal ports of Cassis, La Ciotat and Toulon, believing them to be healthier. In addition, Marseille levied heavy port taxes on the class of a ship, its tonnage, destination and cargo, usually 1 to 4 per cent of its value, with additional taxes on spices, drugs, cooking oil, honey and alums, as well as cargo taxes by weight, on goods in transit, harbour entry and maintenance fees, dockage and anchorage fees, judicial and military fees. Heavy taxes, war, piracy and plague hindered the growth of Marseille's foreign trade until the late seventeenth century.[26]

In modernizing Marseille, Colbert swept away many of these taxes by edict in March 1669 to make the city a duty-free port. Goods entering Marseille for local consumption or trans-shipment were not subject to royal customs duties, and about half of the other taxes were eliminated. The 1669 edict gave Marseille a virtual monopoly of the Levant trade by making other French ports pay a 20 per cent tax on Levant goods that had not come through the city. The Spanish war ended in 1659, and Louis XIV's wars did not disrupt Mediterranean trade. Plague outbreaks and piracy subsided, and Marseille's trade began to flourish. Its export of woollen cloth to the Levant, for example, grew at the rate of 4.6 per cent a year during the late seventeenth century. Soon the city's ships were sailing past Gibraltar toward the sugar-producing Caribbean islands, the French Atlantic and the northern European ports. Marseille, Bordeaux, Nantes and Saint-Malo all experienced a sudden spurt of commercial and urban growth during the late seventeenth century.[27]

Commercial success stimulated industrial growth, and manufacturing flourished, although Marseille was always more a mercantile than an industrial city. The first sugar refinery appeared at Marseille in 1671; its owner was a wholesale merchant and shipowner who had surplus capital. By 1683, there were two sugar refineries using 1,200,000 pounds of raw sugar a year and, by the 1730s, the city was annually processing 6,000,000 pounds, 80 to 90 per cent of which was re-exported. Soap manufacturing was just as successful, and there were 30 soap factories in Marseille by 1720. Other industries included the manufacture of textiles, leather, shoes, hats, bonnets, candles, glass, ceramics, bricks, tiles, jam, candy, crates, boxes and barrels. Marseille was unable to compete with Lyon in the production of silk, or with Languedoc in woollen cloth. But it imported the art of colour-dyeing from Italy, and after 1648 it used raw cotton from the Levant and dyes from the New World to produce colourful printed cotton cloth.[28] The commercial and industrial success of Marseille created a need for more workers, who were drawn in from the surrounding countryside attracted by higher wages. They in turn increased urban consumption, and stimulated market-gardening and wine production in the terroir, food production in Basse-Provence and the Rhône river valley, and fishing and salt-making along the coast. Far from exploiting the countryside, cities such as Marseille supplied the markets and jobs vital to rural prosperity.

Marseille's economic success generated wealth, creating an urban elite of prosperous merchants and manufacturers. This was an open elite whose ranks were filled by those who had money, and its membership turned over rapidly. There was greater social mobility in cities. There had been only four merchants in Marseille in 1595, who had fortunes of more than 300,000 écus (900,000 livres), and another five with fortunes of more than 100,000 écus (300,000 livres). A hundred years later, however, there were about 250 to 275 wealthy wholesale merchants in Marseille, and another 100 or so retail merchants and merchant-manufacturers. Jean-Baptiste Bruny was one of the wealthiest, with a fortune of 2,242,179 livres at his death in 1723. A merchant worth 200,000 livres in 1686 was considered rich.[29]

Urban elites everywhere in France, for instance, at Montpellier and Aix-en-Provence, increased steadily in size and wealth during the sixteenth and seventeenth centuries. Urban notables at Dijon were 4.7 per cent of the population in 1450, and 23.4 per cent in 1750. At Saint-Malo, 35 individuals in 1710 had fortunes of 400,000 to 1,000,000 livres, while 75 had fortunes over 200,000, and 142 had fortunes over 100,000. The urban elite of Saint-Malo was nearly as large and wealthy as that of Marseille. Members of these elites eagerly sought to join the nobility by purchasing titles, fiefs and ennobling offices. Jean-Baptiste Bruny of Marseille, for instance, purchased the fiefs of Lourmarin and Saint-Cannat as well as the barony of La Tour d'Aigues. The numbers of newly ennobled soared until the mid-seventeenth century when the rate dropped.[30] Everywhere wealthy elites took control of municipal government to become self-perpetuating political oligarchies.[31]

Tension and conflict accompanied urban growth. Violence flared in a number of French towns and cities during the first half of the seventeenth century, but tapered off after 1660. Marseille, for example, experienced serious revolts against royal authority in the 1590s, 1640s and 1650s. Causes of these urban revolts were complex, but included miserable living conditions for the poor whose numbers soared; glaring inequalities between the rich and poor who lived in close proximity; domination of the municipal government by a small, wealthy elite; and heavy taxes levied by this elite and the crown. Urban elites had their own grievances, including royal attacks on their privileges, and heavy royal taxes. Their discontent made them willing participants, even leaders of urban revolts, which took the form of spontaneous popular protests, elite protests and mixtures of the two.[32] The crown interfered regularly in the operation of municipal governments, but had to satisfy at least some of the demands of governing urban elites in order to achieve peace and stability. The important role of the state in the development of urban commercial and industrial capitalism needs to be remembered.[33]

The Annalistes have concentrated upon commercial and manufacturing cities like Marseille, and produced some excellent case studies if few synthetic overviews. Their critics, however, charge that they have overlooked other types of cities and patterns of urban development.[34] Not all cities doubled in size because of commercial and industrial growth. Provincial capitals and regional administrative cities are a case in point. They expanded because of the development of the early modern state, and the resulting increase in the number of royal officials. Royal government in the early sixteenth century had included about 4,000 royal officials, whose number had increased tenfold by 1660. Most of these offices were venal, that is, they were sold by the crown, and their numbers were inflated for fiscal reasons. Provincial capitals like Dijon, Rouen, Rennes, Grenoble and Aix-en-Provence, and regional administrative cities like Montpellier, Caen and Nantes, grew in population and surface area because they were residences of royal officials. Even a commercial and industrial city like Marseille was home to a large number of royal military personnel. The army quadrupled its effective during the seventeenth century, and the navy more than doubled after 1660. Garrison and fleet towns grew rapidly in size as a result. The population and area of Toulon, for instance, nearly doubled after it became the base for the Mediterranean sailing fleet and galleys. The state had become a big consumer of urban goods and services.[35]

Regional administrative cities expanded as well because of an increase in the number of resident clergy. New religious houses founded during the Catholic Reformation sprouted like mushrooms in the open spaces near the city walls. There were 53 founded in Paris between 1610 and 1661; 17 in Rouen between 1600 and 1660; and 19 in the small towns of the Trégorois between 1600 and 1703. In Aix-en-Provence, there were approximately 65 religious foundations by 1695, including 29 religious houses with 1,136 members of the regular and secular clergy. Resident clergy were comparatively more numerous in Aix than in nearby Marseille. The church, like the state, had become a big consumer of urban goods and services.[36]

Nobles increasingly lived in provincial capitals like Aix-en-Provence, regional administrative cities like Montpellier and aristocratic cities like Arles, which had 300 nobles in residence in 1660 and, of course, Paris and Versailles. Even Marseille had a resident nobility, although they were comparatively fewer than in Aix. Roland Mousnier has observed, 'In the 17th century the nobility seem to have been big spenders. A *gentilhomme* (noble) had to *faire largesse* (be generous with money) – it was one of his social characteristics.' A noble lifestyle required lavish spending as an outward indication of rank, and nobles ruined themselves with displays of conspicuous consumption, spending more money when they were in town.[37] Cities became places of aristocratic residence and stylish display. Thomas Platter noted that the merchants' wives of Marseille wore silk stockings just like nobles' wives, but that they demonstrated more wealth than taste. He wrote, 'Thus, while their sleeves and corsage are of red taffeta, velvet, or silk, their skirts are of the same stuff, but yellow, grey, or blue, which makes them look like parakeets.' Nobles, and would-be nobles who imitated their lavish spending, became enthusiastic consumers of urban services and goods. Marseille's ships supplied a growing urban market for luxury goods.

The seventeenth century witnessed the birth of a new consumerism that would become a characteristic of eighteenth-century urban life.[38] The dress, food and entertainment of the leisure classes became increasingly elaborate during this century. When Madame de Sévigné visited Marseille in December 1672, she attended a formal reception hosted by the municipal government, dined with the bishop at his new residence to the sound of music, danced at a masked costume ball given by the city's governor and lunched on the galleys' flagship after a convict had performed acrobatic tricks on deck. The menu of the six-course banquet welcoming Madeleine de Scudéry's brother to Marseille included partridges and ortolans; shellfish soup; fresh fruit; jellies, preserves and jams; a variety of side-dishes; muscat, mulled wine and lemonade. In 1687, the intendant of the galleys gave a soirée in his new, luxuriously furnished town house (now the city hall) that featured three balls in different rooms, a light supper for the ladies and an opera in several acts.[39]

Those who could afford to do so filled the theatres, while travelling theatrical companies appeared regularly at the French language theatre of Marseille. Permanent theatrical companies flourished in Paris during the late seventeenth century, but there were not sufficient audiences to support resident companies in the provincial cities until the next century. The Provençal language theatre was very popular because most Marseillais spoke only Provençal. Madeleine de Scudéry complained that she would have to make return social calls to 42 houses of the city's elite, and that only 6 or 7 of the women spoke French. After 1685, operas by Lully were regularly performed at the newly founded Marseille Academy of Music where opera ballets, comic operas and concerts were also performed. There were organ concerts in the city's churches, and a municipal string ensemble played in public. Dancing was popular. Thomas Platter wrote that he watched a tournament in the city streets by the masked, costumed nobility on horseback, followed by street dancing for the people and private balls for the wealthy. He wrote, 'All the evening I saw masqueraders going through the streets to the sound of music . . . a great many good-for-nothing fellows amused themselves by throwing oranges, just as we throw snowballs.' Cargoes of oranges arrived frequently at this time of year, and over-ripe oranges were plentiful and cheap, so there was always orange-throwing during Carnival. Performances by street entertainers, and displays of exotic animals and freaks, were popular everywhere. There was greater literacy and more books in cities, whose inhabitants became known for their sociability. Urban proximity and wealth created a lifestyle different from that in the countryside.[40]

Public civic ceremonies drew big crowds, including the installation of new members of the city government, their marriages and funerals, receptions for visiting dignitaries, the ascension of a new king to the throne, the birth of a dauphin, royal entries, visits by the king and other members of the royal family, military victories and peace treaties. There were parades with floats, processions of notables through the streets to the sound of trumpets, drums, musket fire, violones and oboes with fireworks and bonfires at night.

Quasi-civic religious holidays included the Fête-Dieu (Corpus Christi Day) when all ships in the harbour doused their lights and removed their pennants. A procession formed on the quays to wind its way through the old city. The religious confraternities marched first to the sound of flutes and tambourines, then young girls by twos in white wearing flowers and singing hymns, followed by children dressed as cherubs and angels. The guilds came next, the butchers' guild leading a bull garlanded with flowers and covered with a tapestry on which a child sat in a sheepskin representing John the Baptist. After the ceremony, the slaughtered bull was roasted and given to the poor. The clergy came last, swinging censers and chanting. Church bells were rung, cannons fired and the procession ended at the quays where sailors waited for the concluding ceremony. The 21 July festival of Saint Victor, the city's patron saint, featured a float in the form of a boat constructed by the fishermen's guild that carried the saint's relics from the Abbey of Saint-Victor through the streets and back to the abbey. Flowers thrown by passersby and from windows covered the float. Carnival lasted a week and attracted big crowds as did public executions. There was always something to see and do in a city.[41]

As the provincial capital, a seat of sovereign judicial courts, and a residence for nobles and clerics, Aix-en-Provence displayed a pattern of growth different from that of neighbouring Marseille. Aix was not a commercial or industrial city, but its population increased from 22,000 or 23,000 in 1630, to about

27,500 in 1695, and 30,500 if its terroir is included. This increase was due to greater numbers of resident officials, nobles, clerics and their servants, not to economic expansion. Aix had a comparatively large number of domestic servants, who were 27 per cent of household heads in the census of 1695.[42] Aix and Marseille provide contrasting models of seventeenth-century urban growth and expansion.

URBAN GROWTH AND SOCIAL CHANGE

The foregoing case study has illustrated some general trends in urban growth and development. The population and surface area of Marseille more than doubled, and its enlargement was carefully planned. After 1670, its commerce and manufacturing increased, and rural immigrants arrived in droves to seek employment. A small, wealthy elite dominated the municipal government, and became avid consumers of material luxuries. Rich and poor alike eagerly attended public spectacles and entertainments, and a distinct urban lifestyle flourished based on proximity and sociability. Urban solidarities of neighbourhood, work and sociability proliferated because of rapid urbanization and rural immigration. These ties were dependent upon density, which was an essential urban characteristic, and differed from rural solidarities in having a basis other than village and seigneury. Rural solidarities among those living off the land were challenged by urban solidarities among those living on wages and profits in close proximity within cities.

Members of the urban working classes were surrounded by webs of neighbourhood relationships based on familiarity and daily contact. Neighbours were physically close, the result of high density urban living, and neighbourhoods were defined by sight and sound, extending as far as one could see or hear from a house or shop, including the street in front and the courtyard behind. Households overlapped with workshops, and there was no difference between house and street. The working classes of Marseille were grouped in neighbourhoods in the old city by occupation, kin and village of origin. Two-thirds of the Marseillais were still living in the old city in 1789; the wealthy lived in the new city. Streets were named for the trade of their inhabitants, a nearby tavern or inn, a fountain or well at the corner.

There was a high rate of mobility, with new faces constantly appearing, but there was always a core of permanent residents, who had inherited their fathers' trades, intermarried and were willing to welcome kin and friends from their home village. Those who moved away tended to be unmarried recent arrivals without kin or friends. There was segregation by occupation, but neighbourhoods could also be mixed, especially in non-industrial towns.[43] Neighbourhoods were urban villages, and neighbours were kin, friends, acquaintances from home and work colleagues who shared the same space and habits, helped to bring up children, intervened in family quarrels, lent what was needed, provided help in emergencies, and were always around for a chat. Self-image and the inseparable image of others were based on what the neighbours thought and said, and neighbourhood gossip determined public reputation and honour. A dense mesh of neighbourhood relationships characterized urban life.[44]

Taverns were popular meeting places for men. Eating and drinking provided an excuse for conversation and day-to-day sociability. Taverns varied greatly in size, décor and clientele, but regulars could be found there at any time of the day, having a bowl of soup or a glass of wine, smoking a pipe and playing cards or throwing dice. Peak hours were lunch and dinner; peak days were Sundays and holidays. Brawls, crime, street riots and even revolts emanated from the taverns, which were closely watched by the police. Workingmen and neighbourhood regulars rubbed shoulders with rogues and crooks because taverns were also the haunts of gamblers, prostitutes, thieves and burglars. Guild ceremonies, masonic meetings, journeymen celebrations and private parties were held there, and second-hand dealers came around looking for customers; taverns were the flea markets of the day. Women, who only went to taverns with male relatives, met their female friends and neighbours in shops, markets, streets and at public fountains or wells.

Coffee houses, or cafés, which sold coffee, tea, chocolate and wine, were a leisure-class version of the taverns. Introduced to Marseille from Turkey in 1644, coffee was still a new, expensive drink that was growing in popularity. In cafés, men talked about politics over a cup of coffee, read newspapers and played chess.[45] Leisure-class sociability also included attending salons, academy meetings, theatres, musical events, literary societies and social circles of all kinds. The Academy of Arts and Sciences became a centre of Marseille's intellectual life, while Academies of Music and of Painting, Sculpture and Architecture were established.[46] In towns, there were more opportunities to form ties of sociability.

Work-related, corporate ties included membership in guilds. Most artisans joined guilds, which proliferated in Marseille during the seventeenth century. Masters had their own associations, or confraternities, affiliated with churches and religious orders. Journeymen could join these, but they also formed their own associations known as *compagnonnages*. Masters, journeymen and apprentices shared the bond of working together in the same workshop, although this was an impermanent bond because disputes were frequent, and workers often changed employers.[47]

Artisans lived in Marseille's old city, and in the late sixteenth century were mostly employed in textiles, leather tanning, construction and fishing. Ship-building increased during the seventeenth century, and the port and its ship-yards kept other workers busy. With increased production for export after

1670, Marseille became a big manufacturer of beaver hats; the pelts came from Canada. The city also made red woollen fezzes or caps, which it sold by the thousands in North Africa. By 1700, there were 100 hat workshops employing 700 men and 2,500 women; the hat trade employed 10,000 people all together. By 1710, there were 300 beaver hatmakers alone in Marseille, of whom one-quarter were master artisans, and three-quarters were journeymen, mostly immigrants. Journeymen had to move around to find permanent places as masters. Marseille's shoemaking trade was larger than that of Paris, and the shoe manufacturers owned big workshops employing 50 or more journeymen, who made shoes for export to southern Europe and the colonies. The production of *faïence*, glazed, coloured earthenware, also flourished in Marseille. The city's largest trades and guilds were those of the shoemakers, tailors, bakers, hatters, textile weavers, framework knitters, wigmakers, tanners, iron-workers and coopers. Provence, however, had fewer guild members than elsewhere, and they became comparatively even fewer as mass manufacturing and rural immigration increased.[48]

Other corporate, work-related ties included membership in associations, known as companies, of royal officials, clerks, lawyers, notaries and doctors, and in joint-stock companies. The latter in Marseille included the Coral Company of Africa, which dated from the sixteenth century and imported coral from the Barbary states, Corsica and Sardinia to use in making jewellery. After the Canada Company collapsed, the Company of the Indies had the monopoly on the importation of beaver pelts for hats. The Mediterranean Company was founded in 1685 to produce silk textiles, but failed in 1735 because of competition from Lyon. Five different Marseille companies were formed to trade with the Levant between 1669 and 1690. At first few Marseillais invested because they lacked commercial capital. But the revival of trade generated more capital, and Marseillais invested heavily in the last two companies.[49] Work-related ties based upon the pursuit of an occupation or a career, especially if they were corporate, provided a social and legal identity. These ties brought privileges and benefits, as well as duties and obligations, and they overlapped with the urban solidarities of neighbourhood and sociability, and the universal solidarities of family, kin and household.

Social changes in seventeenth-century Marseille reflected similar changes occurring elsewhere in France. Early modern cities were microcosms of social change. There was a proliferation of wealthy, non-noble urban elites, who sought ennoblement and eagerly imitated the nobility in style-conscious, conspicuous expenditure. There was more social mobility in towns than in the countryside. The distinct urban lifestyle included a new consumerism and new forms of sociability based on proximity and a concentration of wealth. Neighbourhood, sociability and work-related ties were a significant difference between rural and urban life, and contributed to a distinct urban identity.

Suggested reading

William Beik, *Urban Protest in Seventeenth-Century France* (Cambridge, 1997); idem, 'Louis XIV and the Cities', *Edo and Paris*, ed. James McClain *et al.* (Ithaca, 1994), pp. 68–85.

Philip Benedict, *Cities and Social Change in Early Modern France* (London, 1989); idem, 'More than Market and Manufactory: The Cities of Early Modern France', *French Historical Studies*, 20 (1997), 511–38.

Thomas Brennan, *Public Drinking and Popular Culture in Eighteenth-Century Paris* (Princeton, 1988).

James Farr, *Hands of Honor. Artisans and Their World in Dijon, 1550–1650* (Ithaca, 1988).

Robert Fox and Anthony Turner, eds, *Luxury Trades and Consumerism in Ancien Régime Paris* (Brookfield, Vt, 1998).

David Garrioch, *Neighbourhood and Community in Paris, 1740–1790* (Cambridge, 1996).

T.J.A. Le Goff, *Vannes and its Region. A Study of Town and Country in Eighteenth-Century France* (Oxford, 1981).

Robert Isherwood, *Farce and Fantasy. Popular Entertainment in Eighteenth-Century France* (New York, 1986).

Robert Muchembled, *Popular Culture and Elite Culture in France, 1400–1750*, tr. Lydia Cochrane (Baton Rouge, 1985).

Daniel Roche, *The People of Paris*, tr. Marie Evans (Berkeley, 1987); idem, *The Culture of Clothing*, tr. Jean Birrell (Cambridge, 1994); idem, *The Decencies of Life*, tr. Brian Pearce (Cambridge, 2000).

Robert Schneider, *Public Life in Toulouse, 1462–1789* (Ithaca, 1989).

J.K.J. Thomson, *Clermont-de-Lodève, 1633–1789* (Cambridge, 1982).

Cynthia Truant, *The Rites of Labor. Brotherhoods of Compagnonnage in Old and New Regime France* (Ithaca, 1994).

CHAPTER 5

THE NOBILITY

During the last decades of Louis XIV's reign, the royal court at Versailles numbered as many as five thousand people, of whom only a few hundred or even a few dozen, were influential at any given moment. The court had no institutionalized power but, because it surrounded the king and his ministers who exercised power, the court became a pressure group with an impact on decision-making. The duc de Saint-Simon compared its operation to a game of billiards, which was a popular court entertainment. He noted in his memoirs that he sought for his own reasons to arrange the marriage of Mademoiselle, the king's great-niece, to her first cousin, the duc de Berry, the king's grandson, through the influence of Père Le Tellier, who was the king's Jesuit confessor, and a number of court ladies. They convinced the king to agree to the marriage. Saint Simon compared the manoeuvre to a game of billiards because the first ball moved the third ball through the action of the second ball, in this case the king's confessor, the Jesuits and the court ladies. It is both ironic and significant that the new duchesse de Berry was drunk in public only a few days after the marriage, led a dissolute life, and disappointed all hopes that Saint Simon had placed in her. The operation of the court, like the outcome of a game of billiards, was unpredictable.[1]

The royal court has been compared to a large pyramid where individuals manoeuvred for position based on rank, title and fortune. The only variable was the king himself at the summit who could change the places of those beneath him whom he favoured. Madame de Motteville, a lady-in-waiting to Anne of Austria, noted that '. . . the longing for favour is an indivisible chain which attaches everyone to the king . . . and few ever willingly detach themselves'. Madame de La Fayette remarked that 'the court gravitated around ambition. Nobody was tranquil or indifferent – everyone was busily trying to better their position by pleasing, helping or hindering someone else.' Anticourt pamphlets compared the royal court to a marketplace, and condemned the frenzied search for place and patronage by greedy, ambitious courtiers. A flood of manuals on how to behave at court were really guides on how to succeed, and were widely read by nobles seeking royal favour.[2]

As a national meeting place for the nobility, and for the king and the nobility, the royal court was a vast stage where everyone was on display.

Going to court was socially prestigious, and nobles went to court to see and be seen. Dramatic self-presentation was a form of self-marketing that could help to secure the patronage needed for advancement. The competition for advancement was probably most intense at the court of Louis XIV. Cardinal Mazarin on his deathbed had advised the young king to distribute patronage himself, so the nobility would look to him for favours, a policy that would strengthen the monarchy, and Louis had taken his advice, maintaining a close control himself over the distribution of royal patronage. The king demanded obedient service from his courtiers, but he rewarded them generously.[3]

Royal palaces were more accessible to the public in the seventeenth century than the presidential palace of the Elysée is today. All that was required was for ladies to be in court dress with an escort, and for gentlemen to be wearing a sword, the symbol of noble rank. The porter would hire out swords to those who had 'forgotten' their own. If properly dressed, the guard at the gate would let you pass without a second glance, and once through the gate, you could stroll at will through the grounds and main rooms without any kind of supervision, which explains the throngs of sightseers who filled the royal palaces, quite apart from the hordes of tradesmen, workmen and servants who were everywhere. There were always people loitering in the corridors, on staircases and behind pillars. It was easy to see the king, harder to speak to him and even harder to secure his attention.

For a noble new to the court, the best way to attract the king's attention was to be stationed by a well-known courtier where the king was likely to pass, and then hand him a petition or even speak to him. A group of citizens of Angers had decided to establish an Academy of Arts and Letters in 1685, only to discover that they needed royal letters of authorization. They asked Monsieur Grandet, the mayor of Angers, to go to Versailles to present a petition to the king requesting the letters. The governor of Anjou would ordinarily have been the courtier to ask for help, but he was Louis de Lorraine, comte d'Armagnac, who was known for his reluctance to make appeals to the king. Fortunately, Grandet was acquainted with one of Louis XIV's gentlemen-in-waiting, Chevais du Boullay, who agreed to station him near the royal table at dinner. The king ate alone before his standing courtiers. Grandet, a new face at court, could easily be seen in the crowd because he was a tall, good-looking man, and Louis asked who he was. Making inquiries, the comte d'Armagnac agreed to present him to the king after dinner the next day. The king granted him a private audience, and authorized the letters he needed. Grandet would never have succeeded so quickly without the help of Chevais du Boullay and the comte d'Armagnac.[4] Many petitioners had to spend months at court.

Daniel Chamier, a Protestant minister from the Dauphiné, went to the court at Fontainebleau in November 1607, to obtain royal letters authorizing a Protestant college at Montélimar of which he was to be rector. He hung about the corridors of the château, hoping to meet Henri IV in a chance encounter, and joined the throng of courtiers watching the king dine. He followed the royal hunting party through the forest of Fontainebleau, and trailed along behind the king in his walks through the gardens. Finally, he gave up and asked the Protestant noblemen at court for help. The duc de Bouillon arranged an interview for him with the king and, after five costly months at court, he received the letters of authorization he needed in March 1608.[5]

Nicolas de Beauvais-Nangis went to court for the first time in 1599, in search of high office in the king's household or the royal army, which he expected to receive because his father knew the king personally. He returned home after only a few weeks, but he went to court again in 1600 and in 1601. He wrote in his memoirs that Henri IV, who had been friendly at first, soon cooled and became distant; kings had to endure the endless importunings of their courtiers. Ignored, Nicolas left court again. He wrote that he disdained associating with lesser nobles like himself, and wanted to be among the great nobility, but despaired of ever having the opportunity to do so because of 'not being well dressed, nor having the means to be free and easy with money, nor being able to offer open-handed hospitality as they did'.[6] Money was needed to cut a good figure at court, and the Beauvais-Nangis fortune was modest.

Personal magnificence was considered a visual expression of rank and status, and great nobles from wealthy, illustrious old families were expected to live extravagantly. High rank required personal grandeur, a large household and lavish hospitality, and great nobles lost prestige when they did not live in this manner. A duke who did not live as a duke should live was not really a duke. The *grands*, great court nobles, were at the top of the noble hierarchy, and were usually titled (duke, count, viscount, baron). They were followed by sword nobles, sometimes titled, whose families had medieval origins but smaller fortunes, and untitled provincial sword nobles from less distinguished, less wealthy families who have been called 'the second nobility.'[7] Then came robe nobles whose families had been ennobled by officeholding within the last century, and at the bottom of the hierarchy were newly ennobled gentlemen, and self-proclaimed nobles, who were not really nobles at all.

Nicolas's father was able to secure him a minor office in the king's household for a salary of 1,200 livres, but this was not enough to allow him to live at court. Life at court was expensive. A noble at Henri III's court, living modestly, could manage on 2,000 livres a year. But, if he wanted horses, servants and to live in style, he needed an income of at least 10,000 livres a year and, if he wanted to live sumptuously in great style, he needed more than 100,000 livres.[8] In order to remain at court, Nicolas needed a royal pension to supplement his household salary and meagre income. His father worried that he lacked the temperament to succeed at court because he was neither patient nor obsequious. Nicolas himself admitted that his unwilling-ness to fawn and toady, and his ineptness at intrigue, hindered his advance-ment. He did not really like the royal court. Many provincial nobles disliked the corruption, licentiousness and extravagance of court life. Roger de Rabutin, comte de Bussy, was both bored and depressed by its frivolous pastimes. He seldom went, and was not promoted because he lacked the court patronage necessary for a successful army career.[9]

Nicolas went to court five times in as many years before he solved the problem of how to attract the king's attention. He cultivated men whom Henri IV liked, including the ducs de Bouillon and Montbazon who were the king's friends, and the baron de Vitry who was his guard captain. Nicolas was bathing with Vitry in the Seine across from the Arsenal one day when Henri went by in a boat. Someone in the boat pointed him out, and the duc de Montbazon mentioned his need for a pension. The king said that he should speak to him about it. Nicolas scurried that evening to find a place in the front row of courtiers surrounding the king, who spoke to him during dinner because a royal favourite, the duc de Bouillon, put in a good word. When the king withdrew to his private apartments after dinner to play tarot, he gave Nicolas a candle to hold so he could see the cards. Someone brought him a letter from one of his mistresses, and he told Nicolas to bring the candle closer so he could read it. Nicolas discreetly turned his head away in order not to read over his shoulder, a tactful gesture that pleased the king, who gave him an annual pension of 1,000 écus (3,000 livres), so he could remain at court.[10]

Noble honour required serving the king by fighting for him and attending his court, but going to court could also be profitable. Etienne d'Hozier, a Provençal gentleman who was captain of the town of Salon, made nineteen trips to court between 1572 and 1607 as a provincial deputy. He made useful connections while there, and found places for his brother in the royal guards and his son in the king's household, which Nicolas de Beauvais-Nangis had been trying to do. The king, among all the great noble patrons in France, was the most profitable to serve, and ambitious nobles, like Nicolas, were obsessed by the thought of attending court to seek advancement through royal favour.[11] So, what type of institution was the royal court, and how influential was it?

THE ROYAL COURT

The centre of court life was the king's household, surrounded by the separate households of the royal family. Nobles came to court to serve in these royal households, which increased steadily in size. François I's household in 1523 had 540 members, while Henri IV's had grown to about 1,500 in 1595. Louis XIV's household was 1,864 in 1651, and about 4,000 by 1657. Marie de Médicis's household had 464 members in 1606 and, when Anne of Austria married Louis XIII in 1615, she brought with her a household of 250. The household of Gaston, duc d'Orléans, Louis XIII's brother, numbered about 400 in 1648; that of Philippe, duc d'Orléans, Louis XIV's brother, nearly 500 in 1663, and over 1,000 in 1669; his wife's numbered more than 200. Nobles sought places for their children in royal households as a way of educating and socializing them, and providing opportunities for them to make useful connections. Household offices were venal, but the king could make a gift of the purchase price. Household members did not serve continuously; most served three or six months out of twelve in a rotation system that doubled the number of nobles attending court. They were a large number: Henri III's court in the late sixteenth century had 8,000 members, while Louis XIV's a century later had over 10,000 members, about half of whom were noble.[12]

Great court nobles filled the higher household offices, lesser-ranked nobles the lower offices and a horde of non-nobles the menial positions. Beyond this permanent core was a vast, amorphous mass of visitors temporarily at court. Great nobles resided at court after 1660, but their numbers were comparatively small. They filled about 250 high offices in the king's household, and were fewer in the other royal households, perhaps a total of 300. The more numerous lesser nobles serving in the lower household offices resided at court temporarily, coming and going because of the rotation system. There were perhaps 200,000 nobles in France during Louis XIV's reign, about 1 per cent of the population, and at any given moment about 5,000 of them were at court, although the rotation system would have doubled this number. During Henri III's reign, the percentage of nobles regularly at court, or belonging to families in which someone was employed at court, ranged from a low of 2.19 to a high of 12.09 per cent among the nobility of the nine different regions studied, averaging 7.25 per cent. In the late sixteenth century, therefore, between 7 and 8 per cent of the French nobility went to court regularly. A century later, about 70 families of the Provençal nobility, or 15 per cent of that province's 500 noble families, went to court either regularly or at least occasionally. In 1698, 15 of 95 families of the high Breton nobility, or approximately 15 per cent, went to court at least occasionally. The actual percentage of nobles attending court would have been smaller than 15 per cent, however, because only adult males usually went; women, children and the elderly did not often go. So, perhaps 10 per cent of the 200,000 nobles in France went to court either regularly or occasionally during the late seventeenth century.[13] The overall number of nobles going to court, therefore, was small. Most provincial nobles seldom if ever went.

For centuries, the royal courts had moved from place to place. Henri IV's court was an armed camp that only settled down after he was securely on the throne. Louis XIII's court moved frequently during wartime; otherwise, he spent much of his time at his hunting lodge of Versailles. The royal court from 1600 through the mid-1660s usually spent the winter at the Louvre in Paris, visiting nearby Fontainebleau, Saint Germain, Chantilly and Versailles during the summer. But after the death of his mother in 1666, Louis XIV spent more and more time at Versailles, which he enlarged into an impressive royal palace. On 6 May 1682, he moved there permanently with his increasingly formal, elaborate and sophisticated court.[14]

Characterized by carefully planned spectacles in which Louis endlessly recreated himself as king, his court became a cultural trend-setter and an arbiter of noble styles, tastes and manners to a greater extent than any previous royal court. Louis XIV was a generous patron of the arts, and his courtiers became influential consumers and patrons of elite culture.[15] By setting standards of taste and behaviour, they helped to shape noble values and attitudes. Court noblewomen, for instance, exerted a civilizing influence far beyond their numbers. Always in the minority, perhaps 20 to 25 per cent of those in attendance, they transformed court life by making it more courteous and less immoral, and they demanded refined behaviour from those whom they advanced.[16]

Although only 10 per cent of the nobility may have gone to court, the ripple effect spread the court's influence to a much larger number. The high-ranking, prestigious nobles who attended court regularly were imitated. Trend-setters in their own provinces, they became conduits of court styles and manners, and the novelties they brought back from the court were eagerly copied by nobles who wanted to be fashionable. Provençal noble society provides examples of this diffusion of court culture. Madame de Venel, the governess of Mazarin's nieces, lived at court, but returned home to Aix from time to time to see her husband. On one of these occasions, she redecorated their town house in the new court style of white and gold, which was widely imitated. The Cardinal had given her a monopoly on icehouses in Provence worth 20,000 livres a year. The use of ice was an Italian refinement that was introduced at court around 1650, and quickly became popular.

Court entertainments were much imitated. Raffles were introduced from Italy at about this time, and became a favourite court amusement. At a dinner Cardinal Mazarin gave for the royal family, the guests drew slips of paper on which the name of an object appeared; on this occasion, there were no blank slips. The prizes included crystal candlesticks, mirrors, small tables, perfumes, gloves, scarves, ribbons, fans and several diamonds. Madame de Sévigné's daughter, newly arrived from court, began to hold raffles at Aix, and a short time later the salons of nearby Beaucaire were holding raffles, which then appeared everywhere in Provence. The comtesse de Rochefort reported with glee that she had won a pair of gloves and six panels of lace. Another favourite court pastime, especially among the ladies, was gambling at cards for high stakes. Soon, a gambling craze had swept France, and Provençal ladies were making social calls carrying packs of cards.

The lavish receptions of courtiers were also widely imitated. During the 1630s, the Parisian guests of Léonard Goulas had arrived to the sound of music, and then watched a comedy in the *grande salle*. Afterwards, there was a supper with meat and fruit dishes, and then they returned to the grande salle for a ball. When the night was well advanced, the doors were thrown open at the end of the ballroom, and everyone entered a brilliantly lit room, blazing with candles in crystal chandeliers and silver wall sconces, for a repast of sweets and desserts. This event sounds exactly like the soirée that the intendant of the royal galleys gave as a housewarming party at his new Marseille mansion in 1687. Louis XIV's renovation project at Versailles inspired numerous provincial imitations, and the building arts flourished in Provence with significant construction at Marseille, Aix, Toulon, Avignon and Tarascon during the late seventeenth century.[17] Court culture was influential. What role did the court play in transforming the traditional social role and identity of the nobility? What other forces besides the court were responsible for this transformation in the lives of French nobles?

THE COURT, THE KING AND THE NOBILITY

Norbert Elias has argued that a civilizing process of 'courtization' turned the French nobility from warriors into courtiers during Louis XIV's reign. The king adopted an elaborate code of manners at court to tame the nobility by forcing them to pay him exaggerated respect, deference and obedience, and the nobility internalized this rigid courtesy code. The king controlled the court, which formed and shaped noble culture, and the manners and tastes of the court nobility influenced those of the provincial nobility.[18] It has been suggested that 'courtization' may have begun at Louis XIII's court. If so, it only became fully developed at his son's court because Louis XIII's court was notorious for its disorganization, crudeness and informality. It has also been suggested that the new civility may have originated in the urban culture of Louis XIII's cities rather than at his court.[19]

Maurice Magendie has argued that a new code of honour regulating noble conduct appeared at the court of Louis XIV after 1661. The new civility emphasized courtesy and sociability. Honour (*honnêteté*) now became politeness, good taste and social adaptability, while an honourable gentleman (*honnête homme*) became someone who knew and observed the social conventions; he was well-mannered, discrete, charming, well-spoken and adaptable. This new civility originated in the Parisian salons presided over by noble hostesses who insisted upon witty, intelligent conversation and good manners, and from there spread to the royal court.[20] The increased elegance and splendour of Louis XIV's court encouraged the adoption of this more easygoing approach to life, and nobles everywhere were soon practising the new civility. As a result, their behaviour became less crude and violent. When the new civility was adopted as a code of conduct by the rest of society, the result was greater peace and stability for France.[21]

This interpretation has been challenged, however. The royal court's influence as a force for social change has been questioned. Ellery Schalk has pointed out that there was a significant social and cultural gap between the court and the provincial nobility, and that this gap became wider as time went on.[22] Schalk insists that the court had little or no influence on noble behaviour during the late sixteenth and early seventeenth centuries. Dominated by Italian culture, the royal courts of Henri III and Henri IV became intellectual islands remote from the provincial nobility, whose interests were primarily military. The significant transformation in noble manners began in the 1590s, well before Louis XIV's personal reign, and it occurred independently of the royal court. This transformation was a result of the separation of the military profession from noble rank; a growing noble interest in education and culture; and a greater emphasis upon birth as the only determinant of rank.[23]

How influential, in fact, was court culture of the late sixteenth and early seventeenth centuries? The answer depends on when chivalry ceased to be influential, and on whether the Italian culture of the royal courts had an alienating effect on the nobility. Schalk has argued that a decline in the influence of chivalry, plus a remote royal court, made possible a transformation of noble behaviour beginning in the late sixteenth century.[24] It has been suggested, however, that the influence of chivalry may only have lessened after 1661, and that significant changes in noble behaviour may only have occurred afterward during the personal reign of Louis XIV.[25] Which view is correct?

Anti-court pamphlets provide the evidence for Schalk's interpretation, but how accurately do pamphlets reflect the reality of social change? Literary texts do not always provide an accurate record of social and cultural change. Court noblewomen, for example, are seldom mentioned in the pamphlets and never positively, but their civilizing influence has been widely recognized. Most sixteenth-century nobles were illiterate or quasi-literate and, if their interests were primarily military, then how accurately would pamphlets reflect changes in their attitudes? These texts and their authors would seem to represent the views of an educated minority rather than a majority. Not all nobles were soldiers; in fact, only a small percentage pursued regular army careers during the sixteenth century. Most served in the irregularly summoned provincial militia, and many never went to war at all. There has been, moreover, considerable disagreement among historians about the nature of the differences, if any, between court and provincial nobles. Finally, Italian influence in France was not limited to the royal court, but was strong throughout southern France, especially in the Rhône river valley including Provence, the Comtat, Languedoc and the cities of Lyon, Avignon and Marseille, which had large Italian populations. There were famous French noble families of Italian origin by the seventeenth century. The isolation of an Italianate royal court has perhaps been exaggerated.[26]

Schalk has quite rightly challenged Elias's insistence on the royal court's use as an instrument to control the nobility. Widely regarded as oversimplified, Elias's interpretation exaggerates the court's influence, and ignores other important forces affecting the nobility. The court's use as an instrument of control rests on the assumption that there was a fundamental opposition between the king and the nobility, which has been challenged in recent years. The nobility may also have cooperated with the crown for reasons other than the new courtesy code.[27] They may have cooperated in the hope of securing advancement.

The distribution of patronage was a rationale everywhere in Europe for the existence of royal courts. Newly arrived nobles in search of patronage quickly adopted court manners, dress and speech to avoid appearing ridiculous, and to escape provoking snobbish laughter. Looking and sounding like a country bumpkin did not attract patrons. Voluntarily altering their appearance and manners to conform to those of the court, nobles changed their attitudes and values as well, especially if they stayed at court for a while. The steadily increasing noble traffic to and from the royal court spread the courtly ethic into the provinces. Nobles were not coerced into obedience by having to obey a rigid courtesy code at court, but rather they cooperated voluntarily, adopting court mores and manners in order to advance. This was the case at Henri III's court in the late sixteenth century, and at Louis XIV's court a century later. Historians have overlooked the implications of the court's function as a marketplace. The distribution of patronage at court was a significant factor influencing noble behaviour.[28]

Historians agree that the behaviour of nobles during Louis XIV's reign became more courteous and less violent, but they disagree on the court's role in causing this change. Did court nobles adopt the new code of manners voluntarily or involuntarily? Was the new civility responsible for the decline in noble violence, or were there other more important causes? Did the new civility develop at the royal court and, if so, at whose court? Did it develop instead in Parisian and provincial salons as part of the new urban culture? Historians do not agree on the answers. What other forces besides the royal court were responsible for transforming the social role and identity of the nobility during the seventeenth century?

THE CHANGING ROLE OF THE NOBILITY

A flood of newcomers helped to transform the nobility's traditional role and image. The high rate of ennoblement was caused by an increase in the size and wealth of urban elites, and by the development of the early modern state. Wealthy urban elites claimed noble rank because they could afford to live a noble lifestyle, while new robe nobles filled the ranks of an expanding royal bureaucracy. This influx of non-nobles began to change the nobility's social and self-identity. In response, old sword nobles insisted upon birth as the only determinant of rank, and demanded public recognition of their rights and privileges. Traditional noble solidarities of honour, rank, royal service, clientage and seigneury (land and its ties) changed, and new noble solidarities of career and sociability appeared.

Nicolas's father, Antoine de Brichanteau, first marquis de Beauvais-Nangis, came from a prestigious old family of the Brie sword nobility. He had fought for the crown during the religious wars, accompanied Henri III to Poland, and was rewarded in 1575 with a captaincy in the royal guards. Later, as a reward for his loyalty to Henri IV, his seigneury of Nangis was elevated to a marquisate. Nicolas, to his sorrow, was never as successful. He wrote in his memoirs that he could not afford to buy an office in the king's household, but he did secure the captaincy of a light horse company in the regiment of Champagne. His father was disappointed; he had hoped for a higher office for his oldest son. Nicolas wrote bitterly that money, favour and ambition were needed for success in a military career. He did not secure advancement in 1623 because of a lack of favour. Having rejoined Louis XIII and his court at Fontainebleau that year, he discovered that someone had vilified him in his absence, and that the king was not pleased to see him. So, he stayed only one day and went home for the rest of the year. Nicolas's memoirs are full of similar excuses for his failure to advance as far as he thought he should. Proud of his family's military record, he was disappointed by his own lack of achievement. Nobles put ambition first, and sought advancement through royal service, which was often military, at least until mid-century. They pursued military careers from ambition, honour and a desire for *gloire*, or martial glory. The search for glory, fame and renown based upon great military exploits, was a goal of noble life, despite the fact that most nobles lived quietly in the country and never went to war.[29]

Henri de Campion's memoirs recount the highlights of his military career, which began in 1634 when he entered the service of Gaston, duc d'Orléans. An ambitious younger son from an impoverished old Norman noble family,

Campion soon left the duke's service to join the regiment of Normandy, which was fighting on the northern frontier under the command of the provincial governor, the duc de Longueville. Later he left the royal army to enter the service of François de Vendôme, duc de Beaufort, and became involved, reluctantly, in his plot to assassinate Cardinal Mazarin in 1643. When the plot was discovered, Campion had to go briefly into exile, and then he entered the service of Beaufort's father, César, duc de Vendôme, who did not reward him as he had expected. So, he returned to the Normandy regiment where he was promoted to lieutenant-colonel, and he remained there until he retired.[30]

Henri de Campion had become the client of a great noble in revolt against the king, and had served his patron loyally without regarding this behaviour as treasonous or dishonourable. Campion was able to separate his service to a patron from his loyalty and obedience as a royal subject because of the contemporary failure to distinguish between private and public. Clientage was a personal, private relationship. It was a bond of reciprocal, if unspecified, obligations between unequals cloaked in a language of courtesy emphasizing loyalty, honour, affection, service, generosity, respect and gratitude. Participants viewed, or at least described, their motives and actions in these terms, even if the reality was different. So, Campion considered his loyal service to a patron as private behaviour that was separate from his public obedience to the king, and thus honourable.[31] Army command provided officers such as Henri de Campion with the patronage to reward clients, and clientage was as prevalent in the army as it was at the royal court.[32]

During Louis XIV's reign, competent, professional soldiering became nearly as important as birth, wealth and connections in securing promotions. A new professionalism emerged that emphasized training, skill, experience, discipline and obedience. The changing technology, expanding scale and increasing bureaucratization of armies transformed the nature of military service. Nobles now began to pursue permanent careers in hierarchical, bureaucratized royal armies, and their letters home were filled with talk of supplies, equipment and troop movements. They wrote less about glory, honour and personal ambition, although they still hoped to serve under a colonel with enough influence at Versailles to get them promoted. Connections at the royal court, either to the king, his family or to great court nobles, were the most important factor in a successful military career. The crown asserted a monopoly on public violence during Louis XIV's reign, restricting warfare to royal military campaigns. Nobles no longer fought independently of the state, while the new professionalism lessened the brutality of noble officers toward their subordinates. Duelling was banned and, although it continued illicitly, its frequency lessened. The officer corps of the royal armies was staffed mostly by nobles, but they no longer had a monopoly on soldiering, and they no longer served in the private armies of great nobles as Henri de Campion had done.[33]

The royal service of Claude Bazin, sieur de Bezons, illustrates the emergence of new professional standards in administration. Claude's grandfather had been bourgeois, a doctor on the faculty of medicine at the University of Paris, and the family had been recently ennobled by royal letters. Claude's government career included intendancies in Soisson (1646–8), Catalonia (1648–9), Bourges (1650–1) and Languedoc (1653–73). The intendants were essential cogs in the machinery of the new royal bureaucracy. A protégé of Michel Le Tellier, who was the minister for war, Claude Bazin de Bezons was a veteran army intendant, that is, he was a bureaucrat, not a soldier. Named provincial intendant in Languedoc in 1653, he requested a transfer after seven years. Le Tellier approached Cardinal Mazarin on his behalf, but was refused. Le Tellier wrote to Claude that '. . . because you are more useful for the king's service in Languedoc, he [the Cardinal] had decided that he could not produce it for you'. Mazarin had refused, not from a lack of favour, but in the best interests of the royal service because Claude's competence and efficiency were needed where he was.[34] This was a new, more professional approach to administration. Careers in the royal army, navy and bureaucracy created a new professionalism and new career loyalties among nobles.

Nicolas de Beauvais-Nangis and Henri de Campion belonged to medieval families of the sword nobility. In contrast, Claude Bazin de Bezons came from a recently ennobled family of Parisian administrators. Claude was a robe noble, so-named for the robes worn as a symbol of royal officeholding. Many royal offices ennobled, and most robe families had been ennobled within the previous century. The robe nobility emerged as a significant social group during the seventeenth century. Robe nobles were literate, educated their children and staffed the expanding royal bureaucracy. Their numbers grew rapidly until at least the mid-seventeenth century.[35]

Noble rank had been traditionally regarded as hereditary, that is, based on birth, medieval in origin and inseparable from soldiering. Sword noble families of medieval origin such as the Beauvais-Nangis and Campion had produced soldiers for generations. This understanding of nobility changed, however, when increasingly noble rank had been recently acquired through letters of ennoblement, officeholding, marriage, purchasing fiefs or titles and living nobly, that is, simply assuming noble rank by living a noble lifestyle, which required wealth. Financiers and other monied men moved easily into the nobility because they could afford to live the same lifestyle. The assumption of noble rank by members of the wealthy urban elites became so frequent that Louis XIV ordered a national investigation lasting from 1666 to 1674. Those claiming noble rank had to present documentary proof to royal investigators or cease claiming it. What nobility meant became even more confusing when the army was full of non-nobles who sometimes became officers. Eventually, a royal edict in 1750 made military service as an officer ennobling without royal letters, and it became a means of social mobility.[36]

After the mid-seventeenth century, there was a gradual slowing in the rate of entry into the nobility. Because ennobling royal offices were hereditary, fewer of them came on to the market, and entry into the robe nobility began to close, while the number of ennobling municipal offices declined. Louis XIV's inquiry into false nobles invalidated the claims of some individuals who had assumed noble rank by living nobly, and the king issued fewer royal letters of ennoblement. The result was a decline in the rate of ennoblement in the late seventeenth century, although the extent and permanence of this decline is debated by historians.[37] The underlying problem was that noble families tended to die out, sometimes after only a few generations, and had to be replaced by new blood for the nobility to survive. The Beauvais-Nangis, for example, became extinct in the early eighteenth century. Although historians disagree on whether the nobility actually declined in size as a social group, they agree that there were fewer and fewer noble families of medieval origins, and that the growing intermarriage between sword and robe blurred the distinctions between them.[38] This confusion about the meaning of noble rank made changes in noble behaviour easier.

Sword nobles considered the influx of non-nobles threatening because they feared debasement of their rank. They insisted upon birth as the only determinant of rank, and demanded public reinforcement of their traditional rights and privileges. They were afraid that monied upstarts would turn the social hierarchy on its head, and debase noble status, privileges and power, a view expressed by Fénélon, Saint-Simon and Boulainvilliers among others. Financiers were routinely depicted as self-made men of lowly origins, although most were ennobled and came from the urban elites or royal administrative families.[39] The widespread adoption of the new civility, and the increasing importance of competence and merit in army promotions, did nothing to allay noble fears of debasement. Noble protests became loudest during the last decades of Louis XIV's reign when the danger had lessened and the rate of entry was slowing.

Molière's comedy, *Le Bourgeois Gentilhomme* (1670), satirized the social pretensions of monied upstarts. A middle-aged, would-be gentleman, Monsieur Jourdain, who is newly rich, hires tutors to teach him how to dress and behave like a noble, and they gleefully make a fool of him. His tailor dresses him in skintight red velvet breeches, a navy coat with flowers, a plumed hat, a big, curly wig and shoes so tight he limps. His dancing master teaches him how to bow by having him walk backward with a skip and a hop to bow, then forward slowly to bow three more times, the third time to knee level. By this time his tutors are guffawing, his maid is laughing so hard she is bent over and his giggling wife tells him that he has become a joke, although he will not listen. The play was one of Molière's most successful comedies.[40]

The roots of the so-called 'seigneurial reaction', which occurred during the eighteenth century, reached back into the last decades of Louis XIV's reign. Seigneurs or big landowners insisted on a stricter enforcement of their dues and rights, for instance, forest, water and judicial rights. Rents had fallen off and they were seeking to maximize their revenues by collecting all that was due them. The reduction in seigneurial revenues caused by the demographic crisis and heavy royal taxation may have been more severe in the north than in the south. During the eighteenth century, landowners went even further, and began to rediscover and enforce seigneurial dues that had been allowed to lapse or had never been strictly enforced. Their eagerness to impose long-forgotten dues worsened their relations with the peasantry.[41]

A gradual weakening in traditional noble ties now occurred. Large noble households began to shrink in size during the late seventeenth century, and nobles disappeared from household service, which was increasingly regarded as subservient.[42] High-ranked nobles, who were often at court, no longer spent much time in the provinces, and their absence weakened their patron–client ties to lesser provincial nobles whom they no longer saw or knew. Personal bonds between the greater and lesser nobility also changed because the economic conditions linking them had changed. Great nobles had become more dependent on royal patronage distributed at court, and as landowners they were no longer willing for practical reasons to give material benefits to lesser provincial nobles in exchange for service. Because loyal service to great noble patrons no longer carried as much hope of profit, provincial nobles were more reluctant to serve them as clients. Although both were still interested in maximizing their feudal revenues, the economic interests of the greater and lesser nobility had diverged.[43] Landlord absenteeism gradually loosened seigneurial ties. Nobles living in town became strangers to their peasant tenant farmers, and the personal bonds between them became attenuated. The 'seigneurial reaction' worsened the situation by making their relationship more adversarial.[44] Weaker clientage and seigneurial ties made it more difficult for great nobles to field private armies, a significant social and political change.

Increasingly, the differences between nobles were determined by their levels of education and culture. Noble literacy increased during the seventeenth century, although as a group nobles were never known for their intellectualism. Sword nobles always regarded the more literate robe as *arriviste*. The manners, dress and speech of nobles, as well as their cultural interests and skill at conversation, were influenced by the extent of their schooling, and whether they spent part of the year in town. Noble attendance at salons, academies and theatres in nearby towns created new interests and ties of sociability.[45] Over twenty groups of writers, their friends and patrons, including many nobles, met in Paris during the early seventeenth century. They ranged from the well-established Dupuy circle and Mersenne's academy to smaller, more ephemeral groups. Besides the celebrated salon of Madame de Rambouillet, there were nearly a dozen other salons meeting regularly to discuss literature and language. Some had a reputation for erudition, others for frivolity; some were full of robe nobles; others included financiers and newly ennobled gentlemen. Provincial literary circles, salons and academies attended by nobles flourished, too.[46] The new civility increased noble sociability, while noble activities, interests and self-identity were no longer limited to soldiering. This change contributed to the decline in noble brutality and violence.

Henri de Campion was a third son without money of his own. He used his winnings from gambling at cards and trictrac (backgammon) to pay his expenses, although he was not as lucky at dice. He wrote in his memoirs that the money he lost at dice slowed his promotion within his regiment because he could not afford to spend winters at court in order to acquire the patronage needed for advancement. Nicolas de Beauvais-Nangis was obsessed by his own lack of money, which he mentioned constantly in his memoirs. He wrote that during the winter of 1611/12, he participated in numerous tournaments, tilting matches and competitions at court for which the clothes and equipment had cost him 2,500 écus. He could ill afford this because his pension, although recently increased, only came to 1,200 écus a year. He wanted to accompany the duc de Mayenne to Spain to arrange the marriage of the king's sister, but could not afford the journey. He did not buy an office of camp marshal because the cost would have ruined his family.[47]

Seventeenth-century nobles were always bemoaning their lack of money. An earlier generation of historians took them at their word, believing that there had been a significant reduction in noble revenues during the sixteenth century. This 'crisis in seigneurial revenues' supposedly created a large group of impoverished nobles with serious economic problems, an interpretation compatible with that of a 'seigneurial reaction'.[48] Revisionist historians, however, have challenged the notion of a nobility in economic decline. They emphasize the flexibility, adaptability and economic viability, even prosperity, of seventeenth-century nobles, who efficiently managed their lands or had someone do it for them, expanded their landholdings whenever possible and refused to allow their estates to become fragmented by inheritance. By the eighteenth century, nobles, too, were producing for a market economy. Family fortunes were prudently managed, and enlarged by financial and commercial wealth from carefully arranged marriages. Town nobles invested in trade, manufacturing, urban development, the colonies, government bonds, tax-collecting and banking, although not always in their own names. Nobles everywhere enjoyed a modest prosperity and many thrived. Although some were in straitened circumstances, they were in the minority.[49] This revisionist interpretation has been widely accepted by English-speaking historians. It has been challenged, however, in the case of Brittany. In this province, the higher-ranked nobility may have been more adaptable and prosperous than the lesser-ranked nobility.[50] Was this the case in other provinces, too, or was it typical only of Brittany?

Seventeenth-century nobles successfully adjusted to significant changes in their traditional social role and identity. They absorbed and assimilated a large number of non-nobles, whose resources they used to rejuvenate their own, and thus accepted in private what they refused to admit in public – that noble rank could be acquired by a variety of means, and was no longer the result of birth, medieval in origin or military in function. Noble service to the king now included serving in his government as well as fighting for him and attending his court. Nobles demonstrated a new professionalism in their military and administrative careers, adding competence and efficiency to their traditional values of ambition, honour and martial glory, and they developed new career ties and loyalties. The noble literacy rate rose, and the growing urban residence of nobles encouraged new cultural interests and ties of sociability. Nobles were becoming more courteous and cultured, less bellicose and violent, and the long-term result of their new civility was greater peace and stability for France. By undergoing a significant change in their traditional role and identity, the nobility played a pioneering role in setting new standards of behaviour for their society.

Suggested reading

Joseph Bergin, *Cardinal Richelieu. Power and the Pursuit of Wealth* (New Haven, 1985).

Jonathan Dewald, *Aristocratic Experience and the Origins of Modern Culture* (Berkeley, 1993); idem, *Pont-St-Pierre, 1398–1789* (Berkeley, 1987); idem, *The European Nobility* (Cambridge, 1996).

Norbert Elias, *The Court Society*, tr. Edmund Jephcott (New York, 1983); idem, *The Civilizing Process*, vol. 1, *The History of Manners*, tr. Edmund Jephcott (New York, 1978), vol. 2, *Power and Civility*, tr. Edmund Jephcott (New York, 1982).

Robert Forster, *The House of Saulx-Tavanes* (Baltimore, 1971); idem, *The Nobility of Toulouse in the Eighteenth Century* (Baltimore, 1960).

Robert Harding, *Anatomy of a Power Elite. The Provincial Governors of Early Modern France* (New Haven, 1978).

Emmanuel Le Roy Ladurie, 'Versailles Observed: The Court of Louis XIV in 1709', *The Mind and Method of the Historian*, tr. Siân and Ben Reynolds (Chicago, 1981), pp. 149–73; idem, 'In Normandy's Woods and Fields', *The Territory of the Historian*, tr. Ben and Siân Reynolds (Chicago, 1979), pp. 133–71.

Mark Motley, *Becoming a French Aristocrat. The Education of the Court Nobility, 1580–1715* (Princeton, 1990).

Orest Ranum, 'Courtesy, Absolutism, and the Rise of the French State, 1630–1660', *Journal of Modern History* 52 (1980), 426–51.

Jacques Revel, 'The Uses of Civility', *A History of Private Life*, vol. 3, *Passions of the Renaissance*, ed. Roger Chartier, tr. Arthur Goldhammer (Cambridge, Mass., 1989), pp. 167–202.

Ellery Schalk, *From Valor to Pedigree. Ideas of Nobility in France in the Sixteenth and Seventeenth Centuries* (Princeton, 1986); idem, 'The Court as "Civilizer" of the Nobility', *Princes, Patronage, and the Nobility. The Court at the Beginning of the Modern Age*, eds Ronald Asch and Adolf Birke (Oxford, 1991), pp. 245–63.

CHAPTER 6

THE EARLY MODERN STATE

The king's ministers were notorious for their rudeness to provincial deputies. The Provençal Estates sent Léon de Trimond to Brignoles in May 1630 to present a petition to the king requesting that he lower taxes. Trimond and his fellow deputies were admitted at noon to the bishop's palace where Louis XIII, who was returning from military campaign in Italy, was dining with Cardinal Richelieu and several other ministers. The deputies removed their swords and knelt while one of them read their petition. The minister of finance, the marquis d'Effiat, made faces and whistled throughout their presentation and, when they had finished, the king said curtly that he had listened to their demands, now they were to leave. Richelieu snapped, 'Get up and go!' They were told they had 24 hours to leave the city.[1]

Deputies from the Parlement of Rouen had just begun their presentation in November 1641, when Chancellor Séguier rudely interrupted them to announce loudly that he could tell them nothing, and that they should ask favours from the king. Then he walked out of the room and down the stairs, with the bewildered deputies trailing along behind. He never looked back, and the snubbed deputies returned to their Paris lodgings. When the Rouen parlementaires went to see Sublet de Noyers, secretary of state for Normandy, they did not even get a chance to speak. Noyers abruptly said, 'Messieurs, seeing you here I understand well what you want without you telling me. I am your servant, as I am to all men, and will do what I can for your happiness.' With that, he walked out the door and down the staircase. Following, they found themselves in the street![2]

Jacques de Parades de L'Estang, a consul of Arles who was sent as a deputy to court in 1662 to protest against royal taxation, had an experience that was just as humiliating. He and his fellow deputies had an interview with Brienne, secretary of state for Provence, who promised to arrange an audience for them with the king. They also had interviews with Colbert, minister of finance, and Le Tellier, minister of war. Then the Provençal intendant came to court. Suddenly, the deputies found that interviews with Brienne and Colbert were harder to obtain, and shorter and nastier when they did occur. Parades de L'Estang remarked that threats, rudeness and bad manners seemed natural to Colbert, whose coldness inspired Madame de Sévigné to call him

'Mr North', and Guy Patin 'the man of marble'. Colbert kept his pale features immobile, and maintained a strict silence during interviews. His staring, deep-set, dark eyes under thick eyebrows made his lack of response unnerving. When at last the Arles deputies saw the king, they were promptly dismissed and sent home. The Provençal intendant, who was responsible for collecting taxes, had discredited them before they ever saw the king.[3]

Jacques de Parades de L'Estang, whose noble family dated from the four-teenth century, was a member of the Arles city government for more than three decades.[4] Old sword noble families such as his claimed to have a monopoly on the office of first consul, but their claim was challenged by the newer nobility, who had been relegated to the office of second consul. Four elected consuls served as the executive branch of the Arles city government, and one hundred elected councillors as the legislative branch. Noble squab-bling over municipal officeholding became so intense that the provincial governor had to intervene twice to restore peace. There was trouble again in 1643 when the newly elected second consul refused to serve, saying that to do so would debase his rank. Jacques joined a delegation of old nobles sent to ask the governor to suppress the office of second consul, and noble resent-ment at Arles exploded into violence.

During Mardi Gras, on 8 February 1644, a group of young nobles in favour of suppression, Jacques among them, were eating and drinking in a tavern when someone produced the headgear of the second consul's office and stuck it on the end of a pole. Well in their cups, laughing and joking, the young men paraded the pole past the city hall, and through the streets until they reached the Rhône where they threw it into the water with loud jeers. Domin-ated by the newer nobility and outraged at such blatant public disrespect, the city council issued warrants for their arrest as rebels, started a judicial inquiry and called out the local militia to patrol the streets to prevent a recurrence.

Jacques de Parades de L'Estang, who was nowhere to be found when his arrest warrant was served, was walking past the city hall the next day when he met an elderly gentleman coming the other way. Mardi Gras was tradi-tionally an occasion for satire and ridicule, and Jacques was wearing a sword. So, as an insulting jest, he pulled out his sword and made several passes at the old man, who recoiled in fear. This was reported to councillors in the city hall, who threw open the doors and rushed out to the old man's rescue, led by the first consul waving a cane. The local militia came running into the square and, in the mêlée, Jacques was knocked to the ground and stabbed through the arm, although not seriously hurt. The first consul prevented further violence, and dispersed the crowd.

The provincial governor and intendant arrived a few days later to calm tempers. The governor insisted that the quarrelling factions reconcile by em-bracing publicly in front of the city hall, and refused to suppress the office of second consul. Ten days later, he issued an ordinance removing several city councillors from office and naming new consuls by royal letters, and in May he named all new city councillors. For years the governor and intendant had been working as a team to pack Provençal municipal governments with their own supporters to secure cooperation with royal tax demands. The noble squabbling at Arles had given them the pretext to do so yet again.[5]

What had happened at Arles in 1644 was commonplace in France during the seventeenth century. The crown recognized the traditional privilege of municipal elections, but frequently intervened to suspend elections and name its own hand-picked candidates to office in royal letters delivered by the provincial governor or intendant. Internal disputes weakened municipal resistance to royal intervention. The crown also changed election procedures, and altered the structure of municipal governments, to break the monopoly of uncooperative urban elites on officeholding. The crown sought greater control over municipal governments to lessen opposition to taxation, and everywhere urban elites in vain protested at royal encroachments on their power and privileges.[6]

This is the standard explanation for what happened at Arles, although there may be another interpretation. Jacques de Parades de L'Estang and his faction of sword nobles were seeking to convince the governor and intendant to sanction their control over the Arles city government. The sympathies of the governor, the comte d'Alais, a great court noble who was a grandson of Charles IX, were obvious. He forced the first consul to apologize to Jacques for the pike wound he had suffered at the hands of the local militia, while the intendant, François Bochart de Champigny, revoked the city council's arrest warrants and nullified its judicial inquiry into the events of 8 February. Jacques and his faction were seeking to use royal authority to their own advantage in municipal politics, and were willing to offer fiscal cooperation in exchange. With their encouragement, the consuls and city councillors reinstated the levy of an unpopular tax they had previously suspended. As a reward, the governor appointed Jacques consul by royal letters in 1645.[7]

This incident illustrates the complex, ambiguous nature of the nobility's relationship with the crown. Did the nobility cooperate with the crown and its provincial representatives, the governors and intendants, in governing, or did they live up to their traditional reputation for unruliness, disobedience and violence? Was Parades de L'Estang an irresponsible sword noble, who had harassed an elderly man as a silly prank and participated in drunken political high jinks, or did he help the governor secure obedience from an uncooperative city government? Was there a fundamental opposition between a coercive, controlling early modern state and the provincial nobility, whose privileges and powers it was eroding, or did the state offer sufficient rewards to secure the voluntary cooperation of nobles such as Parades de L'Estang and Trimond, who collaborated because it was in their best interests to do so?

THE TRADITIONAL INTERPRETATION

The early modern state, that is, the authority and power of the king and his government, were a basic force for social cohesion and unity. This chapter presents both sides in a current controversy over the coerciveness of the state in governing, which is significant because the use of force can be divisive. Was the early modern state dominating and controlling, or was it less intrusive, more flexible and willing to compromise with nobles and institutions? Historians are still debating the answer. The widely accepted view of a strong state has been challenged in recent years by revisionists, who insist the state's power has been exaggerated. The traditional and revisionist interpretations are presented here, with the suggestion that they are more compatible than they may seem at first glance. It is hoped this chapter will provide readers with some insight into how generally accepted historical interpretations are reached.

Roland Mousnier and his students,[8] and English-speaking historians,[9] have argued in favour of a strong state, and their view has been widely accepted. The central government at Paris expanded its authority and power at the expense of provincial institutions and elites who were coerced into obedience.[10] The state reached its apogee during Louis XIV's reign to become the first bureaucracy in Europe with the biggest army and the most lucrative tax revenues.[11] How did it become so large and powerful?

War, specifically its cost, was a major factor in its development.[12] The constant warfare in which France participated from 1550 to 1715 has already been mentioned.[13] War became so prevalent that there were significant changes in military strategy and tactics.[14] The rapid expansion of the French army from the constant warfare, and the cost of the army's maintenance and deployment, made necessary a massive increase in taxation.[15] The crown also created and sold royal offices to augment its revenues, thereby substantially increasing the number of royal officials, especially financial officials.[16] The unpopular new taxes and offices provoked widespread opposition, which the new intendants suppressed with a heavy hand.[17]

The nobility rebelled against royal policies. Sword nobles led popular revolts against increased royal taxation, which they resented for reducing the peasants' ability to pay their own rents and dues. Robe nobles protested at the crown's creations of new offices, which threatened the value of their own offices. The intendants punished disobedient nobles by suspending them from office, exiling them, imprisoning them, forcing them to sell their offices, and destroying their property. They disciplined institutions by packing them with new members, suspending their functions, suppressing their privileges and powers, and weakening their authority through the creation of competing new jurisdictions. The provincial governors sent royal troops to occupy rebellious towns, and punished peasants in revolt by devastating the countryside; rebel leaders were publicly executed.[18] The governors and intendants delivered royal edicts suppressing the provincial Estates for hindering tax collection, and the crown refused to summon an Estates General after 1615 because of its financial obstructionism. The governors and intendants delivered royal edicts creating new judicial courts, or new chambers in existing courts, which allowed the crown to fill its coffers while disciplining unruly high courts.[19]

For a century, great noble provincial governors had distributed patronage to create their own large clienteles used as private armies. Increasingly, however, governors were absent from the provinces, either because they were at court or serving in the royal army, and resident intendants assumed their power and authority.[20] Absenteeism weakened noble seigneurial ties with peasant tenant farmers, and patron–client ties with other nobles. Ministerial clienteles were created in the provinces to compete with those of the governors and great nobles, and royal patronage was increasingly distributed at court, forcing nobles to come to court if they wanted to advance. Weaker traditional ties and less control over patronage sapped the great nobles' ability to field private armies, which was a social change with significant political consequences.[21]

State-sponsored representations of royal power were used to awe the nobility into obedience. Power symbolism appeared everywhere, in rituals and ceremonies, architecture and the decorative arts, pamphlet and historical writing. Rituals and ceremonies glorifying the monarchy included the royal family's rites of passage, such as marriages, funerals, baptisms; *Te Deum* masses of celebration; the king's coronation; *lits de justice* when the king appeared in person to force acceptance of royal edicts; progresses or tours by the king through the provinces; and royal entries into cities, especially Paris.[22] Versailles's architecture and decoration were meant to demonstrate royal might and majesty. Court spectacles included ballets and masques in which the king appeared as Apollo, Hercules, Zeus and Caesar, while portraits and medals depicted him as a warrior on horseback.[23] Paid pampleteers presented the case for the crown on important issues, while state-subsidized historians wrote Bourbon-pleasing accounts of the past.[24] The crown used political propaganda to overwhelm the nobility into obedience.

THE REVISIONIST INTERPRETATION

An account of the career of Léon de Trimond, sieur d'Aiglun, will illustrate the revisionist argument. Trimond came from a fourteenth-century noble family, and was the wealthiest inhabitant of Les Mées, a little town in the mountains of Haute-Provence. In the late spring of 1649, the Provençal governor, the comte d'Alais, intervened in municipal elections at Les Mées, and appointed new consuls at the request of Trimond, who was hoping that compliant consuls would enable him to win a lawsuit he had brought against the town for taxation of his property. When the Parlement of Aix overturned the governor's appointments, Alais obtained a decree of the royal council reestablishing them. But the official sent to Les Mées to reinstate the governor's appointees was attacked, trussed up like a chicken and delivered to the Parlement of Aix, which imprisoned him. The Parlement and the governor were feuding.

A year earlier in January 1648, the governor, accompanied by three intendants, had forced the Parlement to accept a royal edict creating a second or duplicate high court at Aix, a Semester Parlement, intended to replace the existing Parlement for six months of the year. The sale of its offices was expected to bring the crown 1 million livres. The parlementaires vehemently objected to the Semester, and refused to allow it to function as a court, halting the sale of its offices. Their angry protests culminated in a revolt against the governor and the crown in January 1649. They drove the Semester judges from Aix, reestablished themselves as the sitting high court, and ransacked the house of the Semester's chief justice. Unable to break down the doors, the mob entered through the roof, threw everything out the windows, and murdered the children's tutor whom they found in the house. They paraded the owner's judicial robes through the town on a pike, and sacked the house of the agent selling Semester offices, scattering his personal papers and letters through the streets where they blew about for days. The governor was held hostage until the parlementaires negotiated a settlement with the crown that included the Semester's abolition. Released in March, the governor rode out in the rain to begin raising an army, and the parlementaires did the same. When they sent deputies to discuss their grievances with the rebellious Paris judges, the Aix parlementaires joined the civil war of the Fronde.[25]

Since the governor's intervention at Les Mées was almost certain to exacerbate an already tense political situation, why did he do it? Undoubtedly, wounded pride and a determination to demonstrate his authority and avenge his honour were motives; he had only recently been released from imprisonment. But the governor was also helping a loyal, obedient servant of the crown, Trimond, who had recently bought an office of councillor in the Semester Parlement for 29,000 livres. The angry mob that imprisoned the governor attempted to sack Trimond's house at Aix, and his property at Les Mées was pillaged a few months later. As a wealthy, influential sword noble, Trimond had a large clientele, and he was able to mobilize 36 of his clients to fight for the governor.[26] He would probably have preferred to buy an already existing judicial office, but these were not readily available, so he had to buy a new creation instead. In order to remain a high court judge, Trimond had levied troops to fight for the governor, thus collaborating with the crown because it was in his best interests to do so. He wanted the Semester to become a permanently sitting high court.

Royal propaganda created the myth of an invincible, all-powerful state, but the early modern state was not 'absolute' in the sense of being free from all restrictions in making decisions or enforcing them, whatever royal propagandists might claim.[27] Recent studies, using provincial documentation from Languedoc, Brittany, Dauphiné, Provence and Picardy, have argued that the early modern state relied on local cooperation in governing to a greater extent than the traditionalists have recognized. Misled by royal propaganda, the traditionalists have exaggerated the strength of the early modern state. Relying for their evidence on documentation from the central government in Paris, they have mistakenly adopted a *centraliste* view of the state as tentacled and all powerful, reaching into the far corners of France to extinguish local autonomy.[28] They have overemphasized the state's power and unity.

The actual state of affairs in the provinces was very different from the claims of royal propagandists. The Paris government was small and distant with limited coercive methods at its disposal. So, necessarily, it had to depend upon the voluntary cooperation of local institutions and elites, who collaborated because in so doing they gained access to royal patronage; the crown rewarded their cooperation with benefits that were at the same time incentives. In 1677, 65.6 per cent of Languedoc's taxes went to the crown, but almost all the rest went to provincial elites, who thus had a strong vested interest in royal government. The crown reinforced the authority and power of provincial institutions executing royal policies, and enhanced the prestige of provincial elites, who basked in the reflected glory of the Sun King. The crown received in exchange a steady flow of tax revenues, a smoothly functioning provincial administration, and less resistance to its policies. Languedoc was considerably more peaceful and obedient by the end of the seventeenth century than at the beginning because of the crown's understanding with local elites, who prospered through their cooperation.[29]

A venal system of officeholding encouraged factional rivalry. By Louis XIV's reign, government offices had become the private property of competing, conflicting individuals and families, thus factionalizing the governing elite. The triumph of Louis XIV's government was its ability to resolve these conflicts, while conciliating the elite and governing at the same time.[30] The king restricted his own activities to foreign affairs and warfare, and reinforced the authority and power of local institutions and elites when they collected the tax revenues he needed to conduct war. It has been argued that local demands so limited the nature and scope of Louis XIV's government that it became the opposite of 'absolute' in many ways, and use of the term 'absolutism' has become controversial.[31]

The crown regularly spent much of the tax money collected in Brittany within the province itself. The lion's share went into the pockets of the nobility as pensions, salaries for military and civil offices, and interest payments on loans. Local elites were obsessed by the need for order because they regarded the world around them as unstable and violent, and they cooperated with the crown to assure the maintenance of the status quo, which included their own elite status. The simplest, most effective check on the crown's power to tax was the peasantry's refusal to pay, which had reached staggering proportions by mid-century, and was a major impediment to the state's expansion. The peasantry did not collaborate with the crown.[32] But sometimes the towns did. Dauphiné became the first province to have its Estates suppressed because the third-estate towns, who paid most of the taxes, decided they had nothing to gain from the existing institution. This assembly was dominated by clerics and nobles of the first and second estates, who paid few if any taxes. So, the tax-paying towns cooperated with the crown to suppress the Estates of Dauphiné, hoping to gain more from its replacement.[33]

Most provincial Estates were not as cooperative. Louis XIV's government suppressed some that were uncooperative, and manipulated the others by flattering, bribing, intimidating and bullying their members. Similarly, the royal government placated the recalcitrant Paris parlementaires by catering to their financial and social interests, limiting the evocations of their judicial cases to other courts, asking for their advice and occasionally deferring to their opinions. The crown managed the members of governing elites by using the carrot and the stick separately and in various combinations, according to the circumstances.[34]

The crown regularly used the selective distribution of royal patronage to secure the cooperation of provincial nobles and urban elites. Provincial and municipal institutions, and the central government at Paris, were permeated by networks of personal relationships based on kinship and clientage.[35] To secure institutional cooperation, royal agents manipulated these networks, which were mainly noble in composition, by distributing patronage to their members as a reward for their compliance. Governors and great nobles had been the principal distributors of royal patronage in cities and provinces during the sixteenth century. They were joined in the seventeenth century by intendants, provincial clients of royal ministers, and other regional notables, usually lesser nobles, who enhanced their own power and prestige by distributing patronage to individuals, networks and institutions in exchange for compliance with royal policies. These patronage or power brokers were used by Henri IV to pacify the cities of Picardy after the League, and by Richelieu, Mazarin, Colbert and Louis XIV to secure the voluntary cooperation of

Provençal institutions and elites. Royal government in the seventeenth century rested upon a broader base of elite support than the traditionalists have recognized.[36]

The revisionists have suggested that the power balance between the provincial governors and the intendants needs reexamination. Traditionally, it was thought that resident intendants supplanted absentee governors during the late seventeenth century. The revisionists, however, argue that not all governors were absentee or powerless, and that not all intendants assumed their authority and power. Some governors, even those who were absentee, maintained provincial clienteles and exercised authority in tandem with the intendants. Military commanders in the provinces were often more powerful than the intendants, in part because the intendants were so few in number. There were only 128 provincial intendants appointed for all of France between 1624 and 1661, and their numbers did not increase significantly during the eighteenth century; only 68 intendants were appointed between 1774 and 1789. Because the intendants could not be everywhere at once, they had to rely for assistance upon their subdelegates, local officials who sympathized with local interests. The subdelegates did much of the day-to-day administrative work using their own agents and clients who had their own agendas, and they became more numerous as time went on.[37] The subdelegates' power needs to be considered in assessing that of the intendants. It should be noted, however, that not enough is known at present about governors or intendants during Louis XIV's personal reign to generalize about the power balance between them.[38]

The revisionist interpretation has other problems. The revisionists have assumed that distinctions in noble rank gradually lessened during the seventeenth century, and that nobles shared similar interests.[39] Was this, in fact, the case? Léon de Trimond and Jacques de Parades de L'Estang were both sword nobles who cooperated with the crown to enhance their elite status, but neither was rewarded as he wished. Trimond's Semester office, which had cost him 29,000 livres, was abolished in 1649. He was not reimbursed until 1658, when he received only 25,000 livres. He never sat in the Parlement of Aix, although he bought an office of councillor for his son in 1659 for 80,000 livres.[40] Parades de L'Estang's rewards were even more ephemeral. Elected consul of Arles several times before he was appointed, he was afterward elected several more times. He did not need to be appointed to hold office and, while he received the governor's support, the office of second consul was never abolished.

The revisionists have not recognized the multiplicity of elites nor the diversity of their interests. Parades de L'Estang and Trimond both sought to preserve their elite status, but they did not share the same interests. The municipal squabbling involving Parades de L'Estang was based on differences in rank between old and new nobles. Parades was an old noble, so he defended their interests. Trimond was also a sword noble, but he bought a robe office which he exercised, thus crossing the line into the new nobility whose interests he defended. Provençal nobles, however, like Breton nobles recognized fewer of the traditional distinctions in rank.[41] Neither Parades de L'Estang nor Trimond got what he wanted, and neither had a mutually beneficial alliance with the crown. Did this affect their cooperation? How typical was their experience? Did collaboration inevitably produce rewards? Did all elites prosper through cooperating with the crown?

The traditionalists have insisted that divisions and antagonisms within the nobility persisted well into the eighteenth century. Differences between sword and robe nobles, great court and lesser provincial nobles, feudal nobles and newly ennobled gentlemen caused tension and conflict within the army and at court during Louis XIV's personal reign and later.[42] We have already seen that the growing distance between the greater and lesser nobility was based on their differences in lifestyle. Seventeenth-century nobles may not have been as unified in their interests as the revisionists claim. Did the diversity of elite interests affect the extent to which they cooperated with the crown?

Revisionist documentation comes largely from peripheral provinces where regionalism was strongest, Languedoc, Provence and Dauphiné in the south, Brittany in the west and Picardy in the north. Frontier provinces were notoriously independent and difficult to govern. Did the crown treat frontier provinces differently from those closer to Paris? The crown may have considered consensus-building tactics more useful in distant provinces where it had less control than in provinces nearer Paris and Versailles. If the traditionalists have relied too much on documentation from the central government, perhaps the revisionists have relied too heavily on documentation from the peripheral provinces.

Most historians agree that the royal government was more powerful in 1715 than it had been in 1589.[43] Traditionalists and revisionists disagree on how this happened, but they agree on the centrality of the nobility's role in its occurrence. The nobility's relationship with the crown had changed, and nobles had become less unruly and more obedient. Did the crown use intimidation to coerce the nobility into obedience as the traditionalists claim, or did it distribute benefits to secure their voluntary cooperation as the revisionists claim? Were these tactics mutually exclusive? It may be argued that the traditionalist and revisionist interpretations are not contradictory or conflicting, and that their differences have been exaggerated. In fact, the crown used both coercion and cooptation to secure obedience. These interpretations look at royal government differently because they are based on different sources, demonstrating the crown's use of both the carrot and the stick.

The Audijos revolt in southwestern France during the 1660s provides an example of the crown's simultaneous use of both coercion and cooptation. This revolt against royal taxation was led by a minor Gascon nobleman,

Bernard d'Audijos. The intendant, Claude Pellot, had been using soldiers to crush local resistance to taxation. Audijos's small band of men began using guerilla tactics against royal tax agents, striking suddenly, disappearing and depending upon local sympathizers to shelter them and conceal their movements. Pellot hanged those rebels whom he could find after torturing them, and left their bodies hanging from gibbets to rot. He sent those suspected of sheltering rebels to the galleys. The local nobility supported Audijos because of Pellot's harshness. Eventually, Louis XIV, who was anxious to regain the support of the local nobility, stepped in to withdraw most of the soldiers, pardon the rebels and appoint Audijos colonel in command of a new regiment composed mostly of his own men. Royal taxes in future were levied without resistance. The crown had simultaneously used both coercion and cooptation to secure obedience in the case of the Audijos revolt, which demonstrates that even rebellious, angry nobles cooperated with the crown when it was in their best interests to do so. Noble behaviour became less violent during Louis XIV's reign, not only because the nobility adopted the new civility, but because the crown had successfully used both coercion and cooptation to persuade them to cooperate.[44]

NEW POLITICAL SOLIDARITIES

The prevalence of personal relationships in early modern government created a conflict in priorities when they overlapped as they often did, or when they were used politically as they often were. To solve this problem, the Bourbon monarchy changed the meaning of political loyalty. Noble service to the king was transformed into the loyal obedience of a royal subject, and the self-identity of all social groups, not just the nobility, came to include being a royal subject. Political loyalty to the king was expected to take priority over other personal and political loyalties, although these expectations were not always realized. New political solidarities appeared during Louis XIV's reign, changing how the inhabitants of France saw themselves, and adding a much needed cohesiveness to the body politic.

A crown-centred patriotism had emerged during the sixteenth century to become king-centred during the seventeenth century. Patriotism by Louis XIV's reign had become an awkward, uneasy union of personal and abstract loyalties that combined personal loyalty to the king as an individual, with civic obedience to the king as the head of state, and national loyalty to the king as the embodiment of the nation. Personal loyalties had been primary under feudalism, but intellectuals during the sixteenth century had broadened the feudal emphasis on personal loyalties to include abstract loyalties to state and church.[45] The development of the early modern state in the seventeenth century had accelerated this trend.

The Bourbon monarchy sought to make loyalty to the king as the head of state primary, and subordinated all other personal loyalties to a king-centred patriotism, especially those used politically, for instance, the client loyalty of Henri de Campion. All political loyalties were to be transferred to the king, and loyalty to the king was to take priority over all other loyalties, a process that had already occurred in England. In France, this process had begun during the reign of Henri IV, and was accelerated by the development of the new professionalism and the new civility. Loyal service to a patron in the royal government became synonymous with loyal service to the king and, by the end of Louis XIV's reign, it was no longer possible to serve a patron in rebellion against the king and still consider oneself a loyal subject as Henri de Campion had done.[46]

These changes in the focus and meaning of political loyalty, encouraged by royal propaganda, were responsible for a growing national awareness that centred on the king as the state and nation. Service in the army contributed to this new awareness of France as a national community. André Corvisier has argued that French soldiers in 1709 were motivated to join the army by the king's call to arms in his letter of 12 June, and by the destitution which was caused by the following severe winter. Sent to all provincial governors and bishops, the king's letter spoke of a just war, the honour of the French people and the imminent danger to a kingdom encircled by enemies that had already endured five years of defeats in the War of the Spanish Succession. The king's call to arms produced a flood of volunteers, which Corvisier regards as evidence of a growing national cohesiveness and awareness.[47]

John Lynn disagrees, however. He notes that the ordinary soldier thought of himself mainly in terms of his provincial and regional origins, and so could not have been motivated by patriotism to fight for the national defence. Lynn asks why, if recruits were so eager to fight for their country, did they have to be tied up and marched away under guard, which happened often, for example, to Pierre Prion? He agrees, however, that service in the army helped to encourage a new national awareness. Louis XIV's army, nearly 400,000 strong during the last decades of his reign, was a gigantic melting pot. Recruitment was national in scope, and soldiers came from everywhere to fight against foreign troops. Serving together taught them that they had something in common, that they were French, even if they lived hundreds of miles apart in different circumstances and did not speak the language of Paris and the Île-de-France. Serving in the army created a sense of national community, and the army became an essential instrument of French unification.[48]

A transformation in the meaning of citizenship contributed to the emerging national awareness. The modern notion of citizenship had first appeared in the city-states of fifteenth-century Italy, which had based their citizenship regulations on Roman law. Citizenship was defined as a commitment to the state, demonstrated by permanent residence and fulfilment of a citizen's duties. Frenchmen who went to Italy to study law had carried these ideas home with them, and grafted them on to surviving feudal practice, notably the royal right of the *aubaine*, which allowed the king to seize the property of any foreigner who died in France. Royal lawyers sought to explain in lawsuits why the king should be permitted to do this, and thus who was French, who was not and why and, in so doing, they developed the criteria for citizenship. These criteria changed, however, with the development of the early modern state. Loyal obedience to the king became the most import-ant duty of citizens, who were transformed into royal subjects. Obedience to the king became the necessary proof of citizenship, acquired through choos-ing to live in France and obeying the laws of the state as set down by the king.

The law distinguished between regnicoles, native inhabitants of the kingdom of France, and resident aliens, individuals of foreign birth living in France, mostly in the cities. French nationality was determined by birth, lineage and royal letters of naturalization, so resident aliens could become naturalized citizens. An analysis of the social characteristics of 256 aliens living in Lyon, who obtained letters of naturalization between 1594 and 1724, shows that the typical naturalized Lyonnais was a man over 30, who was married but did not have children. He was a merchant or a craftsman, often a native of Italy, usually from Savoy, which was close to Lyon. He was Catholic, although foreign Protestants did sometimes become citizens through subterfuge, and he had been resident in the city for at least 16 years. Most declared lengthy prior residence as their reason for seeking naturalization. Antoine Mathieu, for example, a craftsman originally from Languedoc, had gone to seek his fortune in Stockholm, where he lived with a Lutheran but did not marry her. They had a son, born in 1650, whom he brought up as a Catholic. He left Stockholm in 1654, and settled in Lyon with his son for whom he purchased letters of legitimation and naturalization. As a craftsman, Antoine was poorer than most resident aliens, who tended to be well off.[49]

Citizenship and naturalization became more restricted during Louis XIV's reign when the king linked citizenship to Catholicism. Property ownership and Catholicism became necessary to obtain letters of naturalization, espe-cially after Louis revoked the Edict of Nantes, which had established religious toleration. The essential question became whether Protestants, who refused to convert as a matter of conscience, were disobedient subjects or not. Even in this case, however, citizenship brought rights that the king could not legally deny if a Protestant were obedient in every other way. The concept of citizens' rights had become so deeply entrenched that not even Louis XIV could completely deprive French Protestants of their rights as citizens. Catholicism was not absolutely necessary for citizenship or naturalization.[50]

Noble critiques of dependency proliferated during the late seventeenth century, probably as a reaction against the king's insistence that his subjects display greater obedience and loyalty. Jacques de Parades de L'Estang wrote in his memoirs that '. . . whatever their intentions, the great and those in authority admit no one to their affections except dependents, and dependence sometimes has a high cost, being detrimental to conscience, honour and your own interests'. Social pressure, specifically the demands of state, family, kin, rank and lineage, caused nobles to seek escape in privacy, intense friendships, romantic love, personal ambition, the pursuit of glory and all sorts of entertainments including gambling. The interests of the individual had become paramount. Individualism, which flourished during the eighteenth century, had its roots in the last decades of Louis XIV's reign in an outpouring of noble memoirs, autobiographies, portraits, novels and letters.[51]

There were significant changes in the understanding of political loyalty during the seventeenth century. Noble service to the king became the loyal obedience of a royal subject, and the self-identity of everyone, not just the nobility, came to include being a royal subject. The Bourbon monarchy insisted upon the priority of loyalty to the king as the head of the state over all other loyalties. At the same time new political solidarities appeared, including a king-centred patriotism, and a new understanding of citizenship as obedience to the king. These political solidarities encouraged cohesion, and contributed to a new awareness of France as a national community. A national identity in the modern sense did not appear until much later. Scholars debate when France became a nation, but they all agree that it was later than Louis XIV's reign.[52] None the less, a king-centred, national consciousness had appeared by the end of Louis's reign, a portent of changes to come, and added another dimension to social and self-identity. By 1715, most of the inhabitants of France regarded themselves as loyal, obedient subjects of a French king.

Suggested reading

Françoise Bayard, 'Naturalization in Lyon during the *Ancien Régime*', *French History*, 4 (1990), 277–311.
William Beik, *Absolutism and Society in Seventeenth-Century France* (Cambridge, 1985).
Yves-Marie Bercé, *The Birth of Absolutism. A History of France, 1598–1661*, tr. Richard Rex (New York, 1996).
Richard Bonney, *Political Change in France under Richelieu and Mazarin, 1624–1661* (Oxford, 1978); idem, *The Limits of Absolutism in Ancien Régime France* (Aldershot, 1995).
Peter Burke, *The Fabrication of Louis XIV* (New Haven, 1992).
William Church, 'France', *National Consciousness, History, and Political Culture in Early Modern Europe*, ed. Orest Ranum (Baltimore, 1975), pp. 43–66.
James Collins, *Classes, Estates, and Order in Early Modern Brittany* (Cambridge, 1994); idem, *The State in Early Modern France* (Cambridge, 1995).

S. Annette Finley-Croswhite, *Henry IV and the Towns. The Pursuit of Legitimacy in French Urban Society, 1589–1610* (Cambridge, 1999).

Albert Hamscher, *The Parlement of Paris after the Fronde, 1653–1673* (Pittsburgh, 1976).

Daniel Hickey, *The Coming of French Absolutism* (Toronto, 1986).

Sharon Kettering, *Patrons, Brokers, and Clients in Seventeenth-Century France* (New York, 1986).

Russell Major, *Representative Government in Early Modern France* (New Haven, 1980); idem, *From Renaissance Monarchy to Absolute Monarchy: French Kings, Nobles, and Estates* (Baltimore, 1994).

Roger Mettam, *Power and Faction in Louis XIV's France* (New York, 1988).

David Parker, *Class and State in Ancien Régime France. The Road to Modernity?* (London, 1996).

Charlotte Wells, *Law and Citizenship in Early Modern France* (Baltimore, 1995); idem, 'The Language of Citizenship in the French Religious Wars', *The Sixteenth Century Journal*, 30 (1999), 441–56.

CHAPTER 7

THE CHURCH

In April 1687, six children of the Robillard de Champaigné family escaped from the Atlantic port of La Rochelle, hidden below decks in a small English eighteen-tonner. Twenty year old Suzanne, the oldest who was head of the family in the absence of her parents, shepherded aboard her five younger brothers and sisters, aged ten to two, and kept them quiet after paying the captain two hundred livres each for their passage. They were French Protestants, or Huguenots, who were fleeing to the Devon coast in search of religious freedom.

The previous evening Suzanne had dressed the children in their best clothes, and taken them for a walk in the town's main square. After a while, they had slipped away to a house on the embankment where they hid in the attic. At low tide about two o'clock in the morning, four sailors arrived to carry them on to the ship on their shoulders. A cask of wine had been emptied and thrown into the sea, and they were hidden in its place, the trap door tarred shut over their heads. The space was so small that their heads touched the ceiling, but they were careful to keep under the beams so that when the inspectors thrust their swords through the planking they were not hit or discovered. It took the ship seven days to reach Falmouth, and they were seasick all the way.

Their forty-two-year-old mother, Marie de La Rochefoucauld de Champaigné, had been unable to join them because she had gone to their country house for the birth of her last child, a daughter, who had to be left behind because she was too young to travel. Marie came into La Rochelle in June 1687, and hid there with her eldest son until early July. Then they walked miles along the coast at night to reach the shallop that took them out to an English ship anchored at sea. They hid in the hold behind some salt for eight days while the ship was in port, and were not discovered by the inspectors. Eight days after setting sail, they reached Falmouth. Ten months later their father, who had remained behind to deceive the authorities, arrived after escaping overland to Holland.

The Champaigné family's escape was unexceptional. In 1685, Louis XIV revoked the Edict of Nantes, which for a century had permitted freedom of worship for Protestants, who thereafter had to leave the country secretly because their emigration had been declared illegal, punishable by prison or the galleys. So, children left without parents; husbands and wives went separately; kin travelled alone or with strangers; and some family members remained behind to confuse the authorities, or because they were too old, ill or weak to travel. Permanent separations were common.[1]

Many of those who emigrated paid a high price. Jean Marteilhe was condemned to the galleys for life at the age of seventeen when he attempted to flee. A native of Bergerac in the west, he had left home in the winter of 1700, and with a friend had walked across France towards the Belgian border in an attempt to reach Holland. But the two boys got lost in the Ardennes forest, had to give themselves up to the fort at Marienbourg in order to survive, were arrested, imprisoned and condemned to the galleys in January 1701. Along with 135 other Protestant convicts, Jean was freed twelve years later at Marseille because, ironically, he had agreed to leave France, and he went to Amsterdam as he had originally planned. Isaac Dumont de Bostaquet, a fifty-five-year-old country gentleman, was stopped by soldiers in May 1687 on the Normandy coast as he and his family were trying to escape aboard an English ship. Faced with imprisonment, the family split up and Isaac managed to escape overland to Holland. When he arrived, penniless, he learned of the death of two of his daughters, the confiscation and sale of his lands, and his condemnation to the galleys for life. Fortunately, his wife and son were able to join him a year later.[2] Emigrants usually went into permanent exile.

As many as 200,000 French Protestants, who numbered less than one million in a population of nearly twenty million, left by sea or land during the 1680s for England, Scotland, Holland, South Africa, Germany, Switzerland and North America in search of religious freedom. Most had lived in a crescent stretching from the western Atlantic provinces across southern France to the southeastern province of Dauphiné in the Alps. The largest number lived in rural Languedoc. The rest lived in Picardy, Normandy and around Paris in the north, and Burgundy and Champagne in the east.[3] Converts to Protestantism, usually Calvinists, had increased rapidly in numbers during the sixteenth century, particularly in towns and among the nobility. Protestant relations with a Catholic monarchy became increasingly strained and finally exploded into violence in 1562. Sporadic outbreaks of fighting between Catholics and Protestants had continued until 1598.[4] The ascension to the throne in 1589 of a Protestant king, Henri IV, founder of the Bourbon dynasty, and his conversion to Roman Catholicism in 1593, effectively brought an end to the fighting, although Henri was never popular with the Catholic majority.[5] The king's issuance of the Edict of Nantes in 1598 marked the formal conclusion of the Wars of Religion. The edict was an act of toleration establishing Protestant religious rights, including freedom of conscience and worship in churches where they had worshiped before 1597; civic rights such as separate schools, their own judicial courts and the opportunity to hold public office; and political rights such as convening public assemblies and maintaining about 200 fortified, garrisoned towns in western and southern France to guarantee their freedom of worship.[6]

The conversion of Henri IV ensured that the Bourbons became Catholic monarchs, that the Roman Catholic Church was the official state church of France and that royalism was Catholicism; the famous formula was 'one faith, one law, one king'. The Edict of Nantes ensured the continuing existence of a Protestant minority, who were unwillingly tolerated by a Catholic majority seeking unity of faith as necessary to national unity. A society that had recently been torn apart by religious warfare regarded dissent as dangerous. Protestants were expelled from the church as heretics, although most Catholics hoped that since they had been baptized as Christians, they could be persuaded to abjure and return. A resurgent, even militant Catholicism flourished in France as an aftermath of the religious wars. Faith was a universal solidarity, but the question was, which faith?

CATHOLIC REFORM

Pope Clement VIII made peace with Henri IV in 1595, and lifted the ban of excommunication from him, although he was unable to insist upon Henri's enforcement of the Tridentine decrees in France. The canons and decrees of the Council of Trent (1543–63) were the official response of the Roman Catholic Church to the Protestant Reformation. The Council sought the restoration of church authority in lands lost to Protestantism, and asserted the jurisdictional and governmental primacy of papal authority. Henri IV for this reason refused to integrate the Tridentine decrees into French law and, like his successors, he refused to accept the assertion of Catholic zealots that the pope's authority was infallible in all matters regarding the church and superior in that to royal authority. A National Assembly of the French Clergy accepted the Tridentine decrees in 1615, but the parlements never registered them to become French law. The Edict of Nantes, therefore, was not challenged and remained in force.

Royal gallicanism, which was based on the 1516 Concordat of Bologna, set limits on papal power in France. By the terms of this agreement with the pope, the king could appoint important members of the secular clergy, including 14 archbishops and about 100 bishops. The parlements, which were always strongly gallican, retained appellate jurisdiction over church affairs affecting French sovereignty, and could reject papal or conciliar decrees they considered damaging to royal authority. The king thus exercised significant control over the church in France. French bishops resisted the claims of papal infallibility by asserting that they owed their offices to God and the apostolic succession, not to the pope, and that, therefore, they had the right to define doctrine for their dioceses and for the church as a whole in general councils. Their attitude was known as episcopal gallicanism.[7] Gallicans, whether royal or episcopal, were hostile to members of religious orders like the Jesuits, who owed primary allegiance to the pope in Rome rather than to the bishop of their diocese. As ultramontanes, the Jesuits advocated the superiority of papal over royal and diocesan authority.[8]

The intense Catholic spirituality that flourished in France during the early seventeenth century fuelled Catholic Reform.[9] Scholars do not agree on exactly when this movement began, but they agree that it came late to France because of the religious wars.[10] It may have had its roots in the Holy Catholic League of the 1590s.[11] Clerical reformers sought to implement the Tridentine decrees with the help of lay Catholic zealots known as *dévots*. The Council of Trent decreed that bishops use episcopal visitation to reform the parish clergy, that seminaries be established to train priests and that monastic life be reformed.

A number of new religious orders were founded. Those for men included, among others, the Jesuits, Capuchins, Lazarists, Oratorians, Sulpicians, Eudists and Fathers of the Christian Doctrine. Originally a Spanish order, the Society of Jesus opened their first house in France in 1540. The Jesuits were highly effective teachers, missionaries, preachers and confessors, who educated the nobility and urban elites, were confessors to the first three Bourbon kings and were probably the most influential religious order in France. The Capuchins, who were introduced from Italy in 1574, had the mission of preaching to the masses and helping the poor and sick. The Lazarists, founded by Vincent de Paul in 1625, became teachers and missionaries. Pierre de Bérulle in 1611 introduced from Italy the order of the Oratorians, who became teachers in seminaries and boys' schools. Jean Eudes had been an Oratorian for twenty years when he founded the Eudists, who were rural missionaries and preachers. The Sulpicians, founded in 1641, devoted themselves to teaching in seminaries and missionary work, and the Fathers of Christian Doctrine or Doctrinaires, an Italian order introduced into France by César de Bus in 1592, conducted catechism classes for children and adults. Education was a top priority for these orders and, by 1710, there were 117 Jesuit schools for boys in France, 72 Oratorian, 78 Lazarist and 48 Doctrinaire.[12]

A medieval literary tradition had long deplored the monastic victimization of young men, and especially young women, who were forced into religious houses without a vocation and held there against their will. Monasteries and nunneries were depicted as vast tombs and prisons, whose inmates languished for life behind thick stone walls, and there was a vivid literature on this subject. The opposite, in fact, was true. There was a great burst of enthusiasm for the religious life during the early seventeenth century, especially among women, who swarmed into convents inspired by the lives of the saints and mystics, and concern for their own salvation. The numbers of regular clergy swelled.[13]

New religious orders for women included, among others, the Carmelites, Dames of the Visitation, Ursulines, Daughters of Notre Dame and Daughters of Charity. The first house of the Spanish order of Carmelite nuns, an enclosed contemplative order, was established by Madame Barbe Acarie at Paris in 1604. Jeanne de Chantal founded the first Visitation house in 1610 at Annecy with the help of François de Sales. The order took its name from its mission of visiting the poor and sick, and later undertook the education of girls. By 1627, there were 30 Visitation houses, which were not originally enclosed, that is, their members went out into the world. The Tridentine decrees, however, ordered the closure of religious houses for women, so Pope Paul V declared the closure of Visitation houses in 1618. The first French house of the Italian order of Ursulines was established at Avignon in 1592 and, by 1700, there were some 320 houses of 10,000 to 12,000 Ursuline nuns in France, who served as teachers and missionaries. The Ursulines established their first convent and school for girls at Quebec in 1639. Also an unenclosed order, their closure was ordered by the church. The Daughters of Notre Dame founded their first house to teach girls at Bordeaux in 1606, and soon their houses stretched across southern France. Louise de Marillac in 1633 founded the Daughters of Charity, whose mission was to care for the poor and sick. Through the efforts of her co-founder, Vincent de Paul, they were able to remain an unenclosed order, an innovation that was soon widely imitated. Increasingly, women joined the new unenclosed orders to do charitable work like hospital nursing instead of the older enclosed orders emphasizing prayer and contemplation.[14]

Reform was also attempted in the older religious orders such as the Benedictines, Cistercians, Carthusians, Augustinians, Dominicans and Franciscans. These orders were charged with misuse of wealth and power; neglect of spiritual and conventual responsibilities; widespread ignorance; excessive legal appeals to papal and royal courts; a tendency for some houses to be noble; and a lack of vocation among noble members, whose presence was often the result of an ugly face, a deformed body, illegitimacy or being a younger child in an impoverished family, which made them unmarriageable or too expensive to set up in a career. Reformers revived medieval forms of observance, and insisted upon monastic obedience to vows of celibacy and poverty, and to the order's rules including those establishing closure, manual labour and a communal life. Daily prayer, examination of conscience and devotional reading in private and in common were emphasized. The full monastic liturgy was celebrated; legal appeals were curbed; a novitiate was established to eliminate those without a vocation; and novices were accepted from a variety of backgrounds. Enforcement of these reforms proved difficult, however, and was never entirely successful.[15] Catholic Reform combined an emphasis on spiritual renewal with a concern for social reform, and one of its most prominent features was a revival of monasticism.

There were a remarkable number of great religious figures during the seventeenth century, but not all clerics were noteworthy. Blaise Dusacq, a curé from Saint-Bonnet-le-Coureau near Lyons, went on trial before the diocesan court in 1684 for misconduct. He habitually swore, gambled, fought with his parishioners, tried to seduce their wives and usually ended the day so befuddled by drink that he fell off his horse and had to be carried home. Arguing over a game of cards with a parishioner in a tavern, he blurted out to a crowd of onlookers what the man had told him in confession. When the wife of a country innkeeper spurned his advances, he left without paying, shouting insults about her to the proprietor as he rode off.[16] Such misconduct had once been common among the parish clergy, but had become increasingly rare by the late seventeenth century because of parish reform.

Reforming bishops conducted regular, unannounced visits of inspection in their diocese, with the authority to correct any abuses they found such as drunkenness or absenteeism. They, and the seminaries they founded, were responsible for improving the quality of parish clergy, who became more disciplined and better educated with greater spiritual commitment.[17] Resident bishops with a strong vocation were needed for successful parish reform. Cardinal Richelieu became interested in the selection of bishops, and under his leadership the monarchy recovered the episcopal patronage it had lost to the nobility during the religious wars. Although there was never a royal policy on the nomination of bishops, their quality improved. Nepotism persisted in episcopal appointments, which were dominated by the nobility, but it had become unthinkable by the 1640s for nobles to be given bishoprics for underage sons, or unnamed, absentee caretakers. Nobles had to provide their sons with a good education if they wanted them to become bishops.[18] Between 1640 and 1660, reforming bishops helped to found more than 40 seminaries to educate the often ignorant parish clergy, schools staffed mainly by the Oratorians, Eudists and Sulpicians. In addition to the schools of the new religious orders, cathedral schools for the laity were founded to replace those destroyed by the religious wars. The church reached many levels of society through education, and helped to raise the literacy rate, particularly among nobles and women. Church schools were instrumental in securing conversions, and education became an important tool of orthodoxy.[19]

Public catechism classes were conducted by the new religious orders, especially the Doctrinaires. Village schools offering catechism classes were established everywhere, usually by lay religious societies, and staffed by the parish clergy or the Brothers of Christian Schools, founded by Jean-Baptiste de la Salle in 1682. Rural missions taught catechism to children and adults. A bishop would announce a mission for several of his parishes, which would be conducted in a designated village by the Jesuits, Capuchins, Lazarists, Eudists, Sulpicians or Doctrinaires. Besides teaching the catechism, they would explain theology, read the scriptures, preach and say mass. The final meeting, attended by the bishop, would feature a religious procession, a first communion for children and the planting of a cross. Rural missions were meant to increase piety and eliminate ignorance.[20]

The dévots, who first appeared during Henri IV's reign, were often former Leaguers. By the 1620s, under the leadership of Pierre de Bérulle and Michel de Marillac, they had become a political party espousing anti-Huguenot policies at home and pro-Habsburg policies abroad, i.e., they were pro-Spanish. The politically active dévots, however, were always a small group. The majority had little or no interest in politics. Instead, they shared similar religious and social aspirations. They sought to infuse every moment and action of their daily lives with God's love, as François de Sales had taught in his widely read devotional work. Cardinal Richelieu for pragmatic reasons tolerated the Huguenots, and formed alliances with Calvinist rulers in order to hobble the Spanish Habsburgs, whose defeat he considered to be in France's best interests. For opposing his policies, Richelieu destroyed the dévots as a political force in 1630, although they continued their religious and social activities for a long time afterward.[21]

The dévots were another distinctive feature of Catholic Reform in France. With both lay and clerical members, they included many reform leaders. Madame Acarie, for example, held a salon whose members included her cousin, Pierre de Bérulle; Philippe Cospeau, bishop of Nantes; the Capuchin Benedict of Canfield, who was her spiritual instructor; and Michel de Marillac. Many of the dévots, like Madame Acarie and her cousin, were robe nobles; a flock of robe ladies, and even some great court ladies, joined her order. Jeanne de Chantal had been a baroness. Pierre de Bérulle was the spiritual director of Vincent de Paul and Jean Eudes, while Jean-Jacques Olier, founder of the Saint Sulpicians, was a disciple of Vincent de Paul, who was the spiritual instructor of Louise de Marillac, the illegitimate niece of Michel de Marillac. A group of well-connected noble ladies gathered around Louise, who had been a member of the household of Marie de Médicis. Her court sponsors included the duchesse d'Aiguillon, Richelieu's niece. Intense piety and close ties among a small Parisian elite, including many women, characterized the first phase of Catholic Reform in the early seventeenth century. Reform spread outward from Paris in an effort to bring Tridentine spirituality to the masses during the mid-seventeenth century, but there was a decline in interest during the late seventeenth century.[22]

Many new devotional confraternities were founded in the seventeenth century. Working-class counterparts of the dévots, these were lay religious brotherhoods who met regularly for sermons, prayers, hymns and mass, and were frequently affiliated with guilds or workingmen's associations. Women could join, and sometimes composed half the membership. Confraternities were sanctioned by the church as religious bodies, endowed with a patron saint and assigned a chapel in the parish church, or a nearby monastery or convent; they were often affiliated with religious orders. They did charitable work and marched in local processions on holy days, as they did in Marseille on Corpus Christi Day. Penitential confraternities flourished in the Midi. Their members wore a hooded shroud, that is, a sack covering their head, body and limbs that was belted with a cord, and had slit openings for the eyes and mouth. They marched on holy days and for funerals, although they were best known for their flagellant processions and passion plays. Other devotional companies included the Holy Sacrament, a secret society founded in the late 1620s composed of both laymen and clerics. The company left no written records, having kept its existence, membership and activities secret, and its interests ranged from charitable work and poor relief to policing public morals and persecuting heretics. By 1660, the Company of the Holy Sacrament had 4,000 members in 60 cities and towns. The *Association d'amis* was another secret religious society, but there were also non-secret societies such as the companies of the Holy Ghost and Rosary. There was a large network of Marian congregations sponsored by the Jesuits, and other sodalities sponsored by the Dominicans. Lay religious societies became widespread as another expression of Tridentine spirituality.[23]

Lay religious societies created ties and solidarities among the Catholic faithful, as did the implementation of Tridentine Reform. These ties included membership in the greater community of Catholic believers, in the French Catholic church with its parishes and dioceses, in both old and new religious orders, in the dévots and in devotional companies. These bonds were among the strongest in French society. They did not include religious dissenters such as Protestants and Jews, or heterodox Jansenists, who had to forge their own solidarities.

THE IMPACT OF CATHOLIC REFORM

Annalistes such as Robert Muchembled have adopted a socio-cultural approach in trying to understand the religious upheavals of the sixteenth and seventeenth centuries. Historians using this approach have been particularly interested in the impact of Catholic Reform on popular religion, that is, on the religious beliefs and practices of the masses. Historians of an earlier generation tended to be more interested in the nature of the Tridentine decrees and how they were implemented.

The northern village of Maroilles near Avesnes possessed a miraculous fountain dedicated to Saint Humbert, who was believed to cure rabies. On

6 September, the saint's feast day, a procession of the sick came from far and wide to be cured. Each infected person had to perform a novena (nine days' devotion), have a mass said in honour of Saint Humbert and receive communion. Nine days in a row he had to recite five *Paters* and five *Ave Marias*, then dine on three slices of bread that had touched the saint's relics and been soaked in pure water. He had to wash his bites in the water, sleep alone in freshly washed sheets, drink only water and eat only cold food. He had to avoid kitchen smoke, manure, sun light and excess activity or emotion, especially anger. If he believed in God and Saint Humbert, he would be cured. Robert Muchembled believes that these rites were the Christian disguise for an older water cult, a set of popular cultural beliefs and rituals that had been absorbed into Christianity at some time in the past and were now denounced as superstition by Catholic reformers. Muchembled believes that the reformers sought to suppress popular religion as a form of popular culture. They wanted to replace older religious beliefs and practices with a new Catholic orthodoxy, which was actually a new form of elite culture coming from Paris. A centralizing monarchy through its control of the church was seeking to impose the culture of the ruling elite on the rest of society.[24]

The agents of this new urban elite culture were the reforming bishops, a reformed parish clergy, rural missions, lay religious societies and the popular literature of blue books, the *bibliothèque bleue*, whose main publishing centre was at Troyes. These little books, printed on blue paper, sold in huge numbers. Books had originally been a form of elite culture, but with the rise in literacy and general growth in the book trade, they reached a much wider audience, and became a means of transmitting new forms of culture. The church seized upon them as a way of replacing popular religion with the new orthodoxy. The publishers at Troyes and elsewhere widely distributed these little blue books advocating a new form of devotion, and thus helped to popularize Tridentine reform.[25] This interpretation has been challenged, however, and it has been argued that the rising literacy rate did not have a real impact on popular religion until the late eighteenth century.[26] ·

Historians of popular culture tend to view Catholic Reform in France as part of a broader elite attack upon popular culture everywhere in Europe during the sixteenth and seventeenth centuries. The repressive efforts of Protestant and Catholic reformers were backed by elites frightened of mass violence. Ruling elites regarded popular religious holidays like Carnival as opportunities for the lower classes to express hostility, and so wanted these events suppressed.[27]

Socio-cultural historians regard Catholic Reform as the successful Christianization of an illiterate, immoral and superstitious peasantry. By rooting out paganism and educating the masses, Catholic reformers introduced the peasantry to orthodox spirituality for the first time.[28] Christianity everywhere in Europe, not just in France, underwent similar changes, and these changes brought reformers into conflict with local customs and institutions such as the family, household and networks of extended kin.[29] Socio-cultural historians have tended, however, to be vague about the origins and beliefs of popular religion, and have depended heavily for their archival evidence upon a wide variety of local studies.[30]

Annalistes and socio-cultural historians have also been criticized for their sweeping generalizations, and for oversimplifying complex subjects such as religion and culture. Critics charge that their use of the terms 'popular religion', 'pre-Christian' and 'pagan' is so imprecise that these terms are meaningless. They have been accused of not defining the nature of popular religion, nor explaining its origins, while their assumption that popular religion was unchanging for centuries until it disintegrated seems unlikely. Robert Much-embled's reduction of the impact of reform to a dichotomy of elite versus popular culture seems 'a caricatural confrontation', in the words of Michel Vovelle. He notes that socio-cultural historians have used as evidence iconography, quantification of artifacts, descriptions of rituals and folklore, none of which is direct, written evidence of religious beliefs.[31] Church historians have traditionally regarded Catholic reform as the effort to implement the Tridentine decrees, a new orthodoxy, and have studied the nature and impact of these decrees. The Tridentine emphasis upon the sacerdotal aspect of the priesthood, for example, was responsible for establishing a greater emotional distance between the reformed clergy and their parishioners. A socio-cultural approach allows the investigation of previously neglected aspects of Catholic Reform, but this approach needs to be combined with the older theological approach to achieve a complete understanding of reform.[32]

There has been a tendency to overstate the impact of reforming bishops. The accepted wisdom is that bishops imposed reform upon the parish clergy, who then thrust it upon their parishioners. But how did the actions of a reforming parish clergy actually affect their parishioners? In the villages around Lyon, reforming priests sought to establish Tridentine spirituality, aid the diocesan hierarchy in its battle against popular religion and calm the urban elites' fear of a turbulent peasantry. The parish priests were educated men of good character, but they developed strained relations with their parishioners. Forbidden to socialize with them as they had done in the past, they now appeared arrogantly determined to dominate village life and force its restructuring to fit Tridentine ideals. The result was tension and conflict, pitting priests against village notables and male youth groups. The Lyon experience indicates that Catholic Reform was a long, slow process fraught with difficulties, and that local resistance often doomed it to failure. The success of reform depended upon popular acceptance, which was greater in the cities than in the countryside.

Rural parishioners in the diocese of Grenoble did not passively accept outsiders' efforts to impose a new spirituality and more restrained forms of behaviour. Instead, they combined these innovations with their own under-standing of religious practice and appropriate conduct. They did not practise a religion centred on the parish priest and the bishop's decrees as reformers wished, but one that also included confraternities, chapels, saints' devotions and family needs. The villagers' acceptance or rejection of reform depended more on the demands of communal village life, and the competition of rival families, than the efforts of a reforming bishop. The experiences of the parishioners of Layrac in the Agenais were similar.[33]

Inspired by the Annalistes, historians for decades have used a socio-cultural approach in trying to understand the impact of Catholic Reform. They have viewed religion as social and cultural, as a body of believers rather than as a body of beliefs, and in so doing they have overemphasized the socio-cultural aspects of religion, neglecting its theological and intellectual aspects. Catholic Reform occurred because of the Council of Trent, and was the impact of new religious ideas upon both rural and urban believers. The traditional intel-lectual approach needs to be combined with the more recent socio-cultural approach for a better understanding of Catholic Reform.

RELIGIOUS DISSENT: THE PROTESTANTS

In June 1615, a small farm and a vineyard belonging to Pierre de Lacger, a Protestant, were burned. Less than two months later, local residents set fire to his estates at Clot and la Planesié. Nearly a decade later, in June 1624, the sudden death of his brother, Jean, prompted an autopsy because the family feared his death was unnatural. In January 1629, their fear of retaliation was realized when troops of the Protestant duc de Rohan, billeted at Pierre's house in Castres, threatened to burn it down until his sister Marie paid them 400 livres. Why were the Lacgers so disliked by their Protestant neighbours?

The Lacgers were a Protestant family of royal officials who had demon-strated their loyalty and obedience to a Catholic king during the duc de Rohan's Protestant rebellion in the 1620s. Pierre was a royal judge at Castres, while his brother Jean was a royal judge in the court for Protestants at Toulouse, and his brother Jacques was a royal secretary at Paris. Jacques openly criticized Protestant political and religious leaders for exploiting popular fears, and he and Pierre joined their influential Protestant patron, the duc de La Trémoille, in denouncing Rohan's 'adventurism'. As a result, Pierre was temporarily imprisoned by Rohan in 1621. The king a few years later gave Pierre an annual pension of 600 livres as a reward for his loyalty, which had included writing reports on Castres. Pierre's conduct deeply angered many Protestants, who considered him a traitor to their cause, hence the attacks. His conduct exemplifies the dilemma of loyal Protestant subjects of a Catholic king intent on destroying their religious freedom.[34]

Both Catholics and Protestants regarded the Edict of Nantes as temporary. Catholics sought its revocation for allowing heresy, and Protestants wanted its expansion to include their full equality. Its provisions were strictly observed for two decades until a devout Louis XIII began a military campaign across southern and western France in 1620 to demolish Protestant fortified towns and châteaux, which he considered a threat. This campaign culminated in the surrender of La Rochelle in 1628, a decisive turning point marking the end of Protestant military and political power. Walls were torn down, and garrisons dispersed. What the king had granted at will, he could revoke at will.

The crown mostly ignored the Protestants from 1630 to 1661. The king's chief ministers, Richelieu and Mazarin, were pragmatists who had to fight wars abroad and at home, and they did not want trouble with the Huguenots. After Mazarin's death, however, an increasingly absolutist Catholic monarchy, pressured by the French church and the papacy, sought to eliminate the separate status of Protestants, whose conversion was considered necessary for peace and stability. Soon, the only legal Protestant schools were those established before 1597. New ones could not be opened, and some of the legal ones were closed. Protestants were forbidden to send their children abroad to attend school, and every effort was made to convert those who went to Catholic schools; the Jesuit colleges were especially efficacious in this regard. Protestant churches were closed if they could not provide documentary proof of their existence before 1597, and even some that could were closed. Separate Protestant judicial courts were abolished, and special taxes were levied on Protestant believers, who were increasingly excluded from public office-holding. Conversions to Protestantism were forbidden, and general church meetings, or synods, had to be held in the presence of royal commissioners. Reaching adulthood and remaining a Protestant became a conscious act of will. Religious affiliation was an important determinant of social and self-identity.

As an absolute monarch, Louis XIV considered himself obligated to punish subjects who were disobedient. Religious dissent was disobedience under the 'one faith, one law, one king' formula, and considered a threat to national unity. Protestants refusing to abjure could be punished and forced to convert to save their immortal souls. This attitude, shared by a majority of the church, culminated in the king's Revocation of the Edict of Nantes in 1685. The practice of Protestantism, legally known as 'the alleged reformed religion', was prohibited. All Protestant churches were closed and destroyed, and their pastors were given two weeks to convert or leave France. Protestant schools were closed; Protestants were forbidden to emigrate; and *dragonnades* were established south of the Loire. Dragoons or cavalrymen were billeted on

Protestants, with the right to pillage freely until their hosts converted, which most did quickly.[35] Some defied the authorities, however, and continued to practice their religion in secret.[36]

Historians debate the extent of Protestant strength in the face of such pressure. An older view considered the Protestants as a nearly spent force by 1685, having been slowly suffocated by the authorities. Demoralized by the growing restrictions on their daily lives, Protestants converted to Catholicism in growing numbers for pragmatic reasons. Incentives included escaping the payment of debts and special taxes; being able to hold public office; and an end to social isolation: conversion allowed the renegotiation of their social identity. By mid-century, nearly all Protestant great nobles, most robe and provincial nobles, and many members of the urban elites had converted. Heavy immigration from a rural Catholic hinterland eroded Protestant strength in the cities, and there was an overall decline in their numbers from a high intermarriage rate, the military campaigns of the 1620s and emigration abroad.[37]

A more recent interpretation, however, regards this view of Protestant weakness and isolation as overly pessimistic. The numbers of Protestants varied greatly from region to region, but overall they declined only about 25 per cent in the century before revocation. The smaller the numbers of Protestants in a community, the higher their rate of conversion, although they were firmly resistant to rural missions. The frequency of pragmatic conversions, and the high rate of intermarriage may also be exaggerated. The intermarriage rate varied considerably from region to region, but was higher in Aquitaine and the centre-west than in Dauphiné, rural Languedoc and the Cévennes, and ceased abuptly after intermarriage was prohibited by royal edict in 1663. Protestant isolation has also been exaggerated. There were extensive cross-confessional ties in Aquitaine and lower Languedoc through kinship, marriage, godparentage, patronage, friendship and sociability as well as ties between neighbours, masters, servants, tradesmen, employees and customers, who all lived together in the same small communities. Gregory Hanlon writes, 'The exclusion and segregation of the Calvinist minority was, properly speaking, impossible. Tolerance was not only common, it was *normal.*' Robert Sauzet insists that Protestantism remained a powerful force in French society throughout the seventeenth century.[38]

Most historians agree that Protestants had a distinct self-identity, although Hanlon insists that only a minority had an 'authentic Calvinist identity', which they were able to maintain in the face of increasing pressure; the majority were more closely linked to the surrounding Catholic community. The foundations of a separate Protestant identity included the close integration of their church and its married pastor into the community, which has been called 'the presbyterian, consistory and synod system', and a widespread commitment to Protestant tenets of faith including high standards of moral behaviour.

There was a strong biblical culture based on the family custom of bible reading in the evenings, which resulted in a higher Protestant literacy rate and a greater knowledge of French in the Midi. Two elements of the Protestant identity are disputed by historians, whether their families displayed more patriarchal authority, and whether their ethic encouraged capitalistic behaviour that tended to accumulate wealth.

There is also a general agreement that Protestants tended increasingly to marry within their own religion. The family was essential in transmitting religious beliefs to the next generation, and women in families were always among the most committed of believers. Protestants in general tended to have a high marriage rate. Two-thirds of the Lacger men married into other Protestant families of the Castrais, and for over eight generations produced medium-sized families averaging five children each. Their godparents were drawn from the same narrow circle of families into which they married. These families formed a dense Protestant thicket of kin who depended upon each other for support and assistance to a greater degree than in the society at large. Raymond Mentzer writes, 'These affinal kin shared common religious beliefs and values, formed business and social ties, undertook one another's political concerns, and together met the external adversary. They eventually formed a solid phalanx of aunts, uncles, cousins and godparents.'

The Protestants' greatness weakness was a self-defeating political attitude, namely their attempt to remain the loyal, obedient subjects of a Catholic monarch intent on destroying their religious freedom, as we have seen in the case of Pierre de Lacger. French Protestants were monarchists, absolutists and gallicans because they considered royal absolutism their best defence against the papacy and a resumption of religious warfare. The conundrum they faced was how to obey an absolute monarch and remain Protestant. They believed that the solution lay in separating their freedom of conscience and worship from their loyalty and duty as royal subjects. Their tragedy was that an absolute Catholic monarchy refused to allow them to make such a separation.[39]

In order to survive, Protestants needed solidarities of their own, based on membership in the greater community of Protestant believers. They developed strong bonds within their own churches, consistories, colloquies and synods, and close ties to family, kin, friends and neighbours who were fellow believers. These solidarities were strong enough to allow them to withstand outside pressure for generations until the king gave them the choice of converting, emigrating or going underground. Most Protestants were obedient royal subjects who quietly practised their religion, got along with their Catholic neighbours and kept out of the public eye, attitudes that allowed them to live unmolested for decades. Their experience illustrates the classic problem of a religious minority within an intolerant society, how to practise their religion and survive. The Protestant solution included widespread community participation in church affairs; regular church attendance with evening services at home; separate religious education; close ties to family and fellow believers; obedience to the state; and outward social conformity.

The Jews, who were a non-Christian religious minority, followed the same strategy. First expelled from France en masse by Philip the Fair in 1306, they emigrated in large numbers to nearby Avignon in the Comtat Venaissin, which was under papal control. Thomas Platter visited the Jewish community at Avignon in 1596. He noted that about 500 Jews lived on one street, which could be closed by gates at either end, and survived by buying and selling clothing, jewellery, shoes, hats, armour and other types of apparel. Platter wrote, 'They are not permitted to buy either house, garden, field or meadow, within or without the town; they are also forbidden to follow any trade other than those I have mentioned, except money-changing. They pay a good price for old clothes. . . . These they repair and renew, for they are almost all tailors, and end by reselling them as if they were new.' He noted that both men and women wore distinctive yellow hats, and that every Saturday, in a church across from the papal palace, a Jesuit preached a sermon of penitence to the Jews, who were forced to attend in turn, a third at a time.[40]

The Jews were expelled from France several more times during the fourteenth and fifteenth centuries. For this reason, Jewish communities tended to be located on the frontiers, namely in the eastern provinces of Alsace, added in 1648, and Lorraine, in 1766; Avignon and the Comtat Venaissin, which only became a permanent part of France in the 1790s; Nice, which was part of Savoy until the mid-nineteenth century; and in some of the port cities, notably Bordeaux, Bayonne and Marseille. Jews in France probably numbered 200,000 to 300,000 in 1700.

Because they were forbidden to own farm land, join guilds, hold public office or practise the professions, Jews tended to congregate together in urban neighbourhoods where they lived by buying and selling goods, and lending money as they did in Avignon. They also practised the crafts of gold and silver smithing, jewellery and clock making, precious stone cutting and lens grinding. They maintained cross-regional, national and international ties with other family members and Jews in similar occupations. These long-distance ties were a solidarity that had the added advantage of offering a refuge in time of trouble. Jews forged close ties within their own community, and family ties were especially important. There was a Jewish subculture, characterized by the separate languages of Hebrew and Yiddish and a large body of religious writings, which stretched across national boundaries to act as a unifying force. Jews were obedient to the state, and tried to blend in socially. They suffered a drain on their numbers from intermarriage and conversion, and eked out an even more precarious existence than the Protestants.[41]

RELIGIOUS DISSENT: THE JANSENISTS

Antoine Arnauld's fourth child, a daughter, born in 1591, was destined for the church at an early age. Her mother gave birth to a total of twenty children, who did not all live, but were too many for the family to support easily. Because convents did not require big dowries, this child took her vows as a nun when she was only nine, assuming the religious name of Angélique. In 1602, just before her eleventh birthday, she became the abbess of Port-Royal, a dilapidated Cistercian convent in the Chevreuse valley just south of Paris. Angélique wrote in her autobiography that she regarded monastic life as an unbearable yoke. Then, in 1608, she had a religious experience, and determined to reform both herself and her convent. She began by insisting upon observance of the rule of closure.

In the autumn of 1609, she learned that her parents were coming to visit. They had been allowed in the past to roam the convent buildings and grounds freely, but now she wrote and told them not to come because she was determined to enforce the rule of closure. They came, anyway, arriving on 25 September, which became known as 'the day of the *guichet*', because they met their daughter at a little window or guichet set in the entry door. She informed them that they would not be admitted. Her father flew into a rage, telling her that, if she did not obey him and open the door immediately she would never see them again, while her mother sobbed loudly. Angélique stood her ground and refused them admittance. She wrote,

> How strange it is that they wanted me to become a nun against my wishes when I was too young; and now that I want to be a nun, they want me to commit a sin by not observing the rule. I will do nothing of the sort. They did not consult me in making me a nun; I will not consult them now that I wish to live like a nun in order to save myself.[42]

Angélique devoted herself with great energy and enthusiasm to reforming Port-Royal and, in 1625, moved the growing community to Paris because the Chevreuse valley was full of swamps and marshes that caused fever. The new Paris community became known as Port-Royal-de-Paris, and the older community as Port-Royal-des-Champs. Then Angélique broke with the Cistercian order, and established her own Order of the Holy Sacrament, which received both papal and royal approval. The new order immediately came under attack, but a theologian of note, the abbé de Saint-Cyran, rose to its defence, and wrote a treatise successfully disarming its critics. He became the community's spiritual adviser until his death in 1643.

The abbé was a close friend of Cornelius Jansen (1585–1638) from their student days together at the University of Louvain, where they had both been strongly influenced by Augustinian theology. Jansen became a biblical professor at Louvain, then bishop of Ypres, and his magnum opus, *Augustinus*, a study of Augustinian theology, was published posthumously in 1641. Through the abbé de Saint-Cyran, Jansen's Augustinianism had a strong influence on Port-Royal, and the Port-Royal supporters of Jansen became known as Jansenists because they defended his theology.

The doctrinal disputes that split the French church during the seventeenth century were considered obstacles to successful Catholic Reform because they encouraged disunity and heresy.[43] The most serious controversy involved the Jansenists, who insisted that Christianity had become corrupted through the influence of scholasticism, stoicism and pagan philosophies such as epicurean-ism. The Jansenists sought a return to the traditions and purity of the primit-ive church, particularly the church of Augustine. They embraced Augustinian theology, adopted strict moral standards and withdrew from worldly distrac-tions into lives of solitary contemplation and prayer. Augustine had believed that man's nature was seriously impaired by original sin, and that he could only be saved through God's grace or unmerited divine assistance. God had predetermined those who would be redeemed by His grace, and they were known as the 'elect'. Their salvation was God's work alone, a doctrine known as predestination. The relationship between man's free will to choose good or evil actions affecting his redemption, and the efficacy of God's grace in achieving salvation, was a complex doctrinal issue that divided the church for centuries after Augustine's death.

The Council of Trent failed to clarify the issue and, in 1588, the Spanish Jesuit Molina published a book attacking Augustinianism. Molina admitted that grace was necessary to achieve salvation, but he insisted that Christians were free to accept or reject God's gift of grace, and that God's grace was not efficacious unless it was freely accepted. This Jesuit-backed doctrine of free will became known as Molinism. The Dominicans, who were rivals of the Jesuits, opposed Molinism so vehemently that the pope intervened in 1598, and issued decrees prohibiting further debate on the subject. The Jesuits in-spired envy, suspicion and contempt in nearly all church circles because of their influence and prestige, and they quarrelled frequently with both the secular and regular clergy. The publication of Jansen's *Augustinus* stirred up the controversy once more, and the Jesuits launched a series of attacks on the book and its defenders, whom they labelled heterodox (unorthodox) and crypto-Protestants. The ultramontane Jesuits became the most committed foes of the Gallican Jansenists. Angélique's father, Antoine, a lawyer, attacked the Jesuits before the Parlement of Paris in 1594, and Angélique's youngest brother, Antoine, published another such attack in 1643. The battle lines were drawn.

Jansenism had its roots in the monastic revival of Catholic Reform and the dévot movement. The abbé de Saint-Cyran was a dévot. So was François de

Sales, who was Angélique's spiritual adviser from 1620 until his death in 1622. The Arnauld family, however, was the heart and soul of Jansenism, and the ties linking them were essential to its survival. Angélique's mother, her sisters and nieces all took vows as nuns at Port-Royal, and most of her brothers and nephews became informally associated with the community as lay members or *solitaires*, who had repudiated the world for an interior contemplative life. At its peak, Port-Royal included thirteen nuns and six solitaires who were members of this family. The Arnaulds, like many dévots, were a prominent family of the Parisian robe nobility; Jansenism was grounded in the robe.[44] It also attracted significant support from members of the court aristocracy such as the duchesse de Longueville and the duc de Luynes. There were Jansenist bishops, the most famous being those of Pamiers, Alet, Angers and Beauvais, and there were Jansenist priests, seminarians and members of religious orders, in particular the Benedictines, Doctrinaires and Oratorians, who were also rivals of the Jesuits.

In 1653, after a decade of controversy, Innocent X, influenced by the Jesuits, formally condemned as heretical five propositions in Jansen's *Augustinus*. Antoine Arnauld replied that, although the pope might be infallible in matters of doctrine, he could err in matters of fact, and had done so in declaring that Jansen had advocated the five propositions in question. In 1656, the Sorbonne, the theology faculty of the University of Paris, and Pope Alexander VII insisted that these five propositions had been held by Jansen. At this point, the Jesuits appealed to Louis XIV for help. In 1661, a royal decree ordered all members of the French clergy to sign a formulary acknowledging their submission to the papal bull of 1653. Many Jansenists refused to sign, and years of persecution followed. Angélique died at this time, aged seventy, just before the struggle over signing the formulary began.

Port-Royal-de-Paris was purged of nuns who refused to sign, and those who remained were placed under the supervision of another order; most later withdrew to Port-Royal-des-Champs. Several male Jansenists were imprisoned, and others went into hiding, moving frequently around Paris to avoid arrest. Attempts to remove the Jansenist bishops were unsuccessful, but the king made certain that no more were appointed at this time. Louis XIV and Pope Clement IX finally reached a compromise with the Jansenists in 1669. The Jansenist bishops apologized in a letter to the pope. A new, more vaguely worded pastoral letter was then circulated, which everyone signed, and ten years of calm followed.

In 1679, at the conclusion of the Dutch war, Louis turned his attention once again to domestic affairs, resuming his persecution of the Jansenists, who fought back with a series of widely circulated pamphlets. In 1701, the Jansenists successfully aroused public opinion on several sensitive issues just as France entered the War of the Spanish Succession. Convinced that Jansenist support in Paris was strong enough to cause the sort of trouble that had crippled Mazarin during the Fronde, Louis decided to take drastic action to suppress the movement. He obtained papal permission in 1709 to close Port-Royal, and expel its nuns and solitaires; even the graves in the convent cemetery were emptied. The Arnaulds and great court nobles were allowed to remove the bodies of their family members, but the rest were dumped into a common grave. The leading Jansenists had already been imprisoned or driven into exile and, in 1711, the buildings of Port-Royal were razed to the ground. Two years later the papal bull *Unigenitus* condemned as heretical 101 propositions of the Jansenist leader, Pasquier Quesnel. This papal bull sounded the death knell of the movement, although its influence lingered on. The Jansenists' fate was partly responsible for the expulsion of the Jesuits from France in 1762.[45] Certainly, there would never have been a Jansenist controversy without the Jesuits.

The Jansenists' most serious problem was their attitude toward authority. Richelieu, Mazarin and Louis XIV were deeply suspicious of a piety that was expressed by withdrawing from the world into silent austerity, which seemed like a rejection of worldly authority. The Jansenists believed that isolation was necessary for effective meditation, but their withdrawal seemed to put the spiritual needs of the individual above the needs of the state and society. The Jansenists' profound sense of individualism, and their intellectualism, made them difficult to control, which Louis considered dangerous. He regarded their recalcitrance, even if it was an expression of conscience, as wilful disobedience. Their elitism and ties to the dévots had made Richelieu distrustful, while their support of the rebels during the Fronde had alienated Mazarin. Their obstinate defence of their controversial theological beliefs angered Louis XIV. The Jansenists suffered from the same fatal flaw as the Protestants. They sought to be the loyal, obedient subjects of a monarchy determined to repress them.[46]

Did the Jansenists hinder Tridentine Reform? Doctrinal disputes made reform more difficult, and Jansenism was the most divisive Catholic controversy of the century. Jansenism was a small elite movement that did not have much influence on the masses in the countryside. The austerity and strict moral standards of the Jansenists repelled ordinary believers, who did not understand Augustinianism. As Catholic rigorists, however, the Jansenists were supported by educated believers who wanted a return to the true church and abhorred dubious innovations. The Jansenists insisted that they were the true heirs of the early church, and that their opponents were the innovators, but this attitude encouraged lay challenges to church teachings including Tridentine reform. Scholars disagree on how successful Catholic Reform was, and on how serious an obstacle Jansenism was to its success, but they agree that both church and state handled dissent badly. Reform produced solidarities that helped the reformers to succeed, while dissent produced solidarities that helped the dissenters to survive. Solidarities of faith were universal among Catholics, Protestants, Jansenists and Jews.

Suggested reading

Joseph Bergin, *Cardinal de La Rochefoucauld. Leadership and Reform in the French Church* (New Haven, 1987); idem, *The Rise of Richelieu* (New Haven, 1991).

Robin Briggs, *Communities of Belief. Cultural and Social Tensions in Early Modern France* (Oxford, 1989).

Barbara Diefendorf, 'Give Us Back Our Children: Patriarchal Authority and Parental Consent to Religious Vocations in Early Counter-Reformation France', *The Journal of Modern History*, 68 (1996), 265–307.

Gregory Hanlon, *Confession and Community in Seventeenth-Century France. Catholic and Protestant Coexistence in Aquitaine* (Philadelphia, 1993).

Philip Hoffman, *Church and Community in the Diocese of Lyon, 1500–1789* (New Haven, 1984).

Mack Holt, 'Putting Religion Back into the Wars of Religion', *French Historical Studies*, 18 (1993), 524–51; idem, *The French Wars of Religion, 1562–1629* (Cambridge, 1995).

Keith Luria, *Territories of Grace. Cultural Change in the Seventeenth-Century Diocese of Grenoble* (Berkeley, 1991).

Raymond Mentzer, *Blood and Belief. Family Survival and Confessional Identity among the Provincial Huguenot Nobility* (West Lafayette, Ind., 1994).

Henry Phillips, *Church and Culture in Seventeenth-Century France* (Cambridge, 1997).

Elizabeth Rapley, *The Dévotes. Women and Church in Seventeenth-Century France* (Montreal, 1990).

Alexander Sedgwick, *Jansenism in Seventeenth-Century France. Voices from the Wilderness* (Charlottesville, 1977); idem, *The Travails of Conscience. The Arnauld Family and the Ancien Régime* (Cambridge, Mass., 1998).

Michel Vovelle, 'Popular Religion', *Ideologies and Mentalities*, tr. Eamon O'Flaherty (Chicago, 1990), pp. 81–113.

Michael Wolfe, *The Conversion of Henri IV. Politics, Power, and Religious Belief in Early Modern France* (Cambridge, Mass., 1993).

CHAPTER 8

THE MARGINS OF SOCIETY

The state's attorney strode into the criminal court of the Parlement of Paris displaying a book of poetry that he declared to be full of blasphemies. He asked the court to halt its sale, and arrest its author, Théophile de Viau. The duc de Montmorency, the poet's patron and protector, wrote the court a letter protesting his innocence, but Viau was found guilty of impiety and given a harsh sentence in August 1624. He was to be taken in a tumbril from the prisons of the Conciergerie to the doors of Notre Dame where, in his shirt sleeves on his knees with bare head and feet, a rope around his neck, carrying a lit candle, he was to confess and to ask forgiveness for having written, published and sold *The Satirical Parnassus*, a book full of blasphemies and abominations against God and the church. Then he was to be taken to the place de Grèce and burned alive, his ashes scattered to the winds. Needless to say, he was nowhere to be found when it came time to execute the sentence. He had been in hiding for months, so he was burned in effigy.

Viau had almost certainly taken refuge in Montmorency's château of Chantilly north of Paris. At the end of August, he slipped away from the château, and headed north toward the frontier, hoping to cross into the Low Countries. But he was arrested outside Saint-Quentin, tied up, brought into town on an old, lame horse and put in leg irons in an underground cell. He was returned to Paris, where he was imprisoned in the Conciergerie in what had been the cell of Ravaillac, the mad monk who had assassinated Henri IV. The cell was dark except for a few hours at noon – he was allowed neither a fire nor candles – and it was cold, wet and crawling with vermin, but the food was adequate. He spent months there until the Parlement of Paris reversed its decision, and banished him for life. Released from prison in September 1625, Viau was given two weeks to get his affairs in order and leave France. But he went into hiding again and, after travelling incognito with Montmorency for a while, he returned to Paris where he suddenly fell ill, slipped into a coma and died in September 1626, at the age of thirty-six.[1]

Théophile de Viau had been born into a Protestant family in southwestern France. His father had been a lawyer in the Parlement of Bordeaux, and his grandfather a secretary of Marguerite de Navarre. The family had been recently ennobled through service to Henri IV. While attending the University of Leyden, Viau became friendly with Jean-Louis Guez de Balzac, who inherited his father's place as principal secretary to the duc d'Epernon. His father also secured a place for his friend as a butler in the household of Epernon's son, the comte de Candale, and Viau became well-known in Parisian literary circles.[2] In June 1619, however, he was suddenly exiled from France for having written poetry that ridiculed the royal favourite, the duc de Luynes. He went into hiding and, nine months later, after he had published an ode in praise of the favourite, the order was rescinded and he was allowed to return to court. Théophile de Viau now entered the service of Luynes, who was an ardent Catholic, so he converted to Catholicism, and remained in Luynes's service until the favourite's death in December 1621. Then he approached Montmorency, and asked to enter his service, having already published poetry in his praise. Household service was a form of cultural patronage, and the poet became a member of the duke's household in 1622. To his misfortune, however, he had already attracted the attention of a Catholic zealot, Father Garasse, a Jesuit who denounced him as an unbeliever and a libertine in a widely read pamphlet that resulted in his imprisonment, banishment and death.[3]

This chapter looks at marginals and misfits like Théophile de Viau, seeking to explain why they did not fit into seventeenth-century society and what happened to them. Other previously discussed outsiders include Protestants, Jansenists, Jews and resident aliens. Freethinkers, rationalists and scientists, who were intellectual nonconformists, and witches, beggars, vagrants and criminals, who were social nonconformists, are discussed in this chapter. Marginals were treated harshly by seventeenth-century society, which was intolerant. There was a large, impoverished underbelly in this society, which did not have much of an institutional safety net, and those without resources suffered. Outsiders and nonconformists had to develop their own solidarities in order to survive.

FREETHINKERS AND RATIONALISTS

The best-known intellectual dissenters of the early seventeenth century were the libertines, although controversy surrounds this pejorative term used by their critics. They were also known as freethinkers because they questioned aspects of church orthodoxy, and were considered sceptics for this reason. The libertines had been influenced by non-Christian Greek and Roman philosophy. Humanist sceptics such as Montaigne had tended to view morality in natural terms, arguing that men formed their beliefs through their experiences independently of church dogma. The libertine François de la Mothe Le Vayer, an admirer of Montaigne, published a book in 1641 in which he argued that nature provided the means by which men might lead virtuous lives whether they were Christian or not. His critics protested that such opinions minimized the necessity of being Christian, endangered readers' souls and encouraged debauchery. Whether or not La Mothe Le Vayer and other freethinkers were orthodox Christians is in dispute, but their critics confused free thought with loose morals, and considered them immoral because their thinking was unorthodox. The word libertine connotes a dissolute lifestyle, which was attributed to them by their critics, who insisted that they spent most of their time drinking in taverns. Théophile de Viau was probably the most notorious freethinker. Most freethinkers, however, did not lead immoral lives.[4]

The traditional interpretation insists that the libertines were sceptics, who concealed their doubts in order to conduct a hidden assault upon church orthodoxy. The libertines attacked the Trinity; the existence of angels, demons and witches; the nature of divine attributes; facts in the lives of saints; relics, processions and exorcisms. Libertines such as Gabriel Naudé and Pierre Gassendi insisted on separating the truths of faith from those of reason, a position known as fideism, which implies that the one contradicts the other. The traditionalists insist that the libertines were immoral hypocrites who undermined church orthodoxy and led lives of debauchery.[5]

This interpretation has obvious flaws. First, it uses the vocabulary and expresses the attitudes of the libertines' seventeenth-century critics, repeating the charges that Father Garasse made against Théophile de Viau. Second, it insists that these writers kept their subversive thoughts to themselves, or expressed them in a coded, deliberately convoluted way rather than being direct and honest in their expression, which if true opens their work to all sorts of interpretations, some of them bizarre. This was, in fact, the technique used by Father Garasse, who constructed libertine thought himself by stitching together isolated lines of poetry out of context, and then attributing the results to Viau.[6]

The traditional interpretation has been criticized by revisionists who emphasize the Christian content of libertine thought. The revisionists challenge the traditionalist attack upon the libertines' sincerity, and argue that they represented a liberal Catholicism opposed to superstitious witch-hunting and fanatical Protestantism. The libertines had no intention of destroying Christianity or undermining church orthodoxy, quite the reverse. They sought to defend the church against its enemies and critics. Their scepticism was more anti-superstition than anti-Christian, and they were more independent free thinkers than sceptics. The libertines were attacking the credulity of men and the mistakes of organized religion rather than Christianity itself.[7]

Atheism in the seventeenth century was considered a form of free thought. Atheism was scepticism about certain aspects of church orthodoxy, including a diminished role for God in the creation of the world, a belief in the spontaneous generation of matter and a denial that Christ's miracles were in any way natural. Holding one or more of these beliefs did not preclude believing in the existence of God, although not necessarily in an orthodox Christian God. Scholars debate whether atheism in the modern sense of disbelief in the existence of God was possible in this century. It has been argued that the conceptual tools for such an atheism did not exist in the sixteenth century, and that atheism was created by theologians themselves in the seventeenth century while attacking the enemies of Christianity, just as Father Garasse had helped to create libertine thought by attacking Théophile de Viau. Atheism in this view existed more in the imagination of theologians than in reality. On the other hand, it has also been argued that atheism actually existed in sixteenth and seventeenth-century Italy, and that a form of atheism had appeared in France by the late seventeenth century. The problem is that scholars do not agree on exactly what early modern atheism was.[8]

Cartesian rationalism, appearing in the second quarter of the seventeenth century, was a form of thought that had far more radical consequences in the long term than freethinking. Influenced by the new astronomy and physics, René Descartes (1596–1650) was a mathematician who created a new system of thought. He had settled in 1625 in Paris where he began to attract a following in the salons. He became uneasy, however, at the fate of Théophile de Viau and other freethinkers, so he emigrated to Holland where he published his *Discourse on Method* in 1637. He wrote in an easy, readable French style to attract the attention of an educated Parisian audience. He was successful, and the Cartesian rationalists became the heirs of the freethinkers. Descartes considered his major work to be his books on mathematics, physics and mechanics, and intended the *Discourse* only as an introduction to his other work to explain how he had reached his conclusions.

In the *Discourse*, Descartes presented his system of critical doubt, which was meant to establish a structure of truths or first principles about the natural world. Descartes wrote that he must doubt all sense evidence as uncertain, except the indisputable truth that he existed, because, if he did not exist, he would not be thinking. His famous words were, 'I think therefore I am' (*cogito ergo sum*). This was the basic truth upon which he intended, with mathematically precise reasoning, to build a system of truths. By deducing logically from one certain principle to another, he thought it possible to deduce everything important about the natural world. His basic truth, 'I think therefore I am', was, in fact, an intuitive maxim. His only other such maxim was that God existed, but whether Descartes himself was an orthodox Catholic or not is in dispute. An inductive, experimental method of discovering truth appeared at about the same time.[9] Both of these methods were used to discover truths about the natural world, and to reject traditional scientific knowledge unless it could be demonstrated rationally. In particular, they rejected the medieval Aristotelian view of the universe in favour of the new Copernican astronomy and the Galilean science using experimentation.[10]

What was completely unexpected was the sudden interest in the new science that now swept Parisian intellectual circles and salons, inspired mainly by the writings of Descartes. The universities and Jesuit colleges continued to teach the old Aristotelian science, and were frequently hostile to the new science. So, knowledge about Cartesian rationalism and physics had to be disseminated privately outside established educational institutions. Informal gatherings were held to present lectures, demonstrations and experiments. Jacques Rohault, who was a teacher of mathematics, held meetings every Wednesday afternoon in Paris to discuss Cartesian physics and perform experiments, while Théophraste Renaudot conducted lectures and demonstrations every Monday afternoon. The abbé La Roque held natural philosophy discussions on Thursday afternoons, while Messieurs le Chevalier Chassebras du Bréau and de Fontenay hosted discussions of the new science and physics on Saturday afternoons. Their gatherings overlapped with the Saturday scientific salons of Mesdames de Guedreville and Bonneveau. Cartesianism and the new science were also discussed in the Parisian salons of Mesdames de la Sablière, de Sablé and de Sévigné, and that of the duchesse du Maine in her nearby château at Sceaux. Men of letters began discussing the new science, while the aristocracy in general, and noblewomen in particular, were fascinated by Cartesianism. Science was discussed in the literary salons of Madeleine de Scudéry and Madame Deshoulières; literature was discussed in the scientific salons of Madame de Sévigné and the duchesse du Maine. The new science, necessarily because of the way it was disseminated, became a sociable discipline.[11]

Besides attending salons and informal lectures, men of science exchanged views through correspondence, visits and travel, collecting and lending books, and attending academy meetings. Marsin Mersenne was a mathematician who conducted a large international correspondence, as did Ismael Boulliau, Pierre Gassendi and Nicolas Fabri de Peiresc, who held an open house for scholars and scientists at his estate near Aix-en-Provence. Correspondents exchanged publications, visited each other and travelled together to visit mutual friends and scholars, which included visits to Paris by provincials and travels to foreign countries. Collecting books, manuscripts, medals, coins and objects of interest for their *cabinets*, or studies, had been popular among scholars for years; scientific meetings were often held in *cabinets*. The best known library in Paris was that of Jacques-Auguste de Thou, administered by the brothers Jacques and Pierre Du Puy who had their own *cabinet*, as did Gabriel Naudé who was Mazarin's librarian. Buying and lending books became an occasion for exchanging views. Regular scientific meetings such as those sponsored by Jacques Rohault, Marsin Mersenne and Théophraste Renaudot were formalized in private academies. Others in Paris included those of Habert de Montmor, who collected books and held academy meetings at his home;

Pierre Bourdelot, who was the physician of the Condé family, and held meetings in their town house; and the duc de Luynes, who had a château at nearby Dampierre. Private academies were followed by state-sponsored public academies such as the *Académie française* (1635) and the *Académie des sciences* (1666) in Paris, and their provincial counterparts. Women could not join the public academies, but they attended meetings of the private academies.[12] The popularity of the new science may have contributed to the declining interest in Catholic Reform by turning the attention of the educated elite in other directions.

Men interested in the new science were unable to make a living by researching, publishing or teaching it; the word 'scientist' had not even been coined. The pursuit of science was not yet considered a profession, and there was still only a modest public interest in it despite its growing popularity among intellectuals. Scientists made a living as judges, lawyers, clerics, doctors, publishers, instrument makers, philosophy and mathematics teachers, clients of nobles and so forth; they did not fit a social type. They were usually self-taught, and came from all over France. The majority were Catholic, although a notable minority were Jansenists and, above all, they were sociable.[13]

Sociability has been defined as the voluntary interaction among individuals of different social standing. In other words, a sociable individual was someone who enjoyed the company of others, including strangers.[14] Although the word was not coined until later, sociability flourished during the seventeenth century because of urbanization, the new civility, Cartesian rationalism and the new science. While civility encouraged relationships based on sociability, it was also important to the development of the new science. To validate the results of experiments, it was necessary to provide an authority for them, which became the credibility of those performing the experiments. If the experimenters were gentlemen, their courtesy and civility was their credibility because gentlemen were known to be honourable, reputable and reliable. The new civility equated good manners with honour, and honourable men never lied or committed fraud.[15]

Seventeenth-century cultural sociability helped to produce the concept of a republic of letters, which became a foundation for the Enlightenment. The republic of letters was an international intellectual community, cosmopolitan, egalitarian and sociable in nature, extending back to the ancient world, and reaching all over Europe to include men of letters and science everywhere. The characteristics of the late seventeenth-century republic, however, may have differed from its mid-eighteenth-century counterpart.[16] Cultural sociability also led to a transformation in political culture through the development of a public political sphere. After 1715, men of learning began to turn their skills of inquiry and debate to the previously neglected topics of public policy and government action, and began to criticize the crown's policies and decisions, which led to public political opinions for the first time.[17] Ties of sociability were vital to the dissemination and development of the new science. These ties helped to create a republic of letters and a public political discourse, and were an essential social solidarity that reinforced shared intellectual interests in the face of an often indifferent, sometimes hostile society.

WITCHES

It has been estimated that there were 100,000 to 110,000 trials for witchcraft in Europe between 1450 and 1750, resulting in 40,000 to 60,000 executions of whom only 20 to 25 per cent of the victims were men. Prosecutions for witchcraft increased rapidly during the decades between 1580 and 1680. Approximately 10,000 of these trials occurred in France, which has been called 'the cradle of the great witch-hunt' because so many of its cases were adjudicated.[18] Why was there a sudden increase in witchcraft prosecutions after 1580, and what caused the equally sudden decline after 1680?

The Grandier case was one of the most notorious of the French witchcraft trials. Urbain Grandier was the curé of Saint Pierre du Marché in Loudun in western France. Although he was handsome, intelligent and eloquent, his caustic wit, arrogance and belligerence caused widespread resentment and, when he began to seduce townswomen, he made deadly enemies. Loudun, a Protestant stronghold, was the target of a conversion campaign directed by Cardinal Richelieu's confessor, Father Joseph. A house of Ursulines was established at Loudun in 1627 to help in this campaign, headed by an ambitious young abbess, Jeanne des Anges. After Grandier refused to become the Ursulines' confessor, Jeanne des Anges declared herself possessed of demons, and under exorcism denounced Grandier as responsible. She fell into trances, and exhibited frightening contortions and convulsions. Demonic possession spread among the Ursulines like the plague, and seventeen more nuns declared themselves afflicted. Under exorcism, they denounced Grandier as their bewitcher, describing him as a dark spectre who terrorized them at night. They screamed lasciviously at the mention of his name, ripped their clothing and threw themselves on the ground, writhing and cursing. Many in Loudun were eager to believe in his guilt.

Grandier was tried for witchcraft in July and August 1634, found guilty by a judge whom Cardinal Richelieu had appointed, and condemned to death. After begging forgiveness at the doors of Loudun's churches on his knees with a rope around his neck, holding a lighted candle, he was taken to the Place de Sainte-Croix, tied to a stake and burned alive after being tortured to force him to confess his guilt and name his accomplices. Grandier's legs were crushed by his torturers, so he had to be carried to his execution on a cart. With his shirt soaked in sulphur, he proclaimed his innocence until the flames enveloped him. Parisian intellectuals and freethinkers like Théophraste Renaudot, Guy Patin and Gabriel Naudé were dubious about the reality of demonic possession, and sceptical about Grandier's guilt. As medical doctors, they were suspicious of cases of possession in convents, attributing the nuns'symptoms to hysteria, erotic impulses, melancholia and mental illness. They recognized that emotional instability and a craving for attention could motivate accusers. Jeanne des Anges became a national celebrity, and was still being exorcised for demons three years after Grandier's death.[19]

Accusations of witchcraft often expressed enmities that were an outgrowth of local or familial feuds and rivalries. Urbain Grandier, for example, was a parish priest who had made powerful enemies. As the member of a Loudun circle of savants, he had become the good friend of another member, one of his parishioners, Louis Trincant, who was a state's attorney. In 1629, Trincant's oldest daughter became pregnant, and named Grandier as the father. He denied it, but rumours swept the town, and Grandier's death was the result of the enmity that developed between him and the Trincants, an important family with many friends and allies. They were not his only enemies.

A year after Grandier's arrival in Loudun, he had insisted that, as a canon of Sainte-Croix, he should take precedence in a church procession over the bishop of Luçon. Although Loudun was in the bishop's diocese, the bishop was participating, not in his episcopal capacity, but as the visiting prior of an abbey in the Loudun diocese. The bishop, of course, was Richelieu. Proud and ambitious, from an old noble family, he was not likely to forget having to walk behind an upstart commoner. Richelieu's successor, who was a close friend, was not likely to forget either, and Bishop de La Rocheposay became an enemy of the young priest. Grandier also quarrelled with other clerics in Loudun including the Capuchins, who were Father Joseph's order, and with René Hervé, the criminal lieutenant who was both judge and police chief.[20]

Historians disagree on the role of the state in witch-hunting, but it is clear that the condemnation of Urbain Grandier could not have occurred without Richelieu's approval. The Loudun authorities were acting with the support of the Paris government. Historians have argued that the increase in witchcraft prosecutions was a result of the judicial and administrative centralization of the early modern state. A centralizing royal bureaucracy in Paris extended its control over local courts, and introduced new judicial methods that included the use of inquisitorial procedures and judicial torture to force confessions. As a result, local authorities began to prosecute witchcraft cases which would previously have been ignored. Judges and other members of the royal bureaucracy, buttressed by a church implementing Tridentine Reform, were at the same time attacking rural superstition. Robert Muchembled has argued that royal officials and rural missionaries sought to suppress witchcraft, a form of popular culture and religion, as part of a process of rural acculturation accompanying statebuilding and Catholic Reform.[21]

Judicial torture was considered necessary to force the truth from unreliable or reluctant witnesses when the penalty was death, and used to force confessions in capital cases; confessions were considered necessary to convict. Torture was not used if other means of gathering evidence were available. The threat of torture always preceded its application, and it was never used on the physically frail. Judges decided its use and form. Common forms of torture concentrated on the body's extremities, either distending and dislocating them as in the rack and strappado, or compressing and crushing them as in thumbscrews and legscrews, which were used on Grandier. In France, those already convicted and awaiting execution could be tortured for information about other crimes and criminals, which happened to Urbain Grandier.[22]

The causal connection between statebuilding and witch-hunting has been challenged, however. Local authorities were usually the moving force in witchcraft prosecutions, and they did not act as agents of the central government in so doing. In fact, it was the Paris government's lack of control over local authorities, and its failure to supervise local courts, that led to the increase in witchcraft prosecutions. A study of witchcraft cases adjudicated by the Parlement of Paris demonstrates that the number of death sentences handed down was less than half the total; sentences were often commuted during appeal; and torture was not routinely used in witchcraft cases. In other words, the Parlement of Paris, the most important high court with the largest jurisdiction, was more reluctant than many provincial courts to prosecute witchcraft cases. It has also been noted that no royal edicts before 1682 even mentioned witchcraft.[23] These different views of the state's role in witch-hunting are not contradictory, however, because they refer to different periods. Local prosecutions increased in France until around mid-century, and then began to decline as the central government became stronger.

Other causes of witch-hunting included scapegoating; misogyny; and religious reform. Everyday occurrences were often incomprehensible, for example, sudden illnesses causing paralysis, blindness or death; birth deformities, miscarriages and still births; children who died overnight; mental illness; accidents of all kinds; damages to crops from weather; deaths of domestic animals from disease. These disasters, however, could be explained by the operation of a witch in the neighbourhood.[24] Witch-hunting provided a release for the fears and anxieties caused by hard times.

Witch-hunting as a form of scapegoating also explains who was accused and why. Seventy-five to eighty per cent of the accused were women, mostly old, poor and alone, widows or spinsters without children or kin, who were believed to resort to supernatural forces because of their weakness. They made good scapegoats because they were isolated, defenceless and unable to fight back. Accusations of witchcraft projected patriarchal social fears on to these women, who were considered troublemakers because they were outside the direct control of husbands and fathers. There was an antifemale bias in early modern society. Women were considered morally weaker and more emotional than men, and thought to suffer from an overwhelming sexual passion that made them easy prey for the devil; it was believed that witches engaged in carnal relations with the devil. Charges of sexual offenses began to accompany accusations of witchcraft. Such charges were increasingly made against innocent women who, unlike freethinkers and rationalists, had not chosen to play the role of witch.

Urbain Grandier was a man accused of witchcraft. Twenty to twenty-five per cent of those accused were men, a percentage that may have been higher in France because so many witchcraft trials there involved demonic possession. Male witches were often clergy. Male witches also tended to be accused of 'unnatural' sexual offenses such as incest, sodomy or bestiality; heresy; serious theft involving murder, banditry or sacrilege (theft from a church); and arson – a firesetter was someone in league with the devil. Witchcraft became another form of heresy and, since it was believed that witches worshipped the devil, they were burned alive to give them a foretaste of the eternal hell they were entering as devil worshippers.

Among men and women accused of witchcraft, there was a high percentage of beggars and vagrants: witch-hunts were a good excuse to rid villages of these undesirables. Everyone thought witches were motivated by malice because they lacked a sense of community, so those on the fringes of a community with little or no stake in it were usually accused of witchcraft. Also accused were habitual quarrellers who had given offense to important people or to everyone in a community. Regarded as troublemakers, they had already been the subject of widespread rumours and gossip. A witch was someone outside the community, or someone who had caused conflict within the community. Urbain Grandier had become notorious as a seducer-priest, an inversion of his church role making him a threat to the community, and he had quarrelled with important people in Loudun. He became the victim of his own reputation for womanizing when he refused to act as the Ursulines' confessor. In their minds, he was a much sought-after individual, even a love object, who had spurned them, and they retaliated by accusing him of witchcraft. Clerics, doctors, midwives, herbalists, cooks and wet-nurses were especially vulnerable to charges of witchcraft.[25]

It has been argued that Protestant and Catholic reform intensified witch-hunting. Reformers had become preoccupied with the devil and his power in the world, which they viewed as a battlefield in a cosmic conflict between good and evil. Witches were the devil's soldiers in the war for souls. The medieval devil had been the anti-type of Christ, teaching hatred rather than love but, by 1600, the devil had become the anti-type of God the Father, a cosmic force demanding obedience. This change enhanced the devil's role, and consequently that of witches. It occurred because of a change in the Christian moral code. The seven deadly sins (pride, covetousness, lust, envy, anger, gluttony and sloth), the basis of the medieval code, were replaced by the ten commandments (beginning with 'thou shalt not'), which focused on obedience. The emphasis shifted from a sinner's reconciliation with God to his obedience to the will of God. Sin now became disobedience, and witch-craft became devil worship, obedience to the devil and heresy. Overzealous reformers, both Protestant and Catholic, regarded themselves as fighting sin, evil, the devil, heresy and idolatry when they detected witches and exorcised demons. The militancy of religious reform intensified witch-hunting.

Not all historians agree. It has been pointed out that there was a low rate of conviction in witchcraft trials in Calvin's Geneva, a city traditionally regarded as severe in its persecution of witches. It has also been pointed out that the Aristotelian naturalism of Thomas Aquinas encouraged scepticism about de-monology, which would have been intensified by Catholic Reform. A liberal Catholicism regarded demonic possession and exorcism as dubious, and witch-hunting as superstition. Regional differences in witch-hunting were so extreme that it can be difficult to suggest one all-encompassing theory to explain the phenomenon satisfactorily. Witch-hunting had more than one cause.[26]

Robert Mandrou has argued that the decline in witchcraft prosecutions after 1680 was the result of what he called 'a spiritual revolution' among the judiciary, first in Paris, then in the provinces. The widespread dissemination of Cartesian rationalism and the new science lessened the judges' belief in demonology and diabolism. Among the educated elite, there was a growing disbelief in the devil's power and his intervention in the world and, con-sequently, in demonic possession and witchcraft. Increasingly, it was recog-nized that occurrences previously attributed to witchcraft had natural causes, and that witchcraft was just superstition, not a crime. This change in attitude among the elite brought an end to witch-hunting. Judges became increasingly reluctant to hear witchcraft cases, an attitude that discouraged their prosecu-tion, and the result was a decline in the number of prosecutions.[27]

Mandrou's interpretation has been challenged, however. A study of witch-craft cases on appeal before the Parlement of Paris from 1565 to 1640 has led Alfred Soman to conclude that changes in the judges' attitude toward witchcraft had little to do with the intellectual revolution of the seventeenth century. These changes had begun to occur before the appearance of Cartesian rationalism, and had less to do with scepticism about the reality of witchcraft as a crime than with the efforts of Paris judges to impose higher standards of criminal justice on the lower courts. The Paris judges increasingly insisted on a higher standard of proof in criminal trials, including free confessions not made under torture or the threat of torture, and firsthand testimony by several unimpeachable witnesses. The enforcement of higher standards of proof in witchcraft trials meant fewer convictions, more sentences overturned on appeal and fewer prosecutions. This was an ongoing change in criminal justice not directly related to the new science.[28]

Robert Muchembled has suggested that these interpretations are not contradictory. Changes in the criminal justice system accompanied the growing disbelief in witchcraft from the spread of Cartesian rationalism and physics. Changes in the criminal justice system were also part of the early modern state's efforts to achieve judicial uniformity. Simultaneously, the implementation of Tridentine reform, and the increase in literacy from the new religious schools, discredited superstition. By the end of the seventeenth century, those in authority at the local level, whether they were judges, lawyers, schoolteachers, doctors or priests, were discouraging the practice of scapegoating through witch-hunting. Like witch-hunting itself, the decline in witchcraft prosecutions had multiple causes.[29]

POVERTY AND CRIME

Chronic, endemic poverty and a soaring crime rate characterized seventeenth-century society. The only resource of the poor was their labour, which was barely enough to keep them alive. Living hand-to-mouth, they were unable to save, and so had no resources to fall back on in time of trouble. With the demographic crisis, their numbers swelled and they became a problem serious enough to demand the state's attention for the first time. Between 40 and 50 per cent of the population by 1700 were poor, and about 50 to 60 per cent of the poor were indigent, that is, destitute and often homeless. About one-quarter to one-third of the population, therefore, were beggars and vagrants with no means of support and no fixed abode. Criminals often came from this group.[30] What methods did Louis XIV's government use to deal with the related problems of poverty and crime, and how effective were they?

Poverty was a cause of crime. Prostitutes, for example, were usually destitute and unemployed, or the near-destitute working poor. In 1648, a procuress named Barbe approached 20-year-old Catherine Jacquelin, an unemployed domestic servant, who was selling wine in the streets of Dijon and starving. Barbe told her that she could do better by 'abandoning herself' to a man of quality, and that she, Barbe, could arrange such a liaison. This began Jacquelin's life of prostitution, which lasted for only 6 weeks before she was arrested, convicted, whipped and banished. Catherine Robin, the 22-year-old daughter of a shoemaker, was arrested by Dijon's authorities in 1649 for streetwalking. She said that her brother had returned from the war and, finding her pregnant after a failed courtship, had kicked her out of the house. Dishonoured, she had wandered Burgundy's roads and, when she could not find work as a servant, she had fallen in with a group of women in similar straits. When these women were arrested for prostitution, they said they had done it 'to stay alive'. Besides whipping and banishment, the punishment usually included public shaming. Claudine Chevenet, a mason's wife, was convicted in 1700 of procuring, and sentenced to be whipped in Dijon's main squares wearing a placard that said 'public procuress', then branded with a hot iron on her left shoulder, and banished from the town for five years.[31]

Contemporaries divided the poor into deserving and undeserving on the basis of whether they worked or not. In the first group were the temporarily unemployed, and those who could not earn enough to feed families unable to support themselves. The deserving poor worked, and so had a place in society, however precarious. They also included those who could not work because they were elderly, ill, crippled, insane, widows with small children and abandoned or orphaned children. In the second group were the undeserving poor, who were able-bodied and could work, but did not. They were the beggars, tramps and criminals; the crimes of the poor were begging, vagrancy, theft, smuggling and prostitution. Having no place in society, the undeserving poor were regarded as a threat to public order, and the rapid growth in their numbers caused anxiety and fear, especially in cities which had a concentration of wealth. There was a high urban crime rate.[32]

Crime was an overwhelmingly male activity: 70 to 80 per cent of urban crimes were committed by males, usually young adults aged 20 to 40, frequently rural immigrants from regions around the city. They tended to be illiterate and unskilled labourers with a high rate of unemployment. Over half the crimes of first-time offenders were petty thefts of clothing and food; it is easy to assume that the motive was deprivation. In addition to theft, women were arrested for female crimes including prostitution, procuring and brothel-keeping; concubinage, often with a priest; licentious behaviour; abortion, infanticide and the abandonment or murder of an unwanted child, usually illegitimate. Women were less likely than men to take to the roads as vagrants, but this did happen.[33]

The state's attorney at Avalon in Burgundy arrested 'a troop of vagabonds' in 1695 for being a threat to public order, and won convictions against six of them. Margueritte Jacquenet was the leader of the troop, which included her son Jean and daughter Jeanne, plus two other unrelated men and an unrelated woman, none married but all living together, so they were also charged with concubinage and licentiousness. Margueritte Jacquenet was condemned to hang; Jean was to spend the rest of his life in the galleys; one of the other men was sent to the galleys for five years; the remaining man and two women were to be present at the execution of their leader and then banished from Avalon for life. Fortunately, their sentences were reduced on appeal. Vagrants often banded together in small groups for the purpose of robbery. Women acted as scouts, decoys and disposed of stolen goods for these gangs, which were feared by the authorities because their members were repeat offenders; branding allowed their identification.[34] Professional criminals had to forge their own solidarities in order to survive.

An interpretation of patterns in early modern crime, based on evidence from Normandy, suggests that sixteenth and seventeenth-century crimes were largely violence against persons, that is, physical and verbal assaults while, in the eighteenth century, crimes against property such as theft and fraud became more prevalent. This interpretation has been criticized, however, because theft was frequent in the seventeenth century, and a high rate of violent crime continued in the Auvergne, Languedoc and southwestern France during the eighteenth century. These regions were rural and backward. Did similar levels of violent crime exist in the cities? Regional considerations seem to have been important in determining the prevalence of types of crimes.[35]

Seventeenth-century punishments for crime were brutal by modern standards, the severity far out of proportion to the crime. Punishment was considered proportional to the social danger the crime posed, not to the damage it caused. The more dangerous the crime, the harsher the punishment, so the penalties for treason and heresy were horrendous, as in the cases of Théophile de Viau and Urbain Grandier. In addition, public shaming and humiliation were widely used. It was hoped that harsh punishment, administered publicly, would deter potential criminals. Since crime was equated with sin, punishment was at the same time both penance and expiation.[36]

The policy of incarcerating the poor dated from the sixteenth century, and was revived by a 1656 royal edict creating a Paris hospital-detention complex known as the general hospital. Edicts created other general hospitals in cities that did not already have them. Within a year, the Paris general hospital housed nearly 6,000 beggars, vagabonds and criminals, among whom were also incarcerated the aged, senile, insane, orphans and prostitutes, all herded together. The edict creating the Paris general hospital ordered the undeserving poor to present themselves at its doors to be given work, and those who failed to do so, and continued to beg or steal, were to be arrested by the police and forcibly confined. Detainees, who had grown in number to 8,000 by 1673, worked long hours to help defray their expenses. General hospitals were workhouses.[37]

A new Paris official, the lieutenant general of police, was created by an edict in 1667, and given the authority to cope with urban problems, including unsafe and badly maintained streets, mountains of filth and rubbish everywhere, unemployment, begging, crime and prostitution. The word 'police' was understood more broadly than it is today, and meant the regulation of nearly every aspect of public life. The power of the police, however, was limited by the fact that they were few in number and lacked funding. Their inefficiency is demonstrated by their inability to control prostitution.

Prostitution was illegal, but the numbers of prostitutes in cities grew at an alarming rate. By 1700, there were at least 40,000 prostitutes in Paris alone, 30,000 of them destitute and on the streets, while prostitution in Marseille and Montpellier had reached epidemic proportions. The police tried, unsuccessfully, to control the activities of prostitutes by restricting them to red-light districts, but they openly solicited everywhere in the public gardens, bath-houses, taverns and theatres, at the city's gates and bridges, and on the grands boulevards. Some of them were protected by the police or acted as police informants. An edict in 1684 ordered the imprisonment in general hospitals of all prostitutes under 25 who were repeat offenders. Another edict ordered that prostitutes found within 8 kilometres of army camps were to have their noses and ears slit; the military authorities were worried about the spread of venereal disease. This edict was not enforced but, by 1703, there were 4,512 prostitutes in the Paris Salpêtrière hospital, about 10 per cent of those in the city. In fact, the police only arrested prostitutes if they had committed other crimes or were known to be syphilitic; in its last stages syphilis can cause madness. The police did not have the manpower to control prostitution.[38]

An edict in 1700 required that all able-bodied beggars return to their places of birth in order to clear the cities. Men failing to comply were to be whipped for first offenses, and women incarcerated in general hospitals. Punishments for second offenses included whipping, pillorying and five years in the galleys. This edict was impossible to enforce. Attempted enforcement in Paris led to beggars fighting in the streets with the police; the edict was a dead letter everywhere else. The Paris police were more effective than most, but they were unpopular because of their brutality and corruption; low wages made them easy to bribe. The police in Languedoc were both ineffective and detested for their abusive arrests and for the harsh summary justice of the police courts.[39]

The crown issued a new criminal ordinance in 1670 codifying the existing tangle of criminal law, and establishing procedures used in criminal trials for a century. Reflecting the crown's concern about the crime rate, trial procedures were weighted heavily in favour of judges, who determined the guilt or innocence of the accused, questioned witnesses, directed the investigation of evidence and decided if judicial torture would be used. There was no formal criminal charge, no cross-examination of witnesses by prosecution or defence, no defence lawyer except in cases of civil fraud and no jury. The ordinance's philosophy of justice was based, not on the fear that an innocent person might be wrongly punished, but that he or she might be guilty and escape punishment, leaving society unprotected.[40]

Enlightenment thinkers regarded the 1670 criminal code as harsh, outmoded and unjust, while historians from an Anglo-American legal background invariably reject judge-dominated inquisitorial procedures. This combined hostility has produced a tenacious myth about the barbarism of criminal justice during the Old Regime.[41] Michel Foucault restated this myth when he began his book on the development of the modern prison system with an account of the horrifying public execution of the regicide Damiens in 1757. Foucault rightly observed that such cruel punishments were not everyday penal practice. Spectacular public rituals of execution, heavy with Christian symbolism, did not occur frequently, although they were massively attended when they did. Foucault contrasted these public spectacles, which were intended to control criminal behaviour through intimidation, with the forms of control replacing them inside prisons. Developing in the late eighteenth and nineteenth centuries, prisons sought to control and reshape inmates' behaviour through the use of reason and voluntary cooperation, although the regimes established were often grotesque, mindless and coercive.[42]

In an earlier book on the creation of insane asylums, Foucault argued that the establishment of the Paris general hospital was a landmark event in what he called, 'The Great Confinement', the state's policy of removing from society all those whom it considered a threat. The uncontrollable, often violent behaviour of the insane made them dangerous, so they were at first confined in general hospitals with beggars, vagrants and criminals, and later in separate asylums. Foucault dwelt at some length on the harsh conditions in public institutions, and their repressive efforts to reform inmates' behaviour. The crown made a serious national effort to bring mendicity under control from 1724 to 1733, rounding up beggars everywhere in France and putting them to work in general hospitals, but this effort was not successful.

Foucault's work is widely recognized as original and influential, especially his 1961 book on madness. His work and that of the Annalistes have inspired most of the recent studies on marginals and the poor. Foucault has been criticized, however, for his schematization, selectiveness in arguments based on non-archival evidence, overgeneralizations and exaggerations for dramatic effect. Revisionist historians have challenged some of his interpretations.[43] It should be noted, however, that Foucault's observations on the state policy of incarcerating social undesirables, and on the secularization of poor relief during the seventeenth century, have been widely accepted.

The revisionists argue that Foucault concentrated on state-sponsored public charitable institutions, and in so doing he overlooked private religious and local charitable institutions that were far more numerous and just as important. He ignored the influence of the Christian charitable impulse, which had been given new vigour by Catholic Reform, and he failed to recognize that most charities were the result of private initiative, not royal policy. He overlooked the diverse origins of 'The Great Confinement', and perpetuated the myth that inmates were mistreated in public charitable institutions.

The origins of 'The Great Confinement' were in Lyon, not in Paris. The model for the general hospital was Notre Dame de La Charité, which was used to confine the poor of Lyon from the day it opened in 1622, and inspired similar hospitals at Orléans (1642), Marseille (1643) and Angoulême (1650). Their forerunners included the poor bureaus established in sixteenth-century cities to supervise the distribution of bread. Numerous religious institutions for poor relief were founded during the sixteenth century, and there was another wave of such foundations with Catholic Reform. Important seventeenth-century charities included those of the Company of the Holy Sacrament, confraternities, new religious orders such as the Daughters of Charity and Lazarists, various municipal institutions and parish poor tax funds administered by local priests. In addition, there was private almsgiving, individual charitable donations and testamentary bequests by both Catholics and Protestants. The dévots founded private charitable institutions, and there was volunteer charitable work by aristocratic and urban elite women. These private initiatives were overlooked by Foucault, who ignored the force of Christian charity as a motive for poor relief. Private initiatives demonstrate that the institutionalized poor were not entirely separate from the rest of society.[44]

The revisionists have also criticized Foucault for not inquiring into the success of the state in implementing 'The Great Confinement'. Some edicts were not enforceable. The edict sending beggars back to their places of origin could not be enforced, and provoked street fighting. It was not unusual for able-bodied beggars to fight with the police who were trying to transport them to general hospitals. The royal government had to depend on local authorities to enforce its policies, and there was significant variation in enforcement. Some edicts were only partially enforced, and some were not enforced at all. Local efforts to administer general hospitals were hampered by inefficiency and negligence, and most hospitals were underfunded, which crippled their efforts. State-sponsored poor relief may have existed, but it was not effective, in part because the state itself was neither as efficient nor as powerful as Foucault believed.[45]

The revisionists insist that Foucault exaggerated the horrors of life in public charitable institutions. Archival-based studies of hospitals do not substantiate this myth, which developed during the Enlightenment as part of the general criticism of Old Regime institutions. The Christian charitable impulse responsible for founding and supporting poor relief institutions also created a genuine concern for the well-being of inmates. Religious institutions were often staffed by nurses from the new religious orders who had dedicated their lives to caring for the sick and poor. The daily realities of life within hospital walls were not as dreadful as Foucault claimed. Inmates developed loyalties to staff members and other inmates, and the hospital represented a surrogate family for individuals whose biological family was unknown or could not support them. Administrators often referred to the whole hospital community as a big family, and to themselves as 'fathers of the poor'. Charitable assistance created social solidarities.[46]

Revisionists have also noted that historians have tended to exaggerate the cruelty of the criminal justice system. Widespread inefficiency and negligence led to considerable laxity in enforcement. There was a high rate of unreported and unprosecuted crime, and sentences were not always enforced, as we have seen in the case of Théophile de Viau. The severity of the sentence was determined by the accused's rank and reputation, whether he was a repeat offender, the nature of his crime and the judge and court before which he appeared. As a result, sentences varied greatly. Non-corporal punishments were the most frequent, especially public shaming; others included fines, damage payments, confiscation and banishment. Also widely used were informal, popular methods of dispute resolution bypassing the courts entirely.

Even when corporal punishments were used, such as whipping or branding, the pain in most instances was temporary and bearable, and sentences were not always vigorously enforced. Whippings were categorized as with or without blood, not by how many strokes, and victims were often strangled first when executed by burning or breaking on the wheel. The use of judicial torture gradually disappeared, although it was only formally abolished in 1780. Its use declined because a new law of proof developed that allowed courts to convict without a confession; some of this new law appeared in the 1670 ordinance. Non-corporal and corporal punishments, combined in various ways, were far more common than imprisonment in the galleys or prisons. The 1670 ordinance was full of ambiguities and omissions, and had little specifically to say about punishment, the details of which were left to local enforcement authorities. In the same way, local judges interpreted the meaning of the ordinance, and their interpretations, determined by local considerations, varied significantly. The Old Regime criminal justice system is usually evaluated in terms of modern standards and practices, and seems barbaric in comparison. But, when it is evaluated in terms of the attitudes and conditions of its own time, it seems fairer and more effective.[47]

Louis XIV's government dealt with the growing problems of poverty and crime by establishing workhouses in the big cities; creating an urban police force to deal with beggars, vagrants and criminals; revising the criminal code; and depending upon harsh exemplary punishment to intimidate potential wrongdoers. None of these solutions was effective. The working poor were able to survive misfortune because they had solidarities on which to rely for assistance in time of need. Beggars, vagabonds and criminals had fewer solidarities on which to rely, or none at all, so they were more vulnerable to misfortune. Beggars lacked the solidarities of work, honour, reputation, sociability and obedience to the state. Vagrants, in addition, lacked the solidarities of family, household, kinship and neighbourhood or village. Marginals might still have the solidarity of church, parish and priest, and the loyalties created by charitable assistance reinforced those of the church. Heretics and witches condemned by the church were the real social outcasts. Intellectual nonconformists such as freethinkers, rationalists and scientists, and social nonconformists such as professional criminals, created their own solidarities. The undeserving poor were marginals because they did not work or have a place in society, but they were far too numerous to be regarded as true marginals on the fringes of society. They belonged instead to a large, impoverished underbelly of society composed of 40 to 50 per cent of the population.

Suggested reading

Robin Briggs, *Witches and Neighbours. The Social and Cultural Context of European Witchcraft* (London, 1996).

Cissie Fairchilds, *Poverty and Charity in Aix-en-Provence, 1640–1789* (Baltimore, 1976).

Michel Foucault, *Madness and Civilization. A History of Insanity in the Age of Reason*, tr. Richard Howard (New York, 1985); idem, *Discipline and Punish. The Birth of the Prison*, tr. Alan Sheridan (New York, 1979).

Anne Goldgar, *Impolite Learning. Conduct and Community in the Republic of Letters, 1680–1750* (New Haven, 1995).

Daniel Hickey, *Local Hospitals in Ancien Régime France. Rationalization, Resistance, Renewal, 1530–1789* (Montreal, 1997).

Olwen Hufton, *The Poor in Eighteenth-Century France* (Oxford, 1974).

Colin Jones, *The Charitable Imperative. Hospitals and Nursing in Ancien Regime and Revolutionary France* (London, 1989).

Joseph Klaits, *Servants of Satan. The Age of the Witch Hunts* (Boomington, 1985).

Brian Levack, *The Witch-Hunt in Early Modern Europe* (New York, 1987).

David Lux, *Patronage and Royal Science in Seventeenth-Century France* (Ithaca, 1989).

Robert Mandrou, *From Humanism to Science, 1480–1700*, tr. Brian Pearce (Atlantic Highlands, NJ, 1979).

Kathryn Norberg, *Rich and Poor in Grenoble, 1600–1814* (Berkeley, 1985).

Robert Rapley, *A Case of Witchcraft. The Trial of Urbain Grandier* (Montreal, 1998).

Julius Ruff, *Crime, Justice, and Public Order in Old Regime France* (Dover, NH, 1984).

Robert Schwartz, *Policing the Poor in Eighteenth-Century France* (Chapel Hill, 1988).

Howard Solomon, *Public Welfare, Science, and Propaganda. The Innovations of Théophraste Renaudot* (Princeton, 1972).

David Sturdy, *Science and Social Status. The Members of the Académie des Sciences, 1666–1750* (Woodbridge, Suffolk, 1995).

SOLIDARITIES AND SOCIAL CHANGE

The rebel forces of Henri II, duc de Montmorency, took the field against the royal army commanded by the maréchal de Schomberg at Castelnaudary in Languedoc on 1 September 1632. Montmorency fought in support of the king's rebellious younger brother, Gaston, duc d'Orléans, a bungler who did not even appear on the field himself. His absence made the outcome a foregone conclusion. The rebels had 3,000 cavalry and 2,000 infantry, who were mostly foreign mercenaries. Schomberg's troops, 1,200 horse and 1,000 foot, were outnumbered 2 to 1, but they were better trained and officered, so they won the day. The battle, which was really more of a skirmish, lasted for only 30 minutes, and the king, coming from Paris, had not even reached Lyon when he learned of his army's victory.

Armored and helmeted like a medieval knight, the thirty-seven year old Montmorency, who was known for his courage and prowess, led an attack on the left wing of the royal army, fighting valiantly with both sword and pistol. He broke through to the seventh rank, expecting his troops to follow him, but they did not. Stabbed and shot many times, with blood gushing from his mouth, he finally went down when his horse was shot from under him and trapped him by its weight. Royal officers, realizing that it was the duke from his gallantry, held back as if they did not want to take him prisoner, preferring to have his men rescue him. They wanted to spare him the shame of capture. Eventually, however, they had to seize him. Taking off his armour, they found him so badly wounded that they thought he was dying. The mortician who later prepared his body for burial found seventeen wounds. He had fought valiantly because he preferred a heroic death on the battlefield to a humiliating public execution for treason.

Montmorency was taken to Toulouse on 27 September, to be tried behind closed doors by the Parlement. The duke was popular, and the king did not want a public protest against his trial. Two days later the duke was found guilty, his presence at Castelnaudary being sufficient to convict him, and he was sentenced to immediate execution. Prominent members of the royal court including the queen, who had accompanied Louis XIII to Toulouse, begged for his life, but the king insisted that the sentence be carried out at once. On 30 September, Montmorency, the last of his line, mounted the newly built scaffold in the empty courtyard of the Toulouse city hall. The gates had been shut, but the crowds outside could still be heard chanting, 'Pardon him! Have mercy on him!' Montmorency had trouble putting his head on the block because of the pain from a throat wound, so he asked to be executed kneeling upright. The executioner cut off his hair, then took off his head with one blow. Afterward, the gates were thrown open, and his head was shown to the silent, waiting crowds. Montmorency was buried in the cathedral of Toulouse, having died with the courage for which he had been known and admired.[1]

Montmorency's behaviour at Castelnaudary contrasts sharply with that of François d'Aubusson, comte de La Feuillade, a half-century later. La Feuillade was thirty years old in 1655, when he got himself noticed as a cavalry captain in the regiment of Gaston d'Orléans, now the king's uncle. A decade later, La Feuillade was named an army lieutenant general, and put in command of 6,000 men whom Louis XIV sent to Vienna to help rescue the Holy Roman Emperor from the Turks. Sometime before this, La Feuillade had visited the abbé de Choisy in Paris, and used the occasion to vent his simmering rage. Pacing back and forth across the room, he threw his hat on the floor, and exploded: 'I can no longer stand it! I've had three brothers killed in the royal service. The king knows that I haven't a penny, and yet he gives me nothing. I am leaving court! I am going home to plant cabbages!' 'Are you crazy?' replied his host. 'Don't you know the king? He's shrewd. He doesn't discard useful courtiers. He may make them wait awhile but, if they'll be patient, he'll heap them with rewards. Wait awhile, and he'll reward you because your services merit it.' This advice did not calm him, so the abbé reminded him of how to be a courtier. 'Be persistent. Appear content and happy, but ask for everything that becomes available. Eventually, the king will give you a pension, and you'll be a *grand seigneur* within two years.' The abbé de Choisy, recounting this incident in his memoirs years later, remarked laconically that La Feuillade had listened, flattered the king assiduously and profited.

In 1667, with the king's help, La Feuillade married wealthy Charlotte Gouffier de Roannez to become the duc de Roannez-La Feuillade and, in 1674, with the king's permission, he and his troops occupied the city of Salins during the military campaign to annex the Franche-Comté. For this action he was named a marshal of France by the king a year later. As a member of the small circle of Louis XIV's personal friends, La Feuillade became known for his obsequiousness. He was responsible in 1685 for constructing the Place des Victoires in Paris to commemorate the royal peace treaties ending the Dutch war. An equestrian statue of Louis XIV was placed in the centre of the square, and on its pedestal were carved the words, 'To the Immortal Man', while lamps were kept burning at its corners twenty-four hours a day. Louis had these lamps removed in 1691, after La Feuillade's death, because he said they reminded him of the lamps in church.[2] La Feuillade was a sycophant who had tirelessly flattered the king in order to advance. Fawning courtiers were plentiful at Louis XIV's court.

Montmorency and La Feuillade illustrate a change in noble behaviour that had occurred during the seventeenth century. In displaying courage and valour on the battlefield, Montmorency exemplified the chivalric ideal of the medieval warrior, which was the model for noble conduct in the early seventeenth century. But the behaviour of La Feuillade, a successful courtier who was charming, eager to please and well-mannered, had become the model by the late seventeenth century. The chivalric influence on noble conduct had waned by the end of Louis XIV's reign, replaced by a new civility emphasizing courtesy and social adaptability. Historians differ about when and why civility developed, but they agree that it was adopted as a code of conduct first by the nobility and then by the rest of society. The new civility made violent behaviour less acceptable.

Historians agree that nobles had become less violent by 1715, but they disagree on why this happened. Besides the new civility, suggested reasons have included the development of the early modern state, the high rate of ennoblement, the resulting transformation in the social role and identity of the nobility, and the accompanying changes in social solidarities. Solidarities were the cohesive forces holding society together, and they included rank, honour and reputation; family, household and kinship; faith and church; state and obedience to the king; seigneurial and patron–client ties; sociability; work-related ties; and regional ties, including village and neighbourhood loyalties. This book has looked at changes in solidarities during the seventeenth century.

One reason for the decline in violence was the changed noble relationship with the crown as a result of the development of the early modern state. Nobles became more cooperative and obedient, although historians disagree on whether this change was forced or voluntary. The crown increasingly distributed patronage to secure noble cooperation, and used intendants and other royal agents to punish recalcitrance, thus successfully combining the tactics of cooptation and coercion. Nobles began to pursue long-term careers in large, bureaucratized royal armies, and a new military professionalism emerged, that is, an emphasis on competence, skill and experience in determining promotion as well as rank. The noble understanding of royal service grew to include administrative careers in the royal bureaucracy, and nobles developed professional and career loyalties. New political loyalties appeared. Noble service to the king was now understood to be the loyal obedience of a royal subject, and inhabitants of France came to regard themselves as the loyal, obedient subjects of a French king.

The nobility experienced an identity crisis during the seventeenth century, the result of having to assimilate a large number of non-nobles. This influx of newcomers transformed the meaning of noble rank. No longer regarded as hereditary or military, that is, medieval in origin, acquired by birth and military in function, noble rank was now often recognized to be more recently acquired through letters of ennoblement, officeholding, marriage, purchase of fiefs and titles, and a noble lifestyle. Nobles were simultaneously becoming interested in something besides soldiering. Their rising literacy rate encouraged new cultural interests, stimulated by their growing tendency to live part of the year in town. Nobles in town began to socialize in coffee houses, salons, theatres, concerts, receptions and academy meetings, and so developed new ties of sociability. Seigneurial ties were weakened by landlord absenteeism, while growing differences in lifestyle between greater and lesser nobles loosened patron–client ties. Weaker ties made it more difficult for great nobles to raise private armies. Traditional noble solidarities of honour, rank, royal service, seigneury and clientage changed, and new noble solidarities of career and sociability appeared. This transformation in the nobility's traditional social role contributed to the decline in violence.

A high rate of ennoblement was a result of the growth in numbers and wealth of urban elites, who assumed noble rank because they could afford to live as nobles did. The population and size of most cities and towns doubled during the seventeenth century. By 1700, the urban population had become 15 to 20 per cent of the total population of France. A flood of rural immigrants into the cities was provoked by the demographic crisis. Destitute, they arrived in search of jobs that were increasingly available in cities after 1670, with the revival of commerce and industry. The mercantile flourishing of port and river cities in the late seventeenth century stimulated manufacturing, and the result was more, better-paid jobs. In rapidly growing cities, half of the population were recent immigrants, mostly from the surrounding countryside. They lived in densely packed neighbourhoods by occupation, kin and village of origin. New forms of sociability appeared, and work-related ties proliferated. Working-class neighbours socialized in taverns, shops and markets, while the leisured classes met in coffee houses, theatres and salons. Work colleagues and acquaintances included members of workshops, guilds, compagnonnages, confraternities, workingmen's associations, professional companies and joint-stock companies. Commercial and industrial expansion created wealth and an urban elite eager to spend their growing wealth on a better lifestyle. The result was a new urban consumerism. A concentration of people and wealth were urban characteristics that helped to create a distinct urban lifestyle.

Traditional rural solidarities of family, village and seigneury were undermined and weakened by the demographic crisis, rural immigration to the cities and landlord absenteeism. Periodically, at least until the 1670s, there were years of demographic crisis when the death rate was twice the average and higher than the birth rate. The causes included disease, famine and war, while the effects included hunger, death and turmoil as peasants fled the countryside. The dislocations caused by the demographic crisis contributed to the high rate of labour mobility. Surplus younger children, especially daughters who lacked dowries and sons who would not inherit, also left home in search of work as domestic servants, agricultural day labourers, apprentices, peddlers, handymen, woodcutters, soldiers, whatever jobs they could find. This was another reason for the high rate of rural immigration to the cities. Frequent or prolonged absences weakened family and village ties, and landlord absenteeism weakened seigneurial ties. The overall effect was to undermine traditional rural solidarities.

Family, kinship and household were universal solidarities. Nuclear families composed of parents and children became increasingly prevalent during the seventeenth century. One cause was the endemic strife within complex families, that is, multi-generational, multi-parent and step-families including extended kin, all living together under one roof. In complex families, there was constant bickering because of the frustrations of daily life, sibling rivalry, disputes over inheritance, arguments over who was mistress of the household and quarrels between authoritarian fathers and dependent sons. Nuclear families with fewer children experienced less tension and conflict, so they became more numerous as children were encouraged to leave home. Rural labour mobility and immigration to the cities were additional reasons for the proliferation of nuclear families. The growing prevalence of small families helped to weaken extended kinship ties and, as a result, duties and obligations to distant kin became more narrowly defined. There was a corresponding decrease in household size.

This was a male-dominated, patriarchal society, but the lives of women were not as restricted and controlled by men as this might imply. The powerlessness of women has been exaggerated. The more essential a woman's contribution to her family's prosperity, the more power she exercised, if informally and indirectly. Besides the obvious contribution of bearing and rearing children, women increased the social status of the families into which they married when their own family had a higher standing, while the dowries of elite women added capital assets to their husbands' fortunes. Women helped in family advancement by finding patrons, arranging advantageous marriages and mobilizing kin resources. Women managed family lands and businesses in place of disinterested, incapacitated or absent husbands. They secured and paid off loans and mortgages, found money for dowries, satisfied creditors, collected debts, raised rents and increased revenues. Women who had access to capital made money by buying and selling real estate, lending money at interest and investing in municipal bonds and consortiums to collect taxes.

Women participated in vital income-producing activities. Besides running households, they helped with the farm work, spun what their husbands wove for middlemen in the cottage textile industry, dealt with servants and day labourers, sold at market what they grew or made and marketed their own labour as domestic servants, midwives, wet-nurses and laundresses. Women ran urban households that were at the same time workshops, and dealt with servants, employees, apprentices, journeymen, customers and neighbours. They worked as saleswomen and cashiers, kept the accounts and ran small businesses of their own, usually in retail commerce, often selling second-hand goods. Solidarities in women's lives included not only family, kinship and household ties, but also work ties created by farm labour, craft production, small-scale commerce and managing family businesses or estates.

Church and faith were universal solidarities, but the question was, which church and which faith? Catholic Reform was implemented in France during the 1590s, while the Edict of Nantes in 1598 granted French Protestants limited religious toleration. The result was the uneasy coexistence of two churches in France, the majority Roman Catholic and the minority Protestant. Protestants were able to survive, despite a growing pressure to abjure and convert, because of their solidarities, which included membership in the greater community of Protestant believers, and in Protestant churches, consistories, colloquies and synods. The Protestant community participated in church affairs, attended church regularly and held evening services at home. Protestant solidarities also included close personal ties to fellow believers who were family, kin, household members, work colleagues, friends and neighbours. Jews, a non-Christian religious minority, survived by developing the same kind of solidarities, to which they added cross-national ties and participation in a Jewish subculture.

Catholic Reform produced solidarities. Besides membership in the greater community of Catholic believers, and in the French church with its parishes and dioceses, Catholic solidarities included membership in religious orders, the dévots and lay religious societies such as confraternities. Catholic solidarities helped to implement Tridentine reform in France. There was, however, a growing demand by the papacy, the French church and the Bourbon monarchy that a uniform Catholic orthodoxy be established. Protestant dissenters were no longer tolerated, and heterodox dissenters such as the Jansenists were suppressed. The Jansenists were able to survive for a century, however, because of the solidarities uniting them, including ties within the Arnauld family, to the dévots and other Catholic rigorists, the Parisian robe nobility, the court aristocracy and other Jansenists. The French church and monarchy insisted upon a uniform orthodoxy from a fear that dissent would produce disunity and turmoil. Unity was achieved at the expense of toleration, however, and its loss produced disunity and turmoil, anyway.

Protestants, Jews and Jansenists were religious nonconformists who developed their own solidarities. Freethinkers, rationalists and scientists were intellectual nonconformists who did the same. Freethinkers questioned aspects of church orthodoxy, while Cartesian rationalists sought to understand the natural world using a deductive system of reasoning. They rejected the medieval Aristotelian view of the universe in favour of that of the new science. Cartesian rationalism became popular among Parisian intellectuals, who developed intellectual solidarities based on shared scientific interests. This intellectual revolution had far-reaching consequences. Witch-hunting, for example, declined as a result of the dissemination of the new science, the adoption of higher standards of judicial proof and the elite's growing rejection of witchcraft as popular superstition.

One-quarter to one-third of seventeenth-century society was destitute and homeless, and there was a soaring crime rate. Beggars, vagrants and criminals congregated in cities, attracted by urban prosperity, and the problems of poverty and crime were serious enough by the late seventeenth century to force the state to take action. Louis XIV's government created general hospitals to incarcerate the undeserving poor who did not work, and were thus considered a threat to public order. General hospitals were also used to house the senile, insane, syphilitic and others who were regarded as a danger to society, and thus had to be removed from it in what has been called 'The Great Confinement'. The state created an urban police force to deal with beggars and vagrants, while the criminal justice system meted out harsh public punishment as a deterrent. None of these solutions was effective. Although poor relief was available through state-sponsored and private charitable institutions, there was not enough to meet the demand.

In fact, this society did not have much of an institutional safety net to rescue those in need. The destitute and homeless had few resources on which they could rely, and so were vulnerable to misfortune. Beggars lacked the solidarities of work, honour, reputation, sociability, patron–client and seigneurial ties, and civic obedience. Vagrants lacked in addition the solidarities of family, household, kinship and neighbourhood or village ties. Individuals sometimes developed solidarities based on charitable assistance, especially when they were inmates of church-related institutions, and professional criminals sometimes forged their own solidarities. The destitute and homeless, however, usually had few solidarities or other resources on which to rely in times of trouble, and they were often treated harshly. Solidarities allowed the survival of marginals who would otherwise have perished.

APPENDIX 1

CHRONOLOGY OF EVENTS

1589	Assassination of Henri III; accession of the Protestant Henri de Navarre to the throne of France; opposition of the Holy Catholic League to his accession; beginning of the War of the League.
1593	Henri de Navarre converts to Catholicism.
1594	He is crowned at Chartres as Henri IV, the first Bourbon king; Paris submits to the new king, followed by other towns.
1595	Reconciliation of Henri IV and Pope Clement VIII.
1598	Edict of Nantes ending the War of the League and the Wars of Religion, and establishing the toleration of Protestants.
1600	Henri IV marries Marie de Médicis.
1601	Birth of the future Louis XIII.
1604–28	War with the Barbary States.
1609	Day of the *guichet* when Mother Angélique, the reforming abbess of Port-Royal, enforces the rule of closure.
1610	Henri IV assassinated by Ravaillac; Marie de Médicis heads the regency government of her young son, Louis XIII.
1614	Opening of the Estates General at Paris, and its last meeting before 1789; the Estates meeting continues through 1615.
1615	Marriage of Louis XIII and Anne of Austria; National Assembly of French Clergy accepts Canons and Decrees of the Council of Trent.
1618	Thirty Years' War begins.
1621	Louis XIII launches a military campaign against the Protestants of western and southern France that continues for 8 years.
1622	General hospital established at Lyon, serving as a model for others.
1624	Richelieu becomes the head of the royal council.
1628	Fall of La Rochelle.
1629	Peace of Alais signed with Protestants; Richelieu becomes chief minister of Louis XIII.
1630	Richelieu defeats the queen mother, Marie de Médicis, and the dévots party to win the full backing of Louis XIII.
1632	The revolt, defeat and execution of Henri, duc de Montmorency.
1634	Introduction of intendants throughout France; trial and execution of Urbain Grandier for witchcraft.

1635	Official opening of the war between Spain and France, and entry of France into the Thirty Years' War.
1636	Abbé de Saint-Cyran becomes affiliated with Port-Royal as its spiritual director. He is responsible for the growing influence of Jansen's theology, and members of Port-Royal become known as Jansenists.
1642	Death of Richelieu; Mazarin joins the royal council; death of Marie de Médicis.
1643	Death of Louis XIII; Anne of Austria heads the regency government for her young son, Louis XIV, with Mazarin as chief minister.
1648	Beginning of the civil war of the Fronde; France secures Alsace.
1651	Proclamation of majority of Louis XIV ending regency; Louis XIV and his mother flee Paris; Mazarin forced to leave France.
1652	Mazarin returns from exile.
1653	Royal family and Mazarin return to Paris; end of Fronde; Innocent X in a papal bull condemns as heretical five propositions in Jansen's *Augustinus*.
1654	Louis XIV crowned at Reims.
1656	Foundation of Paris general hospital.
1659	Conclusion of the war between Spain and France; end of the Thirty Years' War.
1660	Louis XIV marries Marie-Thérèse of Spain.
1661	Birth of the Dauphin; death of Mazarin; beginning of Louis XIV's personal reign without a chief minister; Colbert serves as his finance minister; royal decree ordering all members of the clergy to submit to the papal bull of 1653.
1666	Death of Anne of Austria.
1666–74	National investigation into the legitimacy of claims of nobility.
1667	Creation of the post of lieutenant general of Paris police.
1667–8	War of Devolution; France acquires Lille and part of Flanders.
1669	Edict making Marseille a duty-free port; compromise between Louis XIV, Pope Clement IX and the Jansenists.
1670	Crown issues a new criminal code.
1670–80	Beginning of economic revival and gradual end of demographic crisis.
1672–9	War with the Dutch; France secures the Franche-Comté.
1682	Louis XIV moves the royal family and his court to Versailles.
1683	Death of Marie-Thérèse; conquest of Luxembourg.
1684	Marriage of Louis XIV and Madame de Maintenon.
1685	Revocation of the Edict of Nantes; Protestantism is prohibited throughout France.
1686	Mass emigration of Protestants.
1689–97	War of the League of Augsburg; loss of Luxembourg.

1700   Edict ordering cities cleared of able-bodied beggars.

1701–14   War of the Spanish Succession.

1702–10   War of the Camisards, the suppression of Protestants in the Cévennes mountains of southern France.

1709   Port-Royal closed; king's letter to French people asking for their support in Spanish war.

1713   Papal bull *Unigenitus* again condemns Jansenism as heretical.

1715   Death of Louis XIV; accession of his great-grandson as Louis XV; regency government headed by the young king's uncle.

1715–23   Regency government of Philippe, duc d'Orléans.

1720   Last great outbreak of plague in France at Marseille.

APPENDIX 2

GLOSSARY

These terms were not explained in the text.

colloquy: a meeting of several local Protestant churches to discuss matters of importance.

consistory: a group of important male members of a congregation who assisted the pastor in governing a local Protestant church.

Cour des Comptes: a sovereign fiscal court in Provence that combined the functions of the sovereign judicial courts of the Chambres des Comptes and *Cours des Aides* in judging litigation between the crown and its tax officials, auditing and maintaining fiscal records, hearing final appeals from taxpayers and registering royal edicts affecting its competence.

écu and livre: the livre was the standard monetary unity of account, which meant there was no coin of that name. Generally, 3 livres were the equivalent of 1 silver écu, which was a circulating coin, and 6 livres were the equivalent of 1 gold écu, another coin in use.

Estates General: a representative assembly for all of France that met to approve or reject royal tax requests. The Estates did not have legislative authority, although the king often took their advice and issued royal edicts on its basis. The Estates General met in 1484, 1560–1, 1588, 1614–15 and 1789. This assembly was composed of representatives of the first estate or clergy, the second estate or nobility and the third estate, or everyone else, usually represented by town governments. Regions with Provincial Estates chose two delegates from each estate to send to the national meeting. Delegates took with them grievances and reform requests known as *cahiers de doléances*. The Provincial Estates were provincial representative assemblies meeting by estate to approve royal tax requests. Not every region had Estates, and those regions without them met by parish, often collectively, to select delegates and draw up grievances to send to an Estates General. The king convened and dissolved meetings of the Estates, both general and provincial.

governors: chief royal administrative official of the king in a province, a city or town, a fortress or garrison. The governors represented the king in various local or regional proceedings, and delivered royal edicts, ordinances and instructions to institutions and officials on his behalf.

intendants: royal commissioners whose authority was based on a commission from the king. Intendants were sent on missions to act on the king's behalf. They were usually sent on investigative or administrative missions to the provinces, where they worked with the governors; to the royal armies; and to ports with royal fleets, where they worked with the army or navy officers in command. After 1634, intendants were sent to all the *généralités*, or tax districts, in France where they assumed new, more extensive financial responsibilities. Provincial, army, navy and financial intendants became important permanent members of the new royal bureaucracy.

National Assembly of the French Clergy: periodic national meetings of delegates representing the Catholic clergy at the regional level to discuss financial issues and matters of importance.

Parlement: a sovereign law court of France, that is, the highest judicial court in a regional jurisdiction. The Parlements heard on appeal all important cases; civil cases involving 50 livres or more; and all criminal cases involving the death penalty. Privileged individuals had the right to be heard in the first instance before a Parlement. The Parlements also registered royal edicts and ordinances; without registration, these acts did not have the force of law. The Parlement of Paris, which had the largest jurisdiction, served as the final court of appeal for religious cases, and heard all cases related to peers of the realm or titled lords.

parlementaires: judges sitting by chambers in the French Parlements. They included councillors, or ordinary judges, and presidents, or presiding judges. Their offices were venal, that is, they were purchased from the crown. Upon payment of an annual tax, these offices, which ennobled, could be inherited.

seigneur: a rural landowner who possessed feudal rights and privileges. These included rights of justice over civil and minor criminal matters, water rights, forest rights over forest uses, milling or pressing monopolies, and various other rights. A seigneur (lord) owned a seigneury (manor or *seigneurie*), which was a collection of feudal rights over certain estates or lands and certain individuals. Seigneurial rights and privileges created personal relationships, that is, seigneurial ties, between landowner and the individuals involved as well as with tenant farmers who actually worked the land.

state's attorney: chief royal attorney or *procureur du roi*. All royal courts had at least one royal or state's attorney, who presented the king's cases to the court. The state's attorney often had an assistant or two known as *avocat(s) du roi*. The distinction between them is that between present-day British barristers (procureurs) and solicitors (avocats).

subdelegate: local assistant of an intendant. At first, their authority was based on an informal commission from the intendant, but their office became formal and permanent in the eighteenth century. Usually, subdelegates were also other royal or local officials.

synod: a periodic meeting of delegates from local Protestant churches, either at the provincial level (provincial synod), or at the national level (national synod), to discuss important matters.

Tridentine: anything pertaining to the Council of Trent (1543–63). Tridentine decrees, for example, were the Canons and Decrees of the Council of Trent.

APPENDIX 3

A HISTORIOGRAPHICAL ESSAY

Social history has been the most widely read history inside and outside of France for decades. Annalistes such as Emmanuel Le Roy Ladurie, Pierre Goubert, Robert Mandrou and Robert Muchembled, among others, have dominated its study, and produced some of the most brilliantly imaginative history of the late twentieth century. They have also provoked some of the most trenchant criticism, an indication of their originality. Their work, much of which is now available in English, has had a significant impact upon historical writing in general, and has influenced every page in this book. Their path-breaking interpretations and meticulous archival research have set the agenda and parameters for the study of social history for the last three or four decades. Derivative approaches, inspired by the Annalistes, include the new cultural history, which appeared during the 1980s, and feminist history, women's history and gender analysis, which appeared after 1970. This essay reviews some of the more significant work on French social history published during the last thirty years, including the work of the Annalistes and those whom they have inspired.

The Annalistes took their name from the journal in which much of their work was published.[1] This journal was founded in 1929 by Lucien Febvre, a historian of the Renaissance and Reformation, and by Marc Bloch, a student of rural history and feudalism, who were the leaders of the first generation of Annalistes. Fernand Braudel, known for his study of the sixteenth-century Mediterranean world, effectively became the journal's editor in 1956, after the death of his mentor Febvre, and thus the leader of the second generation.[2] Following his example, the Annalistes have tended to specialize in early modern history, although they have been active in all periods of French history.

Substituting problem-oriented, analytical history for narration and biography, the Annalistes criticized traditional historians for their preoccupation with political events, great men and warfare, for 'writing history from the top down'.[3] They observed that such narrow, event-centred history failed to analyse underlying structures and basic patterns of causation, and declared themselves interested in the whole range of human activities, that is, in a 'total history'. They produced socio-economic studies analysing long-term structures and trends stretching over a century or more, using a profusion of statistics, graphs and charts. The Annalistes were interested in urban and regional history, social and family history, including the history of sexuality, and what they called the history of mentalities, the collective ideas and unconscious assumptions of people, and the ways in which these were expressed in metaphors and symbols. They also investigated marginal groups of people ignored by traditional historians in what they called 'writing history from the bottom up'. Favouring an interdisciplinary approach, they borrowed from sociology, anthropology, psychology, linguistics, demography and geography, and they were fascinated by comparative history, by what differentiated French cities and provinces from each other, France from Europe, and Europe from the non-European world.

The Annalistes were criticized, however, for neglecting the study of political history, the history of elites, the impact of individual personalities upon history and for ignoring institutional, financial, diplomatic and military history. Critics charged that the Annalistes' preoccupation with long-term socio-economic trends, demonstrated quantitatively in exhaustive detail, produced massive studies that were not easy to read. Historians of mentalities were criticized for assuming a homogeneity of thought and feeling that had never existed, because they ignored differences created by rank, gender and change over time. They were also criticized for treating belief systems as autonomous, and for ignoring the individuals and the societies that had created such beliefs.

The current or third generation of Annalistes lack the unity of purpose and method that characterized their predecessors. Their fragmentation has been so great that many of them deny a group or school still exists. Some see themselves as the progenitors of a new cultural history, which developed in the 1980s from the history of mentalities.[4] American historians have begun referring to the 1990s as the post-Annalistes decade for this reason. The multiple interests of the current generation were formed partly in response to the stifling domination of Fernand Braudel. A wave of anti-Braudelianism had swept through French universities and research institutes long before his death in 1985.[5] The contemporary generation is interested in cultural history, family and sexual history, the history of marginals, psychohistory, the historical uses of anthropology, women's history and the history of mentalities expanded to include all aspects of daily life no matter how trivial, for example, dreams, the body, smells and sounds. The current generation has shown less interest in quanitative techniques, macroanalysis and lengthy regional studies. They prefer microanalysis or microhistory using case studies, and have been more open than some of their predecessors to ideas from outside France, especially from the English-speaking world.[6]

American and British historians, independently of the Annalistes but influenced by them, have pursued similar directions in research. They have been interested in cultural and feminist history, women's history, gender analysis and a revived political history with a different focus.[7] The new cultural history uses anthropological methods to decode cultural signs and symbols in order to describe collective mentalities. The social and cultural aspects of human experience are stripped down or deconstructed to expose what lies behind their outward representations. Influenced by literary criticism, cultural historians regard history as a text to be interpreted, and have been less interested in the context, that is, in what lies outside the text. They have emphasized the constructed nature of human subjectivity, and the importance of social, class and gender identities. This approach has been called deconstructionism, post-structuralism or post-modernism.[8]

Influenced by deconstructionist thought, a feminist approach to history has existed since the 1970s. Feminist historians argue that the exploitation of women has characterized a male-dominated society, distorting a history written largely by men, so they seek to strip away these distortions.[9] Towards the end of the 1970s, a different approach to women's history appeared, which explored the historical reality and distinctiveness of women's lives, and sought to make visible the previously invisible presence of women in history.[10] This approach is more widely accepted than that of the feminists. The 1980s saw the development of a third approach known as gender analysis, which looks at the beliefs, values, symbols and practices indicating and creating differences between the sexes.[11] As a result, women's history has generally become more focused on societal concepts of gender and identity.[12] The development of gender analysis has revived an interest in political history, although not in the traditional narrative history. The new political history explores cultural representations of power, power relations and the role of gender in politics. It emphasizes the importance of cultural beliefs and attitudes in political causation, and analyses the role of discourse, symbolism and language in politics.[13]

The current generation of Annalistes, and their English-speaking admirers, have had their critics. They have been accused of relativism, that is, of relinquishing objectivity and the goal of constructing a widely accepted, factual body of historical knowledge in favour of a subjective, culturally constructed view of history. They have been accused of abandoning a unifying, synthetic understanding of human experience for a splintered, fractured view, and of using the methods of anthropology and literary criticism to the extent that they are no longer writing history. Critics note that they have relied less on archival research than their predecessors, and that their work tends to be less fact-centred and more theoretical as a result. Mentalities historians have been accused of focusing their attention on the trivial and bizarre to the extent they have ignored issues central to the human experience, and marginalized historical inquiry to become historians of the trivial. Although cultural historians have been prevalent, if not predominant, for nearly two decades, critics note that they still insist upon describing themselves as 'new' and 'cutting-edge', and dismissing their critics as 'old' and 'traditionalist'.

The English-speaking admirers of the Annalistes have had their own special problems. They seem fascinated by trends and fads, especially those originating in France. Despite their desire to be avant-garde, they adopted deconstructionism as a textual approach after literary critics had abandoned it because of its inherent flaws. Feminist historians have displayed an ideological agenda and an open, admitted advocacy that is reminiscent of historical Marxism. Women's historians have tended to praise women's accomplishments no matter how insignificant, while gender analysts have sweepingly reduced all historical inquiry to the study of gender. Cultural history has engulfed nearly every other field of history, and transformed all of them into the study of culture, which is now impossible to define. A new cultural determinism seems to have replaced the old economic determinism of Marxism. Roger Chartier has declared that the cultural history 'revolution' has got out of hand, especially on the American side of the Atlantic.[14] Equally disturbing is a recent tendency to reject other points of view, and to react to criticism with shrill charges of bias and narrow-mindedness, stifling both inquiry and discussion.[15]

A debate raged during the 1960s and 1970s over the structure of early modern French society, which was traditionally divided into three estates. Most historians have accepted this traditional social division because contemporaries accepted it.[16] But the troubling question has been, what subdivisions existed within the three estates? Roland Mousnier believed that the three estates were subdivided into a hierarchy of groups known as orders, which were ranked according to the esteem, honour and prestige attached to their social and political functions by society. An individual became a member of an order by birth, and by his own actions in acquiring offices, titles, fiefs, royal favour, academic degrees and pursuing an occupation or profession. Wealth alone, or an individual's role in the production of material goods, did not determine rank.

Boris Porchnev, a Marxist, had a different view of early modern society. He believed that individuals were classified by the nature of their wealth and economic activity as members of the feudal elite, the bourgeoisie or the proletariat. Early seventeenth-century popular revolts were anti-feudal, anti-fiscal protests by the masses (peasants in the countryside and workers in the towns) against the power of a feudal state dominated by the traditional ruling classes, the clergy, nobility and monarchy. The bourgeoisie, who invested in the system by buying ennobling offices and fiefs, had in this way betrayed their historic mission of leading a revolution by joining the elite in defending a feudal-absolutist state. France had to wait until the end of the eighteenth century for a bourgeois-led revolution that would destroy the Old Regime.[17]

Mousnier agreed that popular revolts of the early seventeenth century were tax protests by the peasants and urban poor, but he believed that these revolts were led by disaffected nobles whose power had been attacked by the monarchy. The Bourbon monarchy used the new bureaucracy to intimidate and coerce the unruly nobility. Venality, the purchase of ennobling state offices, allowed the monarchy to create a new administrative elite, the robe nobility, whom it used to challenge the power of the old feudal elite, the sword nobility. Mousnier described a society of vertically integrated, culturally determined orders linked by personal ties, and rejected the Marxist view of a society of horizontal, materially based classes engaged in a class struggle.[18] The debate on whether early modern France was a society of orders or classes raged into the 1980s.

Both interpretations were attacked. Critics complained that the historical reality was messier and more complicated than either the Marxist or Mousnier models, which were both too schematized, simplistic and theoretical. Mousnier was criticized for idealizing early modern society by disregarding its economic foundations, and taking contemporary descriptions too literally. Porchnev was criticized for adhering too closely to Marxist ideology. Mousnier attempted, unsuccessfully, to apply his model to other societies around the world and across time, but his model worked best for early modern France.[19] The Marxist model was more successfully applied across time and space, but it did not take into account the unique features of seventeenth-century France, such as the development of the early modern state. The emerging royal bureaucracy was an important force for social change, and historians currently using class analysis have included the state in their interpretations for this reason.[20]

Both models were criticized for describing only a part of early modern society. Mousnier was criticized for ignoring the role of wealth and economic activity in determining social identity, and Porchnev for ignoring cultural factors such as esteem, honour, and prestige. James Collins has observed that these overlapping typologies were complementary rather than mutually exclusive ways of looking at the same group of people. Early modern France was both a society of orders and a society of classes, and Frenchmen were ranked both by the nature of their wealth and economic activity, and by culturally determined categories or orders. In both typologies, the social hierarchy was roughly the same with a propertied local elite at the top and a mass of propertyless indigents at the bottom. Neither the Marxist nor the Mousnier model has been wholly accepted, although J. Michael Hayden is probably correct when he states that Mousnier's description is closer to what most historians have found in the archives.[21]

Mousnier's last great synthesis, *The Institutions of France under the Absolute Monarchy, 1598–1798*, described four simultaneously overlapping societies:

lineages or extended families; fealties or patron–client relationships; orders or estates; and corporations or territorial communities. An individual was a member of all four societies at the same time, and could belong simultaneously to many other groups and subgroups, including those that were incompatible. But Mousnier never adequately explained how these multiple societies and groups interacted, or how they all functioned together to maintain vertical integration.[22] His first chapter described the transition from orders to classes that began during Louis XIV's reign, but did not explain why this transition occurred.[23]

Because Mousnier and his students were interested in political history, they have often been erroneously identified with the traditional school of French historiography, and regarded as different from the Annalistes, although they shared many of the same interests. The Mousnierites are a distinguished group of historians, who have studied what the Annalistes did not study, and their work on elites,[24] revolts,[25] institutions[26] and the church,[27] among other subjects, have made a significant contribution to scholarship. Because of their diverse interests, they have not been easy to categorize, but they are not traditionalists.[28]

Even before Mousnier's death in 1989, the debate over whether early modern French society was composed of orders or classes had quietly faded away. The collapse of Marxist governments during the late 1980s helped to undermine historical Marxism, already regarded by many as too ideological and theoretical. For this reason, some historians have begun referring to the 1990s as the post-Marxist or post-materialist decade. Economic causation has remained important, but economic determinism has been discredited, and class analysis is no longer central to historical inquiry.[29]

Another less structural approach to understanding the nature of early modern society appeared while the Mousnier–Porchnev debate raged. It explored changes in the relations between individuals over time, and shifted the focus away from the structures of society to investigate changing patterns in personal relationships, thereby restoring individuals to history. A shift in focus from structures to relationships had the advantage of making unnecessary the inclusion of a causal theory of social conflict and its effect on the long-term social and political development of France. Both the Marxist and Mousnier models contained such theories, which complicated their discussions of the nature of the social hierarchy. This shift in focus also had the advantage of lessening the Annalistes-inspired emphasis on the quanitative demonstration of long-term structures and trends by introducing a subject difficult to treat in this way. The current generation of Annalistes have, in fact, turned away from their predecessors' obsession with quantitative analysis and long-term structures.

Philippe Ariès, who died in 1984, was one of the originators of this new approach emphasizing the study of personal relationships, although he is better known as a founder of the history of mentalities. Ariès published a social history of the family in 1960 in which he discussed family relationships, values and attitudes. He argued that there were fundamental changes in family relationships during the seventeenth century, including the growing prevalence of the nuclear family, and a greater appreciation of its child-rearing functions.[30] His book had enormous influence, and launched the new field of family history. He followed it with a study of early modern attitudes toward death and dying, and a history of privacy.[31] Ariès regarded early modern society as a maze of overlapping personal relationships, although not much is yet known about these intersecting relationships, some integrated, some incompatible. Historians are only now at the stage of describing the characteristics and functions of relationships, not how they interacted.[32]

Norbert Elias long ago observed that complex webs of interdependent relationships, which he called figurations or configurations, surrounded individuals in early modern French society, especially at the court of Louis XIV. He noted that we know very little about these webs, which need study.[33] Roger Chartier has explained that a figuration is 'a social form of extremely variable intent (made up of a group playing cards together, the patrons of a café, a school class, a village, a city, a nation) in which the individuals involved are linked by a specific mode of reciprocal dependence . . . .'.[34] Denis Richet has expressed his interest in studying 'the relationship between the individual and the group, or between individuals and groups'.[35] Arlette Farge has urged historians to undertake the study of relations between individuals, groups and events.[36] This approach represents a distinct change from the study of social structures by earlier generations of Annalistes, who tended to ignore the study of individual relationships and their impact on historical events.

This book has looked at some of the significant changes in social solidarities during the seventeenth century, an approach pioneered by Robert Mandrou.[37] Solidarities were the personal bonds and loyalties that acted as cohesive forces in holding society together, and helping to determine social and self-identity. Yves Durand used this approach, although he regarded solidarities as personal relationships within a hierarchical society composed of classes, orders and castes.[38] Changes in personal relationships affecting an individual's identity, that is, his understanding of who he was and where he belonged within the ranks of society, have been emphasized in these pages. This approach to social change is indebted to the work of Philippe Ariès, Norbert Elias and Robert Mandrou.

Suggested reading

Philippe Ariès, *Centuries of Childhood. A Social History of Family Life*, tr. Robert Baldrick (New York, 1962).

Yves-Marie Bercé, *History of Peasant Revolts*, tr. Amanda Whitmore (Ithaca, 1990).

Lenard Berlanstein, ed., *Rethinking Labor History: Essays on Discourse and Class Analysis* (Urbana, Ill., 1991).

Peter Burke, *The French Historical Revolution. The Annales School, 1929–1989* (Cambridge, 1992); idem, *The Varieties of Cultural History* (Ithaca, NY, 1997).

M.L. Bush, *Social Classes and Social Orders in Europe since 1500* (London, 1992).

Roger Chartier, *On the Edge of the Cliff: History, Language, and Practices*, tr. Lydia Cochrane (Baltimore, 1997); idem, 'Writing Practices', *French Historical Studies*, 21 (1998), 255–64.

P.J. Coveney, *France in Crisis, 1620–1675* (London, 1977).

Norbert Elias, *The Court Society*, tr. Edmund Jephcott (New York, 1983).

Richard Evans, *In Defense of History* (New York, 1999).

Pierre Goubert, *The French Peasantry in the Seventeenth Century*, tr. Ian Patterson (Cambridge, 1986).

J. Michael Hayden, 'Models, Mousnier, and *Qualité*: The Social Structure of Early Modern France', *French History*, 10 (1996), 375–98.

Emmanuel Le Roy Ladurie, *Carnival in Romans*, tr. Mary Feeney (New York, 1980).

Robert Mandrou, *Introduction to Modern France, 1500–1640. An Essay in Historical Psychology*, tr. R.E. Hallmark (London, 1975).

Roland Mousnier, *Social Hierarchies: 1450 to the Present*, tr. Peter Evans (New York, 1973).

Robert Muchembled, *Popular Culture and Elite Culture*, tr. Lydia Cochrane (Baton Rouge, 1985).

MAPS

1 THE MAJOR PROVINCES OF OLD REGIME FRANCE

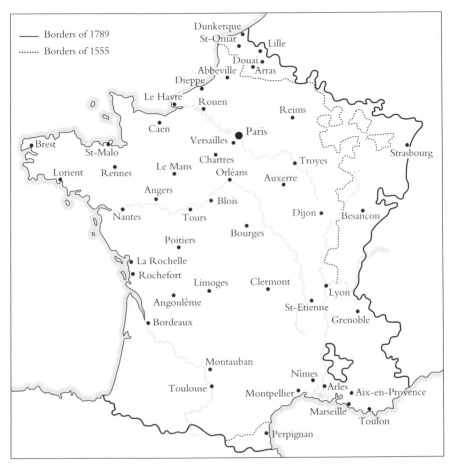

Borders of 1789
Borders of 1555

Dunkerque
St-Omer
Lille
Douai
Abbeville
Arras
Dieppe
Le Havre
Rouen
Reims
Caen
Paris
Versailles
Strasbourg
Brest
St-Malo
Chartres
Troyes
Lorient
Rennes
Le Mans
Orléans
Auxerre
Angers
Blois
Dijon
Besançon
Nantes
Tours
Bourges
Poitiers
La Rochelle
Rochefort
Limoges
Clermont
Lyon
Angoulême
St-Etienne
Bordeaux
Grenoble
Montauban
Nîmes
Toulouse
Montpellier
Arles
Aix-en-Provence
Marseille
Perpignan
Toulon

2 THE MAJOR CITIES OF OLD REGIME FRANCE

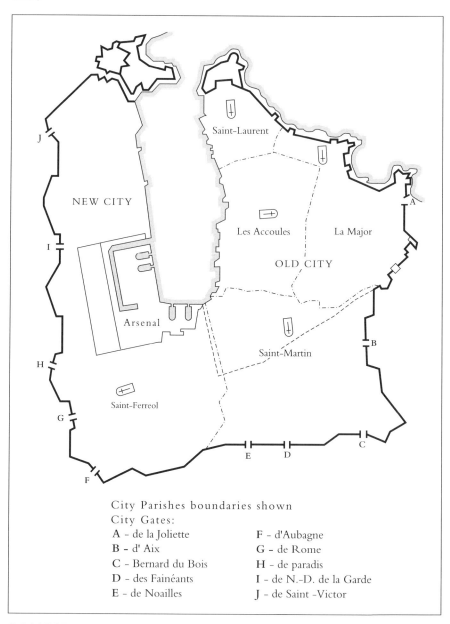

City Parishes boundaries shown
City Gates:
A - de la Joliette
B - d' Aix
C - Bernard du Bois
D - des Fainéants
E - de Noailles
F - d'Aubagne
G - de Rome
H - de paradis
I - de N.-D. de la Garde
J - de Saint -Victor

3 MARSEILLE 1720

NOTES

INTRODUCTION

1. J. Michael Hayden, *France and the Estates General of 1614* (Cambridge, 1974), pp. 98–113.
2. Archives départementales, Bouches-du-Rhône, Aix, J.-H.-L. Hesmivy de Moissac, 'Histoire du Parlement de Provence', 2 vols, I, 428–33, 465; Charles de Grimaldi and Jacques Gaufridy, *Mémoires de la Fronde en Provence* (Aix, 1870), p. 101.
3. François Billaçois, *The Duel*, tr. Trista Selous (New Haven, 1990), pp. 76–9.
4. François duc de La Rochefoucauld, *Mémoires* (Paris, 1925), pp. 195–9.
5. *Mercure françois*, 25 vols (Paris, 1605–44), VI, 268.
6. The work of the English anthropologist, Julian Pitt-Rivers, although often unacknowledged, has significantly influenced the historical understanding of honour. See idem, 'Honor and Social Status', *Honor and Shame*, ed. Jean Péristiany (Chicago, 1966), pp. 21–77; idem, 'Honor', *International Encyclopedia of the Social Sciences*, ed. David Sills, 18 vols (New York, 1968), VI, 503–11; idem, 'The Anthropology of Honour', *The Fate of Schechem* (Cambridge, 1977), pp. 1–17; idem with Jean Péristiany, *Honour and Grace* (Cambridge, 1992). For Pitt-Rivers's influence, see Kristen Neuschel, *Word of Honor* (Ithaca, 1989), pp. 69–102; Bertram Wyatt-Brown, *Southern Honor* (New York, 1982), pp. 25–87.
7. Nicolas Fessenden, 'Epernon and Guyenne: Provincial Politics under Louis XIII' (unpub. PhD dissertation, Columbia University, 1972), pp. 150–67.
8. Arlette Jouanna, 'Recherches sur la notion d'honneur', *Rev d'hist mod et cont*, 15 (1968), 597–623.
9. Philip Benedict, *Rouen during the Wars of Religion* (Cambridge, 1981), pp. 184–6; Henri Drouot, *Mayenne et la Bourgogne*, 2 vols (Paris, 1937), I, 43–55, 80–94, 160–2, 334–48; Frederic Baumgartner, 'Party Alignment in the Parlement of Paris', *Proceedings. West Soc Fr Hist* (1978), 34–40; Sharon Kettering, 'Political Parties at Aix-en-Provence in 1589', *Eur Hist Quart*, 25 (1994), 181–211; Nicolas Le Roux, 'The Catholic Nobility and Political Choice', tr. Mark Greengrass, *Fr Hist*, 8 (1994), 34–50.
10. Robert Mandrou, *Introduction to Modern France*, tr. R.E. Hallmark (London, 1975), pp. 77–138.
11. Yves Durand, *Les solidarités dans les sociétés* (Paris, 1987), pp. 55–111.

CHAPTER 1

1. Molière, *L'Avare*, Act II, scene vi; Act III, scenes viii, ix, x, xi; Act IV, scene ii.
2. Jacques-Auguste de Thou, *Mémoires*, ed. Claude Bernard Petitot, ser. 1, vol. 37 (Paris, 1838), pp. 372–4.

3. Jonathan Dewald, *The Formation of a Provincial Nobility* (Princeton, 1980), p. 252.

4. Barbara Diefendorf, *Paris City Councillors* (Princeton, 1983), pp. 180, 182, 186; Robert Kalas, 'The Selve Family of Limousin', *Sixteenth Cent Journ*, 18 (1987), 147–72; Wendy Gibson, *Women in Seventeenth-Century France* (New York, 1989), p. 47.

5. Dewald, *Formation*, pp. 257–8; Gibson, *Women*, p. 44; Robert Oresko, 'The Marriages of the Nieces of Cardinal Mazarin', *Frankreich im Europäischen Staatensystem*, ed. Ranier Babel (Sigmaringen, 1995), 109–51; Roger Du Chêne, 'Argent et famille au XVIIe siècle', *Provence hist*, 16 (1996), 10.

6. Lucy Norton, ed., tr. *Memoirs Duc de Saint Simon*, 2 vols (New York, 1967), I, 61–3.

7. Jacques Levron, *Les courtisans* (Paris, 1960), tr. Ragnhild Hutton, ed., 'Louis XIV's Courtiers', *Louis XIV and Absolutism* (Columbus, Ohio, 1976), p. 145.

8. Paul Sonnino, *Louis XIV and the Dutch War* (Cambridge, 1988), pp. 38–9.

9. René Pillorget, *La tige et le rameau* (Paris, 1979), pp. 44–9; Jean-Louis Flandrin, *Les amours paysannes* (Paris, 1970), pp. 30–40; Joan Davies, 'The Politics of the Marriage Bed', *Fr Hist*, 6 (1992), 63–95; François Lebrun, *La vie conjugale sous l'Ancien Régime* (Paris, 1975), pp. 21–33. André Burguière *et al.*, eds, *A History of the Family*, 2 vols, *The Impact of Modernity*, tr. Sarah Tenison, vol. II (Cambridge, Mass., 1996), 76–94.

10. Gibson, *Women*, pp. 41–58; Pillorget, *La tige et le rameau*, pp. 49–80; Martine Segalen, *Love and Power in the Peasant Family*, tr. Sarah Matthews (Cambridge, 1983), pp. 14–17; Jean-Louis Flandrin, *Families in Former Times*, tr. Richard Southern (Cambridge, 1979), pp. 145–73; Jonathan Dewald, *Aristocratic Experience* (Berkeley, 1993), pp. 120–4.

11. Lucienne Roubin, 'Male and Female Space', *Rural Society in France*, eds Robert Forster and Orest Ranum (Baltimore, 1977), pp. 152–80; idem, *Chambrettes des Provençaux* (Paris, 1970); Flandrin, *Families in Former Times*, pp. 107–10; idem, *Les amours paysannes*, pp. 108–28, 137–43; Edward Shorter, *Making of the Modern Family* (New York, 1975), pp. 120–48.

12. Robert Harding, *Anatomy of a Power Elite* (New Haven, 1978), pp. 111–17, 143–68; Robert Forster, *House of Saulx-Tavanes* (Baltimore, 1971), pp. 1–54, 120; Jean-Pierre Labatut, *Les ducs et pairs de France* (Paris, 1972), pp. 136–42, 253–4; Dewald, *Formation*, pp. 127–30, 263–8; Guy Chaussinand-Nogaret, *The French Nobility*, tr. William Doyle (Cambridge, 1985), pp. 117–29; Georges d'Avenel, *La noblesse sous Richelieu* (Paris, 1901), pp. 119–20.

13. Jacqueline Carrière, *La population d'Aix-en-Provence* (Aix, 1958), pp. 52, 55; Jacques Dupâquier, *La population française aux XVIIe et XVIIIe siècles* (Paris, 1979), p. 15; Flandrin, *Les amours paysannes*, pp. 178–9; Jacques Depauw, 'Illicit Sexual Activity', *Family and Society*, eds Robert Forster and Orest Ranum (Baltimore, 1976), pp. 145–91; Pierre Caspard, 'Conceptions prenuptiales', *Annales: ESC*, 29 (1974), 989–1008; Jean Delumeau and Daniel Roche, eds, *Histoire des pères* (Paris, 1990), pp. 90–4; Jean-Pierre Bardet, *Rouen aux XVIIe et XVIIIe siècles*, 2 vols (Paris, 1983), I, 320–46.

14. Flandrin, *Families in Former Times*, pp. 4–33; Kristen Gager, *Blood Ties and Fictive Ties* (Princeton, 1996), pp. 16–18; Pillorget, *La tige et le rameau*, pp. 13–14; Lebrun, *La vie conjugale*, pp. 57–74; Segalen, *Love and Power*, pp. 67–8.

15. Flandrin, *Families in Former Times*, pp. 50–92; Emmanuel Le Roy Ladurie, *The Peasants of Languedoc*, tr. John Day (Urbana, 1976), pp. 29–36; Alain Collomp, *La maison du père* (Paris, 1983); idem, 'Famille nucléaire et famille élargie', *Annales: ESC*, 27 (1972), 969–76.

16. Burguière, *A History of the Family*, II, 13–15; Flandrin, *Families in Former Times*, pp. 180–242; James Farr, *Authority and Sexuality* (New York, 1995), pp. 125–33; Emmanuel Le Roy Ladurie, 'Famine Amenorrhea', *Biology of Man*, eds Robert Forster and Orest Ranum (Baltimore, 1975), pp. 163–78; William Langer, 'Infanticide', *Hist Childhood Quart*, 1 (1974), 353–62; Valerie Fields, *Wet-Nursing* (Oxford, 1988); Lebrun, *La vie conjugale*, pp. 90–103, 147–67; Claude Delasselle, 'Les enfants abandonnés', *Annales: ESC*, 30 (1975), 187–218; Alain Molinier, 'Enfants trouvés, enfants abandonés', *Sur la population française* (Paris, 1973), pp. 446–73; Bardet, *Rouen*, I, 263–319.

17. François Lebrun, *Les hommes et la mort en Anjou* (Paris, 1971), p. 114; Carrière, *La population d'Aix*, p. 51; Annik-Pardailhé-Galabrun, *The Birth of Intimacy*, tr. Jocelyn Phelps (Philadelphia, 1991), p. 37; Jacques Gélis, *A History of Childbirth*, tr. Rosemary Morris (Boston, 1991); Bardet, *Rouen*, I, 347–74.

18. Philippe Ariès, *Centuries of Childhood*, tr. Robert Baldrick (New York, 1962); Linda Pollock, *Forgotten Children* (Cambridge, 1983); David Hunt, *Parents and Children in History* (New York, 1970), pp. 32–51; Elizabeth Badinter, *Mother Love: Myth and Reality* (New York, 1981); David Herlihy, 'Medieval Children', *Essays on Medieval Civilization*, eds B.K. Lackner *et al.* (Austin, 1978), pp. 109–31; Arlette Farge, *Fragile Lives*, tr. Carol Shelton (Cambridge, Mass., 1993), pp. 45–51; S. Ryan Johansson, 'Centuries of Childhood', *Journ Family Hist*, 12 (1987), 343–65.

19. Katherine Lynch, 'The Family and Public Life', *Journ Interdis Hist*, 24 (1994), 665–84; Jacques Donzelot, *Policing of Families*, tr. Robert Hurley (Baltimore, 1997).

20. Pillorget, *La tige et le rameau*, p. 55; Lebrun, *Les hommes et la mort*, pp. 127–212, 234, 236, 251; David Troyansky, *Old Age in the Old Regime* (Ithaca, 1989), pp. 12–13; Michel Peronnet, *Les évêques de l'ancienne France*, 2 vols (Lille, 1977), I, 44–5; Pierre Goubert, *Beauvais et le Beauvaisis* (Paris, 1960), p. 63; Laurence Brockliss and Colin Jones, *The Medical World of Early Modern France* (Oxford, 1997), pp. 37–53; Daniel Roche, *The People of Paris*, tr. Marie Evans (Berkeley, 1987), p. 51; W. Gregory Monahan, *Year of Sorrows* (Columbus, 1993), pp. 150–3.

21. Jacques Dupâquier *et al.*, eds, *Marriage and Remarriage* (New York, 1981); Pillorget, *La tige et le rameau*, p. 47; Micheline Baulant, 'The Scattered Family', *Family and Society*, pp. 104–16.

22. Tamara K. Hareven, 'History of the Family and Complexity of Social Change', *Amer Hist Rev*, 96 (1991), 100–8; idem, 'Cycles, Courses, and Cohorts', *Journ Soc Hist*, 12 (1978), 97–109; Jean Cuisenier, ed., *Family Life Cycle* (The Hague, 1977); Martine Seglaen, 'Family Cycle and Household Structure', *Family and Sexuality*, eds Robert Wheaton and Tamara K. Hareven (Philadelphia, 1980), pp. 253–71.

23. Jacqueline Boucher, *La cour de Henri III* (La Guerche-de-Bretagne, 1986), pp. 82–7; Flandrin, *Families in Former Times*, pp. 92–111.

24. Natalie Davis, *Return of Martin Guerre* (Cambridge, Mass., 1989); Robert Finlay, 'Refashioning of Martin Guerre', *Amer Hist Rev*, 93 (June, 1988), 553–71; Natalie Davis, 'On the Lame', ibid., 572–603.

25. Emmanuel Le Roy Ladurie, 'Family Structures and Inheritance Customs', *Family and Society*, pp. 75–103; Lebrun, *La vie conjugale*, pp. 74–8; Roland Mousnier, *Institutions of France*, vol. 1, *Society and the State*, tr. Brian Pearce (Chicago, 1979), pp. 66–78; Robert Wheaton, 'Affinity and Descent', *Family and Sexuality*, pp. 111–34; André Burguière, 'Marriage Ritual in France', *Ritual, Religion, and the Sacred*, eds Robert Forster and Orest Ranum (Baltimore, 1982), pp. 8–23.

26. Burguière, *A History of the Family*, II, 30–76; Alain Collomp, 'Tensions inside the Family', *Interest and Emotion*, eds Hans Medick and David Sabean (Cambridge, 1984), pp. 145–70; idem, *La maison du père*, pp. 113–209; Nicole Castan, 'La criminalité familiale', *Crimes et criminalité*, ed. A. Abbiateci (Paris, 1971), pp. 91–107; Jonathan Dewald, *Aristocratic Experience* (Berkeley, 1993), pp. 69–79; Elizabeth Claverie and Pierre Lamaison, *L'impossible mariage* (Paris, 1982); Arlette Farge and Michel Foucault, *Le désordre des familles* (Paris, 1982).

27. *Passions in the Renaissance*, ed. Roger Chartier, tr. Arthur Goldhammer, vol. 3 of *A History of Private Life*, eds Philippe Ariès and Georges Duby (Cambridge, Mass., 1989), 1–18; Pardailhé-Galabrun, *The Birth of Intimacy*, pp. 33–4.

28. T.J.A. Le Goff, *Vannes and its Region* (Oxford, 1981), pp. 206–15; Malcolm Greenshields, *An Economy of Violence* (University Park, 1994), pp. 73–8, 100–13; Farge, *Fragile Lives*, pp. 42–5; Farge and Foucault, *Le désordre*, pp. 167–73; Edward Wilson, 'Family Honour', *Essays and Studies*, ed. Geoffrey Bullough (London, 1953), pp. 19–40; Jean Péristiany, ed., *Honor and Shame* (Chicago, 1966).

29. Cissie Fairchilds, *Domestic Enemies* (Baltimore, 1984); Sarah Maza, *Servants and Masters* (Princeton, 1983); Jean-Pierre Gutton, *Domestiques et serviteurs* (Paris, 1981); Mark Motley, *Becoming an Aristocrat* (Princeton, 1990); Sharon Kettering, 'Household Service of Noblewomen', *Fr Hist Studies*, 20 (1997), 55–85.

30. Gédéon Tallemant des Réaux, *Historiettes*, ed. Antoine Adam, 2 vols (Paris, 1961), II, 738–9.

31. Jean Cordelier, *Madame de Maintenon* (Paris, 1970), pp. 5–44; Louis Merle, *Constant d'Aubigné* (Paris, 1971).

32. Gager, *Blood Ties and Fictive Ties* (Princeton, 1996); Jean-Pierre Gutton, *Histoire de l'adoption en France* (Paris, 1993); Pardailhé-Galabrun, *The Birth of Intimacy*, p. 34; Delumeau and Roche, *Histoire des pères*, pp. 74, 87–8.

33. Agnès Fine, *Parrains, marraines* (Paris, 1994), pp. 41–91; Françoise Zonabend, 'Baptismal Kinship at Minot', *Ritual, Religion, and the Sacred*, pp. 57–80.

34. Archives du Palais de Monaco, Fonds Grimaldi-Régusse 43–4, livre de raison de Charles Ier de Grimaldi-Régusse; Raymond Mentzer, *Blood and Belief* (West Lafayette, Ind., 1994), pp. 148–51.

35. Zonabend, 'Baptismal Kinship', pp. 62–6; Raymond Ritter, *Catherine de Bourbon*, 2 vols (Paris, 1985), II, 421, 431, 451, 453; idem, *La petite Tignonville* (Bordeaux, 1945), pp. 76, 84, 96, 103–4; Louis de Videl, *Connétable de Lesdiguières* (Paris, 1638), p. 76.

CHAPTER 2

1. Natalie Davis, 'Women on Top', *Society and Culture in Early Modern France* (Stanford, 1975), pp. 124–51; Ian Maclean, *Woman Triumphant* (Oxford, 1977);

Carolyn Lougee, *Le Paradis des Femmes* (Princeton, 1976); Erica Harth, *Cartesian Women* (Ithaca, 1992).

2. Moliére, *The Learned Ladies*, tr. Richard Wilbur (New York, 1977).

3. A. Edward Newton, ed., *The Letters of Madame de Sévigné*, 7 vols (Philadelphia, 1927), IV, 48, V, 226; Frances Mossiker, *Madame de Sévigné* (New York, 1983), pp. 14–16, 58–9, 328.

4. Jonathan Dewald, *Pont-St-Pierre* (Berkeley, 1987), p. 183; Raymond Mentzer, *Blood and Belief* (West Lafayette, Ind., 1994), p. 82; Robert Kalas, 'Noble Widow's Place', *Sixteenth Cent Journ*, 24 (1993), 519–39.

5. Mentzer, *Blood and Belief*, p. 83; Claude Badalo-Dulong, *Banquier du Roi* (Paris, 1951), p. 174; Jonathan Dewald, *Formation of a Provincial Nobility* (Princeton, 1980), p. 257; Raymond Ritter, *La petite Tignonville* (Bordeaux, 1945), pp. 15, 45, 65–8; Sharon Kettering, 'Patronage Power of Noblewomen', *Hist Journ*, 32 (1989), 827.

6. Micheline Cuénin, ed., *Mémoires Madame de La Guette* (Paris, 1982), pp. 43–53.

7. Natalie Davis and Arlette Farge, eds, *Renaissance and Enlightenment Paradoxes*, vol. 3 in *A History of Women*, eds Georges Duby and Michelle Perrot, 5 vols (Cambridge, Mass., 1993), pp. 101–31, 395–435; François Furet and Jacques Ozouf, *Reading and Writing* (Cambridge, 1982), pp. 32–47, 199–206; Roger Chartier *et al.*, *L'éducation en France du XVIe au XVIIIe siècles* (Paris, 1976), pp. 231–47.

8. Pierre-Adolphe Chéruel and Georges d'Avenel, eds, *Lettres du Cardinal Mazarin*, 9 vols (Paris, 1877–1906), vol. IX, pp. 168, 208, 235, 281, 402, 435, 460, 482, 502, 556, 634, 832, 849, 854, 857, 870, 882, 901, 917, 920, 930, 943; Amédée Renée, *Les nièces de Mazarin* (Paris, 1856), pp. 91–6.

9. Kalas, 'Noble Widow's Place', 519–39; Barbara Diefendorf, *Paris City Councillors* (Princeton, 1987), pp. 279–97; idem, 'Widows and Remarriage', *Journ Family Hist* 7 (1982), 379–95; Olwen Hufton, 'Women Without Men', ibid., 9 (1984), 355–76.

10. Wendy Gibson, *Women in Seventeenth-Century France* (New York, 1989), pp. 59–62; Roland Mousnier, *The Institutions of France*, vol. I, *Society and the State*, tr. Brian Pearce (Chicago, 1979), pp. 85–91; Robert Wheaton, 'Affinity and Descent', *Family and Sexuality*, eds Robert Wheaton and Tamara Hareven (Philadelphia, 1980), pp. 111–34; René Pillorget, *La tige et le rameau* (Paris, 1979), pp. 19–42; 81–115; Jacques Poumarede, 'Le droit des veuves', *Femmes et pouvoirs*, eds Danielle Haase-Dubosc and Eliane Viennot (Paris, 1991), pp. 64–76.

11. Mousnier, *Society and the State*, pp. 61–6, 85–91; Sarah Hanley, 'Engendering the State', *Fr Hist Studies*, 16 (1989), 4–27; idem, 'Social Sites of Political Practice', *Amer Hist Rev*, 102 (1997), 27–52; James Farr, *Authority and Sexuality* (New York, 1995), pp. 13–32; Gayle Brunelle, 'Dangerous Liaisons', *Fr Hist Studies*, 19 (1995), 75–103; Zoe Schneider, 'Women before the Bench', ibid., 23 (2000), 1–32; Julie Hardwicke, 'Women "Working" the Law', *Journ Women's Hist*, 9 (1997), 28–49.

12. Barbara Diefendorf, 'Give Us Back Our Children', *Journ Mod Hist*, 68 (1996), 265–307, esp. 272–4; Alan Williams, 'Patterns of Conflict', *Journ Family Hist*, 18 (1993), 39–52, esp. 46–7.

13. Pillorget, *La tige et le rameau*, pp. 39–41; Mousnier, *Society and State*, pp. 61–6; Hanley, 'Engendering the State', pp. 9–11; Farr, *Authority and Sexuality*, pp. 90–123; Beatrice Gottlieb, 'Clandestine Marriage', *Family and Sexuality*, pp. 49–83.

14. Hanley, 'Engendering the State', 4–27; Natalie Davis, 'City Women and Religious Change', *Society and Culture*, p. 72; 'Women on Top', ibid., p. 126.

15. Jean-Louis Flandrin, *Families in Former Times*, tr. Richard Southern (Cambridge, 1979), pp. 145–73; Martine Segalen, *Love and Power in the Peasant Family*, tr. Sarah Matthews (Chicago, 1983), pp. 14–17; Edward Shorter, *Making of the Modern Family* (New York, 1975).

16. Mousnier, *Society and the State*, pp. 85–91; Pillorget, *La tige et le rameau*, pp. 19–42.

17. Gibson, *Women*, pp. 84–96; Alain Lottin, 'Vie et mort du couple', *XVIIe siècle* 102–3 (1974), 59–78; idem, *La désunion du couple* (Paris, 1975); Julie Hardwicke, 'Seeking Separations', *Fr Hist Studies*, 21 (1998), 157–80.

18. Maurice Garden, *Lyon et les lyonnais au XVIIIe siècle* (Paris, 1970), p. 493.

19. Warner Hutchinson, ed., *The Autobiography of Madame Guyon*, tr. Thomas Taylor Allen (New Canaan, Conn., 1980), pp. 6–32.

20. Ruth Kleinman, *Anne of Austria* (Columbus, Ohio, 1985), p. 87; Françoise Bertaut de Motteville, *Mémoires*, ed. Claude Bernard Petitot (Paris, 1824), 2d ser., vol. 36, 356–7.

21. James Scott, *Domination and the Arts of Resistance* (New Haven, 1990), pp. 17–69; Elborg Forster, ed., tr., *A Woman's Life at the Court of the Sun King* (Baltimore, 1984), p. 41.

22. Maclean, *Woman Triumphant*, pp. 1–63; Davis and Farge, *Paradoxes*, pp. 187–374; Farr, *Authority and Sexuality*, pp. 23–32, 45–52, *passim*; Merry Wiesner, *Women and Gender* (Cambridge, 1993), pp. 9–38.

23. Gibson, *Women*, pp. 145–7; Louis de Rouvroy, duc de Saint-Simon, *Mémoires*, ed. Adolphe Chéruel, 13 vols (Paris, 1904–6), II, 31, 354–5; IV, 142, 262, 400; V, 137; VIII, 152–6; Françoise d'Aubigné, marquise de Maintenon, *Lettres*, ed. M. Langlois, 4 vols (Paris, 1935–9), III, 325; V, 6.

24. Forster, *A Woman's Life*, pp. 86–7.

25. Davis, 'Women on Top', p. 145; Davis and Farge, *Paradoxes*, p. 4.

26. Natalie Davis, *Return of Martin Guerre* (Cambridge, Mass., 1983), pp. 31, 50, 60, 68–9, 86, 92, 113, 118; Robert Finlay, 'Refashioning of Martin Guerre', *Amer Hist Rev*, 93 (June, 1988), 555–7; Natalie Davis, *Fiction in the Archives* (Stanford, 1987), pp. 77–111.

27. Elizabeth Rapley, *The Dévotes. Women and Church* (Montreal, 1990), pp. 48–60; idem, 'Women and Religious Vocation', *Fr Hist Studies*, 18 (1994), 613–31; Diefendorf, 'Give Us Back Our Children', 265–307; Marie-Andrée Jégou, *Les Ursulines* (Paris, 1981).

28. Charles Perrault, *Mémoires de ma vie*, ed. Paul Bonnefon (Paris, 1933), p. 223.

29. Williams, 'Patterns of Conflict', 39–52; René La Bruyère, *La marine de Richelieu: Maillé-Brézé* (Paris, 1945), pp. 18–23; Segalen, *Love and Power*, pp. 43–7; Davis, 'The Reasons of Misrule', *Society and Culture*, pp. 97–123; Arlette Farge and Michel Foucault, *Le désordre des familles* (Paris, 1982), pp. 21–154.

30. Forster, *A Woman's Life*, p. 87.

31. Robert Nye, *Masculinity and Male Codes of Honor* (New York, 1993), p. 16; Gibson, *Women*, pp. 63–5; Davis and Farge, *Paradoxes*, pp. 476–80.

32. Carolyn Lougee, *Le Paradis des Femmes* (Princeton, 1976), pp. 113–70; Sara Chapman, 'Patronage as Family Economy', forthcoming *Fr Hist Studies*; Emmanuel Le Roy Ladurie and Jean-François Fitou, 'Hypergamie féminine', *Annales: ESC*, 46 (1991), 133–49; Lucy Norton, ed., tr., *Memoirs Duc de Saint-Simon*, 2 vols (New York, 1967), I, 39–40.

33. Arnaud Chaffanjon, *La marquise de Sévigné* (Paris, 1962), p. 23; Lougee, *Le Paradis des Femmes*, pp. 151–70; Brunelle, 'Mésalliance', 75–103; Joseph Bergin, *Cardinal Richelieu* (New Haven, 1985), pp. 33–4. Professor Bergin notes that he now finds the existence of Isabeau more doubtful.

34. Natalie Davis, 'Ghosts, Kin, and Progeny', *Daedalus*, 106 (1977), 87–114; David Sturdy, *The D'Aligres de La Rivière* (New York, 1986), pp. 165–205; Jean-Pierre Labatut, *Les ducs et pairs de France* (Paris, 1972), pp. 98–142; idem, 'La fidélité du duc de Navailles', *Hommage à Roland Mousnier*, ed. Yves Durand (Paris, 1981), p. 190; Diefendorf, *Paris City Councillors*, pp. 155–209; Sharon Kettering, 'Patronage and Kinship', *Fr Hist Studies*, 16 (1989), 408–35; idem, 'Household Service', ibid., 20 (1997), 55–85; idem, 'Brokerage at the Court of Louis XIV', *Hist Journ*, 36 (1993), 69–87; idem, 'Patronage Power of Noblewomen', 817–41.

35. Segalen, *Love and Power*, pp. 78–113; Olwen Hufton, 'Women and the Family Economy', *Fr Hist Studies*, 9 (1975), 1–22; Jean-Michel Boehler, *La paysannerie d'Alsace*, 3 vols (Strasboug, 1995), II, 1255–6; Lucienne Roubin, 'Male and Female Space', *Rural Society in France*, eds Robert Forster and Orest Ranum (Baltimore, 1977), pp. 152–80.

36. Charles de Ribbe, *Une grande dame dans son ménage* (Paris, 1890), pp. 348–56, 362–9, 375–6; Gibson, *Women*, pp. 101–3; Julie Hardwicke, *The Practice of Patriarchy* (University Park, 1997), pp. 77–142.

37. James Collins, 'The Economic Role of Women', *Fr Hist Studies*, 16 (1989), 436–70; idem, 'Geographic and Social Mobility', *Journ Social Hist*, 24 (1991), 571–2; Cissie Fairchilds, *Poverty and Charity in Aix-en-Provence* (Baltimore, 1976), p. 67; idem, *Domestic Enemies* (Baltimore, 1984), pp. 77–80; William Chester Jordan, *Women and Credit* (Philadelphia, 1993), pp. 53–82; Daniel Dessert, *Argent, pouvoir et société* (Paris, 1984), pp. 364–5.

38. Jacques Levron, *Daily Life at Versailles*, tr. Claire Engel (London, 1968), pp. 70–86; Jacques Saint-Germain, *Les financiers sous Louis XIV* (Paris, 1950), pp. 182–7.

39. Gibson, *Women*, pp. 97–140; Collins, 'Economic Role of Women', 453–63; Natalie Davis, 'Women in the Crafts', *Feminist Studies*, 8 (1982), 47–80; James Farr, *Hands of Honor* (Cornell, 1989), pp. 20, 105; idem, 'Consumers, Commerce, and Craftsmen', *Cities and Social Change*, ed. Philip Benedict (London, 1989), pp. 158–60; André Lespagnol, 'Femmes négociants', *Populations et cultures* (Rennes, 1989), pp. 463–70; Elizabeth Musgrave, 'Women in the Male World of Work', *Fr Hist*, 7 (1993), 30–52; Daryl Hafter, 'Female Masters in the Ribbonmaking Guild', *Fr Hist Studies*, 20 (1997), 1–14.

40. Gayle Brunelle, a forthcoming book entitled, *Enterprising Women, Work, and the Law*; idem, 'Contractual Kin: Servants and Their Mistresses', *Journ Early Mod Hist*, 2 (1998), 372–94; Gregory Hanlon, *L'univers de gens de bien* (Bordeaux, 1989, pp. 100–1; Gay Gullickson, *The Spinners and Weavers of Auffay* (Cambridge, 1986), pp. 162–77.

41. Collins, 'Economic Role of Women', 461–2.

42. Joan Kelly-Gadol, 'Did Women Have a Renaissance?' *Women, History, and Theory* (Chicago, 1984), p. 47; Merry Wiesner, 'Women's Defense of Their Public Role', *Women in the Middle Ages and Renaissance* (Syracuse, 1986), pp. 3, 21; Joan Landes, *Women and the Public Sphere* (Ithaca, 1988), pp. 17–38.

167

43. Dena Goodman, 'Public Sphere and Private Life', *History and Theory* 31 (1992), 1–20.

44. Gibson, *Women*, pp. 197–8; Maurice Magendie, *La politesse mondaine*, 2 vols (Paris, 1923, Geneva, 1970), I, 88–9.

45. Olwen Hufton, *The Prospect Before Her* (New York, 1996), pp. 492–513.

CHAPTER 3

1. Emmanuel Le Roy Ladurie and Orest Ranum, *Pierre Prion* (Paris, 1985), pp. 41–3, 152–3.

2. W. Gregory Monahan, *Year of Sorrows* (Columbus, 1993), pp. 71–5.

3. Le Roy Ladurie, *Pierre Prion*, pp. 43, 153; Monahan, *Year of Sorrows*, pp. 75–8; Marcel Lachiver, *Les années de misère* (Paris, 1992).

4. Le Roy Ladurie, *Pierre Prion*, p. 152; Monahan, *Year of Sorrows*, pp. 30–2, 92–8, 125–53.

5. Pierre Goubert, *The Ancien Régime*, tr. Steve Cox (New York, 1973), pp. 36–41; idem, *Beauvais et le Beauvaisis* (Paris, 1960), pp. 25–82; Pierre Goubert and Daniel Roche, *Les Français et l'Ancien Régime*, 2 vols (Paris, 1984), I, 38–47; Ernest Labrousse *et al.*, *Histoire économique et sociale*, 4 vols (Paris, 1970–82), II, 38–54.

6. Hugues Neveux, Jean Jacquart and Emmanuel Le Roy Ladurie, *L'âge classique des paysans*, vol. 2, *Histoire de la France rurale*, ed. Georges Duby and Armand Wallon, 4 vols (Paris, 1975–6), pp. 185–211; François Lebrun, *Les hommes et la mort en Anjou* (Paris, 1971), pp. 212–79; Jean-Michel Boehler, *La paysannerie d'Alsace*, 3 vols (Strasbourg, 1995), I, 81–293; Laurence Brockliss and Colin Jones, *The Medical World of Early Modern France* (Oxford, 1997), pp. 53–66; Emmanuel Le Roy Ladurie, *Times of Feast, Times of Famine*, tr. Barbara Bray (New York, 1971), pp. 56–60, 129–226; idem, 'Climate', *The Territory of the Historian*, tr. Ben and Siân Reynolds (Chicago, 1979), pp. 287–319.

7. Robert Muchembled, *Popular Culture and Elite Culture*, tr. Lydia Cochrane (Baton Rouge, 1985), pp. 14–22; Robert Mandrou, *Introduction to Modern France*, tr. R.E. Hallmark (New York, 1976), pp. 13–48; Emmanuel Le Roy Ladurie, 'Rétif de la Bretonne', *The Mind and Method of the Historian*, tr. Siân and Ben Reynolds (Chicago, 1981), pp. 211–69; Pierre Goubert, *The French Peasantry in the Seventeenth Century*, tr. Ian Patterson (Cambridge, 1986), pp. 35–43, 92–6, 105–9.

8. Charles Carrière *et al.*, *Marseille, ville morte, la peste de 1720* (Marseille, 1968), pp. 70, 75, 81, 205–13, 301–2.

9. Brockliss and Jones, *Medical World*, pp. 37–42; William McNeill, *Plagues and Peoples* (New York, 1976), pp. 137–40, 170–83; Carrière, *Marseille*, pp. 71, 73, 93, 162–4; Françoise Hildesheimer, *La terreur et la pitié* (Marseille, 1990), pp. 6–10; Jean-Noel Biraben, *Les hommes et la peste*, 2 vols (Paris, 1975), I, 296–8.

10. Brockliss and Jones, *The Medical World*, p. 38; Biraben, *Les hommes et la peste*, I, 119–22, 135–46, 308–9; Carrière, *Marseille*, pp. 106, 201; Hildesheimer, *La terreur et la pitié*, p. 14; Sylvie Mousset, *La peste en Rouergue* (Toulouse, 1992), p. 19; Labrousse, *Histoire économique et sociale*, II, p. 45; Le Roy Ladurie, 'The Unification of the Globe by Disease', *Mind and Method*, pp. 28–72.

11. Emmanuel Le Roy Ladurie, *The Ancien Régime*, tr. Mark Greengrass (Oxford, 1996), pp. 514–51; John Lynn, *Giant of the Grand Siècle* (Cambridge, 1997), pp. 42,

47; Yves-Marie Bercé, *History of Peasant Revolts*, tr. Amanda Whitmore (Ithaca, 1990); Orest Ranum, *The Fronde* (New York, 1994).

12. William Beik, *Absolutism in Seventeenth-Century France* (Cambridge, 1985), pp. 172–6, 218; Malcolm Greenshields, *An Economy of Violence* (University Park, 1994), pp. 158–9; Goubert, *The French Peasantry*, pp. 210–13; Bercé, *History of Peasant Revolts*, pp. 169, 179–80, 190, 196, 242, 328–30; René Pillorget, *Les mouvements insurrectionnels de Provence* (Paris, 1975), pp. 265–71, 505–7, 920–6; Sharon Kettering, *Judicial Politics and Urban Revolt* (Princeton, 1978), pp. 54–5; André Corvisier, *Histoire militaire de la France*, vol. 1, ed. Philippe Contamine (Paris, 1992), pp. 394–408, 435–48; Lynn, *Giant of the Grand Siècle*, pp. 158–60.

13. Le Roy Ladurie, *Pierre Prion*, pp. 45–6.

14. Ibid., pp. 153–7; Pierre Dubois, *Un homme de peste* (Toulon, 1970), pp. 44–5; Carrière, *Marseille*, pp. 69, 183–95; Hildesheimer, *La terreur et la pitié*, pp. 35–66; Danièle Larcena, *La muraille de la peste* (Aix, 1993).

15. Carrière, *Marseille*, p. 72; Biraben, *Les hommes et la peste*, I, 130–1; Hildesheimer, *La terreur et la pitié*, pp. 50–6; Paul Slack, 'Responses to Plague', *In Time of Plague*, ed. Arien Mack (New York, 1991), pp. 111–31.

16. Brockliss and Jones, *The Medical World*, pp. 40–1; Carrière, *Marseille*, pp. 159–95, 263–91; Hildesheimer, *La terreur et la pitié*, pp. 66–142; Biraben, *La homme et la peste*, I, 139–54, 242–6, 309–10.

17. See the historiographical essay for a description of the Annalistes.

18. Jean-Marc Moriceau, *Les fermiers de l'Ile-de-France* (Paris, 1994); Marc Venard, *Bourgeois et paysans au XVIIe siècle* (Paris, 1957).

19. Marc Bloch, *French Rural History*, tr. Janet Sondheimer (Berkeley, 1966); Emmanuel Le Roy Ladurie, *The Peasants of Languedoc*, tr. John Day (Chicago, 1976); idem, *The French Peasantry*, tr. Alan Sheridan (Berkeley, 1987); idem, 'History That Stands Still', *Mind and Method*, pp. 1–27; idem, 'French Peasants in the Sixteenth Century', ibid., pp. 97–122; Pierre Goubert, *The Ancien Régime*, pp. 42–3; idem, *The French Peasantry*, pp. 23–34, 92–109; idem, *Louis XIV and Twenty Million Frenchmen*, tr. Anne Carter (New York, 1970), pp. 38–46; Gérard Bouchard, *Le village immobile* (Paris, 1972).

20. Philippe Ariès, *The Hour of Our Death*, tr. Helen Weaver (New York, 1982). Michel Vovelle, François Lebrun and Pierre Chaunu have also made important contributions to the study of the culture of death.

21. James Scott, *The Moral Economy of the Peasant* (Yale, 1976), pp. 13–34.

22. Muchembled, *Popular Culture*, pp. 14–107; idem, *Nos ancêtres, les paysans* (Lille, 1981), pp. 10–49; Bouchard, *Village immobile*, pp. 212–338; Robert Mandrou, *La France aux XVIIe et XVIIIe siècles* (Paris, 1970), pp. 71–155; Robert Darnton, *The Great Cat Massacre* (New York, 1984), pp. 9–72.

23. For summaries, see Philip Hoffman, *Growth in a Traditional Society* (Princeton, 1996), pp. 12–34; Thomas Brennan, *Burgundy to Champagne* (Baltimore, 1997), pp. ix–xxi; Liana Vardi, *The Land and the Loom* (Durham, 1993), pp. 1–14; Daniel Hickey, 'Innovation and Obstacles to Growth', *Fr Hist Studies*, 15 (1987), 208–40; James Goldsmith, 'The Agrarian History of Preindustrial France', *Journ Eur Econ Hist*, 13 (1984), 175–99.

24. Jacques Dupâquier, *Histoire de la population française*, 4 vols (Paris, 1989), II, 198–9, 203; Georges Frêche, *Toulouse et la region Midi-Pyrénées* (Toulouse, 1975), pp. 101, 682.

169

25. René Baehrel, *Une croissance: La Basse-Provence* (Paris, 1961), pp. 29–30, 232–6, 194–7; Alain Croix, *La Bretagne aux XVIe et XVIIe siècles*, 2 vols (Paris, 1981), I, 174, 353–67; Boehler, *La paysannerie d'Alsace*, I, 172–97; Lebrun, *Les hommes et la mort en Anjou*, p. 231; Goubert and Roche, *Les Français et l'Ancien Régime*, I, 291–312; Gaston Roupnel, *La ville et la campagne* (Paris, 1935), pp. 3–40.

26. Pierre Goubert insists upon the importance of famine in causing the demographic crisis, while Jean-Noel Biraben, François Lebrun and Jean-Pierre Poussou emphasize the effects of epidemics of disease.

27. Goubert, *The Ancien Régime*, p. 38; Le Roy Ladurie, *The French Peasantry*, pp. 267–358; idem, *The Peasants of Languedoc*. Also see Jean Jacquart, *La crise rurale en Ile-de-France* (Paris, 1974); idem, *Paris et L'Ile-de-France au temps des paysans* (Paris, 1990).

28. David Parker, *Class and State in Ancien Régime France* (London, 1996), pp. 28–74; Robert Brenner, 'Agrarian Class Structure', *The Brenner Debate*, eds T.H. Ashton and C.H.E. Philpin (Cambridge, 1985), pp. 10–63.

29. Bercé, *History of Peasant Revolts*; idem, *Revolt and Revolution in Early Modern Europe*, tr. Joseph Bergin (Manchester, 1987); P.J. Coveney, ed., tr., *France in Crisis, 1620–1675* (London, 1977); Roland Mousnier, *Peasant Uprisings*, tr. Brian Pearce (New York, 1970); Le Roy Ladurie, *The French Peasants*, pp. 359–99; René Pillorget, *Les mouvements insurrectionnels*; Madeleine Foisil, *La révolte des Nu-Pieds* (Paris, 1970).

30. Jean Meuvret, *Le problème des subsistances à l'époque Louis XIV*, 3 vols (Paris, 1977–88); idem, 'Monetary Circulation', *Essays in French Economic History*, ed., tr., Rondo Cameron (Homewood, Ill., 1970), pp. 140–9; George Grantham, 'Jean Meuvret and the Subsistence Problem', *Journ Econ Hist*, 49 (1989), 184–200; Hoffman, *Growth in a Traditional Society*, pp. 16–20; idem, 'Institutions and Agriculture', *Politics and Society*, 16 (1988), 241–64; Jean-Laurent Rosenthal, *The Fruits of Revolution* (Cambridge, 1992), pp. 21–36. Also see Steven Kaplan, *Bread, Politics and Political Economy*, 2 vols (The Hague, 1976); idem, *Provisioning Paris* (Ithaca, 1984).

31. Goubert, *The French Peasantry*, pp. 97–147; Boehler, *La paysannerie*, II, 990–1100. For summaries of protoindustrial theory, see Gay Gullickson, *Spinners and Weavers of Auffay* (Cambridge, 1986), pp. 38–67; Tessie Liu, *The Weaver's Knot* (Ithaca, 1994), pp. 1–44; Maxine Berg *et al.*, *Manufacture in Town and Country* (Cambridge, 1983), pp. 16–28.

32. Boehler, *La paysannerie*, II, 1074–5.

33. Brennan, *Burgundy to Champagne*; Vardi, *The Land and the Loom*; Hoffman, *Growth in a Traditional Society*, pp. 35–80; Jean-Marc Moriceau and Gilles Postel-Vinay, *Ferme, Entreprise, Famille* (Paris, 1992).

34. Hoffman, *Growth in a Traditional Society*, pp. 81–192, notes 30, 31, p. 278; idem, 'Land Rents and Agricultural Productivity', *Journ Econ Hist*, 51 (1991), 771–805; Paul Butel, *L'économie française au XVIIIe siècle* (Paris, 1993), pp. 184–99; Boehler, *La paysannerie*, I, 645–835; Michel Morineau, *Les faux-semblants d'un démarrage économique. Cahiers des Annales*, 30 (1971); idem, 'Was there an Agricultural Revolution?', *Essays in French Economic History*, pp. 170–82.

35. Le Roy Ladurie, *Pierre Prion*, pp. 12–15, 40–51.

36. Nicolas Edme Restif de la Bretonne, *La vie de mon père*, ed. Gilbert Rougier (Paris, 1970), pp. 5, 7–8, 17–18, 26, 28, 30–2, 34, 49, 60–3. Also see Emmanuel Le Roy Ladurie, 'Rétif de la Bretonne', *Mind and Method*, pp. 211–69.

37. François Furet and Jacques Ozouf, *Reading and Writing* (Cambridge, 1982), pp. 149–225; Boehler, *La paysannerie*, II, 1811–92; Roger Chartier *et al.*, *L'éducation en France du XVIe au XVIIIe siècle* (Paris, 1976), pp. 3–112.

38. Le Roy Ladurie, 'Rétif de la Bretonne', *Mind and Method*, pp. 214–19; idem, 'The Rouergue through the Lens', ibid., p. 184; idem, *Pierre Prion*, pp. 11–13; Baehrel, *Une croissance*, pp. 250–3; J.K.J. Thomson, *Clermont-de-Lodève, 1633–1789* (Cambridge, 1982), pp. 205–7, 239–40; Olwen Hufton, *The Poor of Eighteenth-Century France* (Oxford, 1974), pp. 26–33; Cissie Fairchilds, *Domestic Service* (Baltimore, 1984), pp. 61–6, 77–85.

39. Jean-Marie Pesez and Emmanuel Le Roy Ladurie, 'The Deserted Villages', *Rural Society in France*, eds Robert Forster and Orest Ranum, trs Elborg Forster and Patricia Ranum (Baltimore, 1977), pp. 72–106.

40. Jean-Pierre Poussou, *Bordeaux et la Sud-Ouest au XVIIIe siècle* (Paris, 1983), pp. 63–150; idem, 'Les mouvements migratoires', *Annales de démographie historique* (1970), 11–78; André Corvisier, 'Service militaire et mobilité géographique', ibid., 185–204; Micheline Baulant, 'Groupes mobiles: la société rurale', *Les marginaux et les exclus*, ed. Arlette Farge (Paris, 1979), pp. 78–121.

41. Dupâquier, 'Mobilité et migrations', *Histoire de la population*, II, 99–174; Bercé, *A History of Peasant Revolts*, pp. 58–70; Abel Poitrineau, *Remues d'hommes* (Paris, 1983); Baehrel, *Une croissance*, pp. 250–3; Hufton, *The Poor*, pp. 69–106; P.M. Jones, *Politics and Rural Society* (Cambridge, 1985), pp. 62–9.

42. Mandrou, *Introduction to Modern France*, pp. 208–18.

43. T.J.A. Le Goff, *Vannes and Its Region* (Oxford, 1981), pp. 61–3, 273–4, 278; Jonathan Dewald, *Pont-St-Pierre* (Berkeley, 1987), pp. 112–16; Boehler, *La Paysannerie*, I, 626; Maurice Agulhon, *La vie sociale en Provence* (Paris, 1970), p. 90; Robert Forster, *The Nobility of Toulouse* (Baltimore, 1960), pp. 152–77.

44. Alain Morel, 'Power and Ideology in the Village', *Rural Society*, pp. 107–25.

45. Venard, *Bourgeois et paysans*, pp. 31–7; Bloch, *French Rural History*, pp. 143–9; Olwen Hufton, *Bayeux in the Late Eighteenth Century* (Oxford, 1967), pp. 75–6.

46. Le Goff, *Vannes and its Region*, pp. 216–28; Cynthia Bouton, *The Flour War* (University Park, 1993), pp. 165–7; David Garrioch, *Neighbourhood and Community* (Cambridge, 1986), pp. 2–6, 12; Jones, *Politics and Rural Society*, pp. 112–44.

47. Hoffman, *Growth in a Traditional Society*, pp. 35–80; Liu, *The Weaver's Knot*, pp. 45–73.

48. Le Roy Ladurie, *Pierre Prion*, pp. 54–6, 71.

49. Daniel Roche, *France in the Enlightenment* (Paris, 1998), pp. 183–5.

50. James Collins, 'Geographic and Social Mobility', *Journ Social Hist*, 24 (1990–1), 564.

CHAPTER 4

1. *Félix et Thomas Platter à Montpellier* (Montpellier, 1892), p. 297. Also see Thomas Platter, *Journal of a Younger Brother*, tr. Seán Jennett (London, 1964); Emmanuel Le Roy Ladurie, *The Beggar and the Professor*, tr. Arthur Goldhammer (Chicago, 1997).

2. Jean-Baptiste Bertrand, *A Historical Relation of the Plague at Marseille*, tr. Anne Plumptre (London, 1805, Farnborough, 1973), p. 24; Wolfgang Kaiser, *Marseille au temps des troubles, 1559–1596*, tr. Florence Chaix (Paris, 1992), pp. 24–7.

3. Platter, *Journal*, pp. 299–300.

4. Bertrand, *A Historical Relation*, pp. 22, 24–5; Charles Carrière *et al.*, *Marseille, ville morte* (Marseille, 1968), pp. 19–20; Kaiser, *Marseille*, pp. 28–9.

5. Platter, *Journal*, pp. 304–5.

6. Ibid., pp. 311, 315–16; Kaiser, *Marseille*, pp. 24, 35–6; Bertrand, *A Historical Relation*, p. 25.

7. Fernand Braudel, *Civilization and Capitalism, 15th–18th Century*, tr. Siân Reynolds, vol. 1, *Structures of Everyday Life* (New York, 1979), p. 479.

8. Kaiser, *Marseille*, pp. 35–7; Charles Carrière, *Négociants marseillais au XVIIIe siècle*, 2 vols (Marseille, 1973), I, 198–9; Philip Benedict, *Cities and Social Change* (London, 1989), pp. 24–5; Edouard Baratier, ed., *Histoire de Marseille* (Toulouse, 1973), pp. 163, 200; René Baehrel, *Une croissance: La Basse-Provence rurale* (Paris, 1961), p. 235. Also see William Sewell, Jr, *Structure and Mobility* (Cambridge, 1985).

9. Marcel Lachiver, *La population de Meulan* (Paris, 1969), pp. 147–65, 193–208; Jean-Pierre Bardet, *Rouen aux XVIIe et XVIIIe siècles*, 2 vols (Paris, 1983), I, 107–21, 347–74; Pierre Deyon, *Amiens* (Paris, 1967), pp. 3–43.

10. Carrière, *Négociants*, pp. 200–3; Baratier, *Histoire de Marseille*, pp. 166–8; Bardet, *Rouen*, I, 211; Jean-Claude Perrot, *Genèse d'une ville moderne: Caen*, 2 vols (Paris, 1975), I, 156–8; Maurice Garden, *Lyon et les lyonnais* (Paris, 1974), pp. 73–4; Jean-Pierre Poussou, *Bordeaux et le sud-ouest* (Paris, 1983), pp. 64–5, 76–8, 100.

11. Emmanuel Le Roy Ladurie *et al.*, *La ville classique*, vol. 3, *Histoire de la France urbaine*, ed. Georges Duby, 5 vols (Paris, 1980–5), pp. 30–1; idem, *The Ancien Régime*, tr. Mark Greengrass (Cambridge, Mass., 1996), p. 306.

12. Philip Benedict, 'Was the Eighteenth Century an Era of Urbanization in France?' *Journ Interdis Hist*, 21 (1990), 179–215; Bernard Lepetit, 'Urbanization: A Comment', 'A Reply', ibid., 23 (1992), 73–95.

13. Gaston Rambert, *Nicolas Arnoul* (Marseille, 1931), pp. 106–57; idem, *Marseille* (Marseille, 1934), pp. 191–243; Félix Tavernier, *Aspects de Marseille* (Paris, 1977), pp. 25–32; Jean-Paul Coste, *Aix-en-Provence* (Aix, 1964), p. 76; Leon Bernard, *The Emerging City* (Durham, 1970); Andrew Trout, *City on the Seine* (New York, 1997), pp. 167–80; Nicolas Cendro *et al.*, *Marseille au XVIIe siècle* (Marseille, 1980), pp. 1–34.

14. Rambert, *Nicolas Arnoul*, pp. 159–86; Tavernier, *Aspects de Marseille*, pp. 33–6; Paul Bamford, *Fighting Ships* (Minneapolis, 1973), pp. 52–67, 173–99.

15. Messrs Rathery and Bouton, eds, *Mademoiselle de Scudéry* (Paris, 1873), pp. 162, 172–3, 27 December 1644; Félix Tavernier, *La vie quotidienne à Marseille* (Paris, 1973), pp. 11, 51–3.

16. Platter, *Journal*, pp. 300–2; Bamford, *Fighting Ships*, pp. 200–49. Also see Jean Marteilhe, *Mémoires d'un galérien*, ed. André Zysberg (Paris, 1982).

17. Jean-Marie Constant, *La société française* (Paris, 1994), pp. 58–62; Daniel Roche, *France in the Enlightenment*, tr. Arthur Goldhammer (Cambridge, Mass., 1998), pp. 174–9.

18. Le Roy Ladurie, *The Ancien Régime*, p. 306. See the above cited works by Jean-Claude Perrot, Jean-Pierre Poussou, Maurice Garden, Jean-Pierre Bardet and Pierre Deyon. Also see Richard Gascon, *Grand commerce et vie urbaine: Lyon et ses marchands*, 2 vols (Paris, 1971); Pierre Goubert, *Beauvais et le Beauvaisis* (Paris, 1960); Alain Croix, *Nantes et le pays nantais* (Paris, 1974); Georges Frêche, *Toulouse et la*

région Midi-Pyrénées (Toulouse, 1975); René Favier, *Les villes du Dauphiné* (Grenoble, 1992).

19. Rathery and Bouton, *Scudéry*, pp. 172, 175, 191; Rambert, *Marseille*, pp. 116–30; idem, *Nicolas Arnoul*, p. 267; Kaiser, *Marseille*, pp. 32–6; Adolphe Crémieux, *Marseille et la royauté* (Paris, 1971), pp. 1–5; Platter, *Journal*, p. 315; Tavernier, *Aspects de Marseille*, p. 11; Gilles Mihière, *Les bastides marseillaises* (Marseille, 1993); Pierre Bianco, *Le terroir marseillais* (Marseille, 1993).

20. Ibid., pp. 51–79; Jean-Paul Coste, *La ville d'Aix en 1695*, 3 vols (Aix, 1970), II, 973–86; T.J.A. Le Goff, *Vannes and its Region* (Oxford, 1981), pp. 205–28; Jean Jacquart, 'Paris: First Metropolis', *Capital Cities and Their Hinterlands*, eds Peter Clark and Bernard Lepetit (Brookfield, Vt, 1996), pp. 105–18; Yves-Marie Bercé, *Histoire des croquants*, 2 vols (Paris, 1974), I, 242–3; Bardet, *Rouen*, I, 198; Gascon, *Lyon et ses marchands*, II, 811–72; André Lespagnol, *Messieurs de Saint-Malo*, 2 vols (Rennes, 1997, 2nd edn), I, 52–70; Annik Pardailhé-Galabrun, *The Birth of Intimacy*, tr. Jocelyn Phelps (Philadelphia, 1988), pp. 19–21.

21. François Bédarida, 'The French Approach to Urban History', *The Pursuit of Urban History*, eds Derek Fraser and Anthony Sutcliffe (London, 1983), pp. 395–406; Le Roy Ladurie, *La ville classique*, pp. 53–107; Deyon, *Amiens*, 145–61, 265–91, 323–38; Jacob Price, *France and the Chesapeake*, 2 vols (Ann Arbor, 1973), I, 5; J.K.J. Thomson, *Clermont-de-Lodève* (Cambridge, 1982), pp. 30–3.

22. Bardet, *Rouen*, I, 216; Favier, *Les villes du Dauphiné*, pp. 22–32; J.K.J. Thomson, 'Variations in Industrial Structure', *Manufacture in Town and Country*, ed. Maxine Berg *et al.* (Cambridge, 1983), pp. 61–91; Cissie Fairchilds *et al.*, 'Forum: Three Views of the Guilds', *Fr Hist Studies*, 15 (1988), 688–730; Christopher Johnson, 'Capitalism and the State', *The Workplace before the Factory*, ed. Thomas Safley and Leonard Rosenband (Ithaca, 1993), pp. 37–62.

23. Henri de Séguiran, 'Procès-verbal . . . de la côte maritime de Provence', *Correspondance de Henri d'Escoubleau de Sourdis*, ed. Eugène Sue, 3 vols (Paris, 1836), III, pp. 226–31; Gaston Rambert, ed., *Histoire du commerce de Marseille*, 6 vols (Paris, 1949–59), IV, 92–118; Tavernier, *Aspects de Marseille*, pp. 37–53.

24. Thomson, *Clermont-de-Lodève*, pp. 138–42; Michel Morineau, 'Flottes de commerce et trafics français en Méditerranée au XVIIe siècle', *XVIIe Siècle*, 86–7 (1970), 136–71; Paul Masson, *Histoire du commerce français dans le Levant au XVIIe siècle* (Paris, 1896), pp. 130–5.

25. Rambert, *Histoire du commerce*, IV, 8–9; Félix Tavernier, *Marseille et la Provence* (Aix, 1960), pp. 174–5; Fernand Braudel, *The Mediterranean*, tr. Siân Reynolds, 2 vols (Berkeley, 1995), II, 865–91; John Wolf, *The Barbary Coast* (New York, 1979), pp. 175–287.

26. Rambert, *Histoire du commerce*, III, 541–52, IV, 8–9, 11, 39–47, 63–73, 88–9; Carrière, *Négociants*, I, 34–48; Tavernier, *Marseille et la Provence*, pp. 178–9; Pierre Guiral, *Histoire de Marseille* (Paris, 1983), pp. 157–8.

27. Thomas Schaeper, 'Government and Business', *Journ Euro Econ Hist*, 17 (1988), 531–57; idem, 'Economic History', *Reign of Louis XIV*, ed. Paul Sonnino (Atlantic Highlands, NJ, 1990), pp. 27–43; Sewell, *Structure and Mobility*, pp. 15–18; Rambert, *Marseille*, pp. 191–208; idem, *Histoire du Commerce*, IV, 204–40; Carrière, *Négociants*, I, 44, 157–92, II, 309–465; Paul Butel, *L'économie française* (Paris, 1993), pp. 22–32; Lespagnol, *Messieurs de Saint-Malo*, I, 235–306.

28. Carrière, *Négociants*, I, 211–12, 237–97, 313–14, II, 876–984; Rambert, *Histoire du commerce*, V, 542–67, VI, 377–410; Paul Masson, *La Provence au XVIIIe siècle*, 3 vols (Paris, 1936), III, 657–707; Baratier, *Histoire de Marseille*, pp. 205–8, 217–19; Robert Stein, *The French Sugar Business* (Baton Rouge, 1988), pp. 113–15; Michel Biehn, *Colors of Provence*, tr. Rosanna Frongin (New York, 1997), pp. 24–7, 68–72, 108–12, 156–9.

29. Kaiser, *Marseille*, p. 59; Carrière, *Négociants*, I, 101, 105–6, 253, 260–9, 272–86; Rambert, *Histoire du commerce*, IV, 498–509; Masson, *La Provence*, III, 659.

30. Frederick Johnson, 'Montpellier', *Cities*, ed. Benedict, pp. 114, 118; James Farr, 'Dijon', ibid., pp. 138–9; Sharon Kettering, *Judicial Politics* (Princeton, 1978), pp. 27–8; Lespagnol, *Messieurs de Saint-Malo*, I, 77–88, II, 171–9; Monique Cubells, 'Usurpations de noblesse en Provence', *Provence hist*, 81 (1970), 281–3; Jean-Marie Constant, 'La mobilité sociale', *XVIIe siècle* 122 (1979), 9; James Wood, *The Nobility of the Election of Bayeux* (Princeton, 1980), pp. 45–55; Rambert, *Histoire du Commerce*, IV, 511–17; Carrière, *Négociants*, 105–6. For merchant ambitions, see Robert Forster, *Merchants, Landlords, Magistrates* (Baltimore, 1980); John Bosher, *The Canada Merchants* (Oxford, 1987).

31. Crémieux, *Marseille*, pp. 834–54; Le Roy Ladurie, *La ville classique*, pp. 157–80; Nora Temple, 'Municipal Elections and Municipal Oligarchies', *French Government and Society*, ed. John Bosher (London, 1973), pp. 70–91; Jacques Maillard, *Le pouvoir municipal à Angers de 1657 à 1789*, 2 vols (Angers, 1984).

32. René Pillorget, *Les mouvements insurrectionnels de Provence* (Paris, 1975); Crémieux, *Marseille et la royauté*; William Beik, *Popular Protest in Seventeenth-Century France* (Cambridge, 1995); Constant, *La société française*, pp. 66–8.

33. William Beik, 'Louis XIV and the Cities', *Edo and Paris*, ed. James McClain *et al.* (Ithaca, 1994), pp. 68–85; Robert Schneider, 'Crown and Capitoulat', *Cities*, ed. Benedict, pp. 195–220; Denis Woronoff, *Histoire de l'industrie en France* (Paris, 1994), pp. 15–68; Johnson, 'Capitalism and the State', pp. 37–62; Charles Tilly, *The Contentious French* (Cambridge, Mass., 1986), pp. 201–44; idem and William Blockmans, eds, *Cities and the Rise of States in Europe* (Boulder, 1994), pp. 1–27, 218–50; Thomas Schaeper, *The French Council of Commerce* (Columbus, 1983); Charles Cole, *Colbert and A Century of French Mercantilism*, 2 vols (New York, 1939); idem, *French Mercantilism, 1683–1700* (New York, 1943).

34. Philip Benedict, 'More Market than Manufactory', *Fr Hist Studies*, 20 (1997), 511–38; idem, *Cities*, pp. 1–64; Josef Konvitz, 'Does the Century 1650–1750, Constitute a Period?' *Journ Urban Hist*, 14 (1988), 419–54.

35. Roland Mousnier, *Le Conseil du Roi* (Paris, 1970), pp. 18–20; idem, *La vénalité des offices sous Henri IV et Louis XIII* (Paris, 1945); William Doyle, *Venality* (Oxford, 1996); Benedict, *Cities*, pp. 24–5; John Lynn, *Giant of the Grand Siècle* (Cambridge, 1997), pp. 43, 47; Geoffrey Symcox, *The Crisis of French Sea Power* (The Hague, 1974), pp. 12–102; Daniel Dessert, *La royale: vaisseaux et marins du Roi-Soleil* (Paris, 1996).

36. Benedict, 'More than Market and Manufactory', p. 529; Cissie Fairchilds, *Poverty and Charity* (Baltimore, 1976), p. 5; Coste, *La ville d'Aix*, I, 45, II, 712, 735–57; Jacqueline Carrière, *La population d'Aix-en-Provence* (Aix, 1958), p. 69; Kettering, *Judicial Politics*, p. 28. Also see Claire Dolan, *Entre tours et clochers* (Aix, 1981).

174

37. Pillorget, *Les mouvements insurrectionnels*, p. 82; Roland Mousnier, *The Institutions of France*, vol. 1, *Society and the State*, tr. Brian Pearce (Chicago, 1979), pp. 168–9.

38. Platter, *Journal*, p. 307; Daniel Roche, *The People of Paris*, tr. Marie Evans (Berkeley, 1987), pp. 127–59; idem, *The Culture of Clothing*, tr. Jean Birrell (Cambridge, 1994); idem, *The Decencies of Life*, tr. Brian Pearce (Cambridge, 2000); idem, *France in the Enlightenment*, tr. Arthur Goldhammer (Cambridge, Mass., 1998), pp. 548–77; Cissie Fairchilds, 'Populuxe Goods', *Consumption and the World of Goods*, eds John Brewer and Roy Porter (London, 1993), pp. 228–48; Robert Fox and Anthony Turner, eds, *Luxury Trades and Consumerism in Ancien Régime Paris* (Aldershot, 1998).

39. Rathery and Boutron, *Scudéry*, pp. 161–2; Edouard Baratier, ed., *Documents de l'histoire de la Provence* (Toulouse, 1971), pp. 198–200; idem, *Histoire de Marseille*, p. 235; Barbara Wheaton, *Savoring the Past* (Philadelphia, 1983), pp. 95–128.

40. Baratier, *Histoire de Marseille*, pp. 184–6, 234–5; Guiral, *Histoire de Marseille*, pp. 165–8; Tavernier, *Aspects de Marseille*, pp. 10, 108–9; idem, *La vie quotidienne*, pp. 131–2; Rathery and Boutron, *Scudéry*, p. 161; Platter, *Journal*, p. 308; Robert Isherwood, *Farce and Fantasy* (New York, 1986), pp. 231–6; Roche, *The People of Paris*, pp. 197–268; Robert Muchembled, *Popular Culture and Elite Culture*, tr. Lydia Cochrane (Baton Rouge, 1985), pp. 108–78; Robert Schneider, *Public Life in Toulouse, 1462–1789* (Ithaca, 1989), pp. 255–75; Pardailhé-Galabrun, *Birth of Intimacy*, pp. 174–212; Roche, *France in the Enlightenment*, pp. 165–8.

41. Tavernier, *Aspects de Marseille*, pp. 85–6; idem, *La vie quotidienne*, pp. 112–17; idem, *Marseille et la royauté*, pp. 44–9; Baratier, *Histoire de Marseille*, pp. 233–4; Trout, *City on the Seine*, pp. 181–92; Schneider, *Public Life*, pp. 141–63; idem, *The Ceremonial City* (Princeton, 1995); Muchembled, *Popular Culture*, pp. 126–52; Arlette Farge, *Fragile Lives*, tr. Carol Shelton (Cambridge, Mass., 1993), pp. 171–225.

42. Carrière, *La population d'Aix*, pp. 33, 85–6; Coste, *La ville d'Aix*, I, 59, 61; II, 731–47, 751–66, 769–76, 959–64; Cissie Fairchilds, *Poverty and Charity in Aix-en-Provence, 1640–1789* (Baltimore, 1976), pp. 9–11.

43. Marcel Couturier, *Recherches sur les structures sociales à Châteaudun* (Paris, 1969); Goubert, *Beauvais*, pp. 281–348; Deyon, *Amiens*, pp. 236–362.

44. Tavernier, *Aspects de Marseille*, pp. 57–9; Kaiser, *Marseille*, pp. 39–128; Roche, *The People of Paris*, pp. 235–47; Pardailhé-Galabrun, *Birth of Intimacy*, pp. 70–2; David Garrioch, *Neighbourhood and Community* (Cambridge, 1986), pp. 16–95; James Farr, *Hands of Honor* (Ithaca, 1988), pp. 156–76; Claire Dolan, 'The Artisans of Aix-en-Provence', *Cities*, ed. Benedict, pp. 174–94.

45. Guiral, *Histoire de Marseille*, pp. 178–9; Garrioch, *Neighbourhood*, pp. 22–7, 180–91; Roche, *The People of Paris*, pp. 248–68; Farr, *Hands of Honor*, pp. 173–6; Trout, *City on the Seine*, pp. 9, 217–19; Jean Leclant, 'Coffee and Cafés in Paris, 1644–1693', *Food and Drink in History*, tr. Patricia Ranum, eds Robert Forster and Orest Ranum (Baltimore, 1979), pp. 86–97; Thomas Brennan, *Public Drinking and Popular Culture* (Baltimore, 1988).

46. Guiral, *Histoire de Marseille*, pp. 178–9; Baratier, *Histoire de Marseille*, pp. 233–6; Tavernier, *La vie quotidienne*, pp. 131–2; idem, *Aspects de Marseille*, pp. 108–9; Pierre Goubert and Daniel Roche, *Les Français et l'Ancien Régime*, 2 vols (Paris, 1984), II, 244–54; David Maland, *Culture and Society in Seventeenth-Century France*

(New York, 1970), chapters 2 and 5; Daniel Roche, *Le siècle des Lumières en province* (Paris, 1978); David Sturdy, *Science and Social Status* (Rochester, 1995); David Lux, *Patronage and Royal Science* (Ithaca, 1989); Maurice Agulhon, *La sociabilité méridionale*, 2 vols (Paris, 1966); idem, *Le cercle dans la France bourgeoisie* (Paris, 1977).

47. Farge, *Fragile Lives*, pp. 104–30; Steven Kaplan and Cynthia Koepp, eds, *Work in France* (Ithaca, 1986), pp. 54–173; Steven Kaplan, *The Bakers of Paris* (Durham, 1996), pp. 155–422; Garrioch, *Neighbourhood*, pp. 97–127; Farr, *Hands of Honor*, pp. 13–75; Michael Sonenscher, *Work and Wages* (Cambridge, 1989), pp. 99–129; idem, *The Hatters* (Berkeley, 1987), pp. 81–96; Cynthia Truant, *The Rites of Labor* (Ithaca, 1994), pp. 48–193; Jean-Pierre Bayard, *Le compagnonnage en France* (Paris, 1978); Emile Coornaert, *Les compagnonnages* (Paris, 1966); Pierre Deyon, 'Manufacturing Industries in Seventeenth-Century France', *Louis XIV and Absolutism*, ed. Ragnhild Hatton (Columbus, 1976), pp. 226–42.

48. Kaiser, *Marseille*, pp. 60–95; Baratier, *Histoire de Marseille*, pp. 202–8; Tavernier, *Aspects de Marseille*, pp. 58–9; Masson, *La Provence*, II, 362–3, III, 666; Sonenscher, *The Hatters*, pp. 32–3, 40, 47–8, 54–5, 139–40; idem, *Work and Wages*, pp. 80, 82, 104–5, 114, 121, 125, 180–3; Maurice Agulhon, *Pénitents et franc-maçons de l'ancienne Provence* (Paris, 1984), pp. 68–85; Marguerite Desnuelle, *La faïence à Marseille au XVIIe siècle* (Aubagne, 1994); Cendro, *Marseille*, pp. 36–50.

49. Mousnier, *Society and State*, pp. 431–75; Kettering, *Judicial Politics*, pp. 216–50; Brockliss and Jones, *The Medical World*, pp. 177–88; Paul Bamford, *Privilege and Profit* (Philadelphia, 1988), pp. 71–82, *passim*; Thomson, *Clermont-de-Lodève*, pp. 140–1; Sonenscher, *The Hatters*, p. 40; Baratier, *Histoire de Marseille*, pp. 204–5; Paul Masson, *Les compagnies du corail* (Paris, 1908).

CHAPTER 5

1. Emmanuel Le Roy Ladurie, 'Versailles Observed', *The Mind and Method of the Historian*, tr. Sîan and Ben Reynolds (Chicago, 1981), pp. 149–73; Louis de Rouvray, duc de Saint Simon, *Mémoires*, ed. Arthur de Boislisle, 43 vols (Paris, 1879–1930), vol. 18, pp. 5–19.

2. Maurice Aymard, 'Friends and Neighbors', *Passions of the Renaissance*, ed. Roger Chartier, tr. Arthur Goldhammer, vol. III, *A History of Private Life*, eds Philippe Ariès and Georges Duby, 5 vols (Cambridge, Mass., 1987), pp. 465–6; *Mémoires of Madame de Motteville*, tr. Katherine Prescott Wormeley, 3 vols (Boston, 1901), I, 205; Madame de La Fayette, *The Princess of Clèves*, tr. Nancy Mitford (New York, 1978), p. 41; Jacqueline Boucher, *La cour de Henri III* (La Guerche-de-Bretagne, 1986), pp. 53–7, 87; Pauline Smith, *The Anti-Courtier Trend* (Geneva, 1966), pp. 11–55, 152–218, 224–6; J.H. Elliott and L.W.B. Brockliss, eds, *The World of the Favourite* (New Haven, 1999).

3. J. Russell Major, *Representative Government* (New Haven, 1980), pp. 629–31; Roger Mettam, *Power and Faction* (Oxford, 1988), p. 197; Bluche, *Louis XIV*, pp. 448–73, 511–35; Nicolas Le Roux, 'Courtisans et favoris', *Hist, écon et soc*, 17 (1998), 377–87.

4. Ragnhild Hatton, ed., *Louis XIV and Absolutism* (Columbus, 1976), pp. 130, 146–7.

5. Daniel Chamier, *Journal de son voyage à la cour*, ed. Charles Read (Paris, 1858, Geneva, 1971 repr.), pp. 21–64.

6. Louis Monmerqué and A.H. Taillandier, eds, *Mémoires du marquis de Beauvais-Nangis* (Paris, 1862), pp. 64, 68, 70–1.

7. Norbert Elias, *The Court Society*, tr. Edmund Jephcott (New York, 1983), p. 64; Jean-Marie Constant, 'La noblesse seconde,' *L'État et les aristocraties*, ed. Philippe Contamine (Paris, 1989), pp. 279–301; Laurent Bourquin, *Noblesse seconde et pouvoir en Champagne* (Paris, 1994); Robert Descimon, 'Chercher des nouvelles voies,' *Rev d'hist mod et cont*, 46 (1999), 11–12.

8. Boucher, *La cour de Henri III*, p. 84.

9. Monmerqué and Taillandier, *Beauvais-Nangis*, pp. 71, 170, 173; Ludovic Lalanne, ed., *Mémoires de Roger de Rabutin, comte de Bussy*, 2 vols (Paris, 1857), I, xviii–xxii; Jacqueline Boucher, *Société et mentalités Henri III*, 4 vols (Lille, 1981), I, 175, 182.

10. Monmerqué and Taillandier, *Beauvais-Nangis*, pp. 92–9.

11. François Bluche, *Louis XIV* (Paris, 1986), pp. 48–73; Arlette Jouanna, *Le devoir de révolte* (Paris, 1989), pp. 80–90; Jean-François Solnon, *La cour de France* (Paris, 1987), pp. 148, 339–72; Boucher, *Société et mentalités*, I, 183.

12. R.J. Knecht, *Francis I* (Cambridge, 1982), p. 89; Jean-Pierre Gutton, *Domestiques et serviteurs* (Paris, 1981), p. 32; David Buisseret, *Henry IV* (London, 1984), p. 94; Solnon, *La cour*, pp. 21, 37–49; Wilmer McCorquodale, 'The Court of Louis XIII' (PhD dissert., Texas, 1994), pp. 43–5, 275–7; Louis Batiffol, *Marie de Médicis*, 2 vols (Paris, 1908), I, 138; Eugène Griselle, *Etat de la maison du roi Louis XIII* (Paris, 1912), pp. 57–82; Ruth Kleinman, *Anne of Austria* (Columbus, 1985), p. 23; Georges Dethan, *Gaston d'Orléans* (Paris, 1959), pp. 351–2; Nancy Barker, *Brother to the Sun King* (Baltimore, 1989), p. 82; Bluche, *Louis XIV*, p. 522; Mark Motley, *Becoming a French Aristocrat* (Princeton, 1990), pp. 18–67.

13. Jean-Pierre Labatut, *Les ducs et pairs* (Paris, 1972), p. 80; Boucher, *Société et mentalités*, I, 177; Manfred Orlea, *La noblesse aux Etats généraux* (Paris, 1980), pp. 53–9; Bluche, *Louis XIV*, p. 522; Paul Masson, *La Provence au XVIIIe siècle*, 3 vols (Paris, 1936), II, 335, 340–1; René Pillorget, *Les mouvements insurrectionnels* (Paris, 1976), pp. 81–3; Jean Meyer, *La noblesse bretonne*, 2 vols (Paris, 1966), II, 867–8.

14. Roland Mousnier, *The Institutions of France*, vol. 2, *The Organs of State*, tr. Arthur Goldhammer, pp. 126–7 (Chicago, 1984); Frederic Baumgartner, *Henry II* (Durham, 1988), pp. 65–6; Buisseret, *Henry IV*, pp. 28–88; Robert Berger, *A Royal Passion* (Cambridge, 1994).

15. Peter Burke, *The Fabrication of Louis XIV* (New Haven, 1992); Jean-Marie Apostolides, *Le Roi-Machine* (Paris, 1981); Louis Marin, *Portrait of the King*, tr. Martha Houle (Minneapolis, 1988); Marie-Christine Moine, *Les fêtes à la cour du roi soleil* (Paris, 1984); Paul Sonnino, ed., *The Reign of Louis XIV* (Atlantic Highlands, NJ, 1990), pp. 195–237; John Rule, ed., *Louis XIV* (Columbus, 1969), pp. 265–301; Solnon, *La cour*, pp. 279–314, 373–417.

16. Boucher, *Société et mentalités*, I, 155–9, 323–9; Solnon, *La cour*, pp. 22–7; Knecht, *Francis I*, pp. 86–92; Wendy Gibson, *Women in Seventeenth-Century France* (New York, 1989), pp. 193–9; Sharon Kettering, 'Brokerage at the Court of Louis XIV', *Hist Journ*, 26 (1993), 69–87.

17. Jean-Paul Coste, *Aix-en-Provence* (Aix, 1967), p. 49; René Borricand, *Les hôtels particuliers d'Aix* (Aix, 1971), pp. 371–2; Charles de Ribbe, *Une grande dame dans*

son ménage (Paris, 1890), pp. 108–11; Jacques Levron, *Daily Life at Versailles*, tr. Claire Engel (London, 1968), pp. 55–86; Charles Constant, ed., *Mémoires de Nicolas Goulas*, 3 vols (Paris, 1832), I, 100–2; Edouard Baratier, *Histoire de la Provence* (Toulouse, 1969), pp. 335–40.

18. Elias, *The Court Society*, pp. 78–213; idem, *The Civilizing Process*, vol. 2, *Power and Civility*, tr. Edmund Jephcott (New York, 1982), pp. 258–70; Daniel Gordon, *Citizens without Sovereignty* (Princeton, 1994), pp. 88–9; Roger Chartier, *Cultural History*, tr. Lydia Cochrane (Ithaca, 1988), pp. 71–94; Stephen Mennell and Johann Goudsblom, eds, *Norbert Elias on Civilization* (Chicago, 1998), pp. 75–94.

19. Orest Ranum, 'Courtesy, Absolutism and the Rise of the French State', *Journ Mod Hist*, 52 (1980), 426–51; Robert Muchembled, *La société policée* (Paris, 1998), pp. 13, 77–122; Solnon, *La cour de France*, pp. 163–249.

20. Maurice Magendie, *La politesse mondaine*, 2 vols (Geneva, 1970 repr.), II, 569–98, 747–90, 837–901; Gordon, *Citizens without Sovereignty*, pp. 116–17; Jacques Revel, 'The Uses of Civility', *Passions of the Renaissance*, pp. 167–202, esp. 192–5; Jorge Arditi, *A Genealogy of Manners* (Chicago, 1998), pp. 122–54; Roger Picard, *Les salons littéraires* (New York, 1943), pp. 19–132.

21. Paul Bénichou, *Man and Ethics*, tr. Elizabeth Hughes (New York, 1971), pp. 189–99; Yves Castan, *Honnêteté en Languedoc* (Paris, 1978), pp. 13–57, 492–529; Guy Chaussinand-Nogaret, *The French Nobility in the Eighteenth Century*, tr. William Doyle (Cambridge, 1985), pp. 65–83.

22. Meyer, *La noblesse bretonne*, II, 861–925; Pierre de Vaissière, *Gentilshommes campagnards* (Paris, 1903).

23. Ellery Schalk, 'The Court as Civilizer', *Princes, Patronage and the Nobility*, eds Ronald Asch and Adolf Birk (New York, 1991), pp. 257–63; idem, *From Valor to Pedigree* (Princeton, 1986), pp. 25–7, 94–144.

24. Ibid.; Arlette Jouanna, 'Recherches sur la notion d'honneur', *Rev d'hist mod et cont* 15 (1968), 597–623.

25. Magendie, *La politesse mondaine*, II, 569–98, 837–901; Bénichou, *Man and Ethics*, pp. 189–99; Maurice Keen, *Chivalry* (New York, 1984), pp. 143–78, 219–53; Orest Ranum, *Paris in the Age of Absolutism* (New York, 1968), pp. 132–66.

26. Mack Holt, *Sixteenth-Cent Journ*, 18 (1987), 445–6; Chartier, *Cultural History*, p. 45; Boucher, *Société et mentalités*, II, 633–7; Smith, *The Anti-Courtier Trend*, pp. 11–55, 152, 188–202, 224–6; Jean-François Dubost, *La France italienne* (Paris, 1997), pp. 151–207; Michel Nassiet, 'La noblesse', *Rev d'hist mod et cont* 46 (1999), 86.

27. William Beik, *Absolutism and Society* (Cambridge, 1985); Jouanna, *Le devoir de révolte*, pp. 391–9.

28. R.J.W. Evans, 'The Court', *Princes, Patronage and the Nobility*, pp. 481–91; Le Roux, 'Courtisans et favoris'; Kettering, 'Brokerage at the Court of Louis XIV'.

29. Monmerqué and Taillandier, *Beauvais-Nangis*, pp. iv–xi, 149, 170, 172–3, 193–4, 210, 244–5; John Lynn, *Giant of the Grand Siècle* (Cambridge, 1997), pp. 251–2; F.E. Sutcliffe, *Guez de Balzac* (Paris, 1959), pp. 113–63; Arlette Jouanna, *Ordre Social* (Paris, 1977), pp. 54–72; Jonathan Dewald, *Aristocratic Experience* (Berkeley, 1993), pp. 15–44, 45; Jean-Marie Constant, *Nobles et paysans en Beauce* (Lille, 1981), p. 158; James Wood, *The Nobility of Bayeux* (Princeton, 1980), p. 85; Bluche, *Louis XIV*, p. 449.

30. Marc Fumaroli, ed., *Mémoires de Campion* (Paris, 1967), pp. 26–33, 49, 149, 154–72, 175–6, 201; Castan, 'Politics and Private Life', *Passions of the Renaissance*, pp. 21–37.

31. Sharon Kettering, 'Gift-Giving and Patronage', *Fr Hist*, 2 (1988), 131–51; idem, 'Patronage in Early Modern France', *Fr Hist Studies*, 17 (1992), 839–62; idem, 'Friendship and Clientage', ibid., 6 (1992), 139–59; idem, *Patrons, Brokers, and Clients* (New York, 1986), pp. 1–39; Mark Greengrass, 'Noble Affinities', *Eur Hist Quart*, 16 (1986), 276–311; idem, 'Political Clientelism before Richelieu', *L'État ou le Roi*, ed. Robert Descimon (Paris, 1996), pp. 69–82; Yves Durand, ed., *Hommage à Roland Mousnier: clientèles et fidélités* (Paris, 1981); idem, *Les solidarités* (Paris, 1987), pp. 152–245; S. Annette Finley-Croswhite, *Henry IV and the Towns* (Cambridge, 1999); Stuart Carroll, *Noble Power during the Wars of Religion* (Cambridge, 1998); Bourquin, *Noblesse seconde* (Paris, 1994); Michel Cassan, *Le temps des guerres de religion* (Château-Gonier, 1996); Katia Béguin, *Les princes de Condé* (Seyssel, 1999); Bernard Barbiche, *Sully: l'homme et ses fidèles* (Paris, 1997).

32. André Corvisier, 'Clientèles et fidélités dans l'armée française', *Hommage à Roland Mousnier*, pp. 213–36; Douglas Baxter, *Servants of the Sword* (Chicago, 1976), pp. 51–9, 202–5; David Parrott, 'Richelieu, the *Grands*, and the French Army', *Richelieu and His Age*, eds Joseph Bergin and Laurence Brockliss (Oxford, 1992), pp. 135–73; Mettam, *Power and Faction*, pp. 45–101; Peter Campbell, *Power and Politics* (New York, 1996), pp. 39–176.

33. Castan, 'Politics and Private Life', pp. 29–37; Lynn, *Giant*, pp. 248–81; Constant, *Nobles et paysans*, pp. 158–89; Philippe Contamine, *Guerre, Etat et société* (Paris, 1972), pp. 536–46; James Wood, *The King's Army* (Cambridge, 1996); François Billaçois, *The Duel*, tr. Trista Selous (New Haven, 1990).

34. Baxter, *Servants of the Sword*, pp. 29 n. 17, 39 n. 42, 57; Richard Bonney, *Political Change in France* (Oxford, 1978), pp. 79 n. 3, 129–30, 154, 439, 477.

35. Roland Mousnier, *The Institutions*, vol. I, *Society and State*, tr. Brian Pearce (Chicago, 1979), pp. 214–35; idem, *La vénalité des offices* (Rouen, 1945); Jean-Marie Constant, *La société française* (Paris, 1994), pp. 40–7; David Sturdy, *The D'Aligres de La Rivière* (New York, 1986); Monique Cubells, *La Provence des Lumières* (Paris, 1984), pp. 309–55; François Bluche, *Les magistrats du Parlement de Paris* (Paris, 1960), pp. 242–69.

36. Pierre Goubert, *The Ancien Régime*, tr. Steve Cox (New York, 1974), pp. 153–92; Robert Descimon, 'Nobility of the Robe', *Changing Identities*, ed. Michael Wolfe (Durham, 1997), pp. 95–123; idem, 'La haute noblesse parlementaire', *L'État et les aristocraties*, pp. 358–86; Jean-Marie Constant, 'La noblesse seconde', ibid., pp. 279–301; idem, *La vie quotidienne de la noblesse* (Paris, 1985), pp. 104–31; Mousnier, *Society and State*, p. 131; Anne Blanchard, 'La noblesse languedocienne', *Sociétés et idéologies*, eds J. Fouilleron *et al.*, 2 vols (Montpellier, 1996), I, 15–35; Wood, *The Nobility of Bayeux*, pp. 20–68; Chaussinand-Nogaret, *The French Nobility*, pp. 23–42; Françoise Bayard, *Le monde des financiers* (Paris, 1988), pp. 421–49; Meyer, *La noblesse bretonne*, I, 5–442; Lynn, *Giant*, pp. 87, 263, 307, 323; Arlette Jouanna, *L'idée de race*, 3 vols (Paris, 1976); Georges Huppert, *Les Bourgeois Gentilshommes* (Chicago, 1977).

37. Michael Fitzsimmons, 'New Light on the Aristocratic Reaction', *Fr Hist*, 10 (1996), 418–31; David Bien, 'La réaction aristocratique', *Annales ESC*, 29 (1974), 23–48,

505–34; idem, 'Manufacturing Nobles', *Journ Mod Hist*, 61 (1989), 445–86; William Doyle, 'Was There an Aristocratic Reaction?', *Past and Present* 57 (1972), 97–122; Constant, *La société française*, pp. 35–7; Mousnier, *Society and State*, pp. 126–31.

38. Jonathan Dewald, *The European Nobility* (Cambridge, 1996), pp. 15–59; Descimon, 'Chercher des nouvelles voies,' 10, note 22; Chaussinand-Nogaret, *The French Nobility*, pp. 2–3, 28–30, 36; Wood, *Nobility of Bayeux*, pp. 69–86; Meyer, *La noblesse bretonne*, II, 927–1016; Donna Bohanan, *Old and New Nobility in Aix* (Baton Rouge, 1992), pp. 133–4; Cubells, *La Provence des Lumières*, pp. 91–104.

39. André Devyer, *Le sang épuré* (Brussels, 1973), pp. 243–77; Harold Ellis, *Boulainvilliers* (Ithaca, 1988), pp. 17–30; Chaussinand-Nogaret, *The French Nobility*, pp. 14–20; Daniel Dessert, *Argent, pouvoir et société* (Paris, 1984), pp. 82–109.

40. Donald Frame, ed., tr. *The Misanthrope and Other Plays by Molière* (New York, 1968), pp. 213–94.

41. Pierre de Saint-Jacob, *Les paysans de la Bourgogne* (Paris, 1960), pp. 173–209; Guy Lemarchand, *La fin du féodalisme* (Paris, 1989), pp. 17–37, 145–51, 163–75; Hilton Root, *Peasants and King in Burgundy* (Berkeley, 1987), pp. 155–204; Jean-Laurent Rosenthal, *The Fruits of Revolution* (Cambridge, 1992), pp. 21–36; John Markoff, *The Abolition of Feudalism* (University Park, Pa, 1996), pp. 16–64.

42. Philippe Ariès, 'Le service domestique', *XVIIe siècle*, 32 (1980), 415–20; Cissie Fairchilds, *Domestic Enemies* (Baltimore, 1984), pp. 4, 15–17; Jonathan Dewald, *Pont-St-Pierre* (Berkeley, 1987), pp. 20–7; Elias, *The Civilizing Process*, vol. I, *The History of Manners*, pp. 160–8; Orest Ranum, 'The Refuges of Intimacy', *Passions of the Renaissance*, pp. 207–63.

43. Dewald, *Pont-St-Pierre*, pp. 109–12; idem, *The European Nobility*, pp. 43–6; Richard Bonney, *Political Change* (Oxford, 1978), pp. 306–7, 447; Sharon Kettering, 'The Decline of Great Noble Clientage', *Canad Journ Hist*, 24 (1989), 157–77; Chaussinand-Nogaret, *The French Nobility*, pp. 43–64; J. Russell Major, *From Renaissance Monarchy* (Baltimore, 1994), pp. 304–10; Constant, 'La noblesse seconde', pp. 279–301; Bourquin, *Noblesse seconde*.

44. T.J.A. Le Goff, *Vannes and Its Region* (Oxford, 1981), pp. 61–3, 273–4, 278; Dewald, *Pont-St-Pierre*, pp. 112–16; Jean-Michel Boehler, *La paysannerie d'Alsace*, 3 vols (Strasbourg, 1995), I, 626, II, 1360–3; Maurice Agulhon, *La vie sociale en Provence* (Paris, 1970), p. 90.

45. Constant, *La société française*, pp. 31–3; idem, *La vie quotidienne de la noblesse*, pp. 161–88; idem, *Nobles et paysans*, pp. 239–57.

46. Chaussinand-Nogaret, *The French Nobility*, pp. 65–83; Meyer, *La noblesse bretonne*, II, 1135–1244; Dewald, *Pont-St-Pierre*, pp. 189–99; idem, *Aristocratic Experience*, pp. 69–103, 174–203; Robert Schneider, 'Self-Censorship and Men of Letters', *Toqueville*, in publication, pp. 17–18; Elizabeth Goldsmith, *Exclusive Conversations* (Philadelphia, 1988); Roger Chartier *et al.*, *L'éducation en France* (Paris, 1976), pp. 147–206; Motley, *Becoming a French Aristocrat*, pp. 16–168.

47. Fumaroli, *Mémoires de Campion*, pp. 96–7; Monmerqué and Taillandier, *Beauvais-Nangis*, pp. 121, 170, 211.

48. Vaissière, *Gentilshommes campagnards*; Lucien Romier, *Le royaume de Cathérine de Médicis*, 2 vols (Paris, 1922); Henri Drouot, *Mayenne et la Bourgogne* (Paris, 1937); Gaston Roupnel, *La ville et la campagne* (Paris, 1955); Davis Bitton, *The French Nobility in Crisis* (Stanford, 1969); Guy Bois, *The Crisis of Feudalism* (Cambridge, 1985).

49. Schalk, *From Valor to Pedigree*, pp. 209–10; Emmanuel Le Roy Ladurie, 'In Normandy's Woods and Fields', *The Territory of the Historian*, tr. Ben and Siân Reynolds (Chicago, 1979), pp. 133–71; Dewald, *Pont-St-Pierre*, pp. 159–89, 213–51; Robert Forster, *The Nobility of Toulouse* (Baltimore, 1960); idem, *The House of Saulx-Tavanes*; Constant, *Nobles et paysans*, pp. 105–9, 127–30; J. Russell Major, 'Noble Income, Inflation, and the Wars of Religion', *Amer Hist Rev*, 86 (1981), 21–48; Mark Greengrass, 'The Landed Fortune of Constable Anne de Montmorency', *Fr Hist*, 2 (1988), 371–98; Meyer, *La noblesse bretonne*, I, 445–590, II, 591–860; Dessert, *Argent, pouvoir et société*, pp. 341–78; Chaussinand-Nogaret, *The French Nobility*, pp. 84–116.

50. Michel Nassiet, *Noblesse et pauvreté* (Bannalec, 1993); Jean Gallet, *La seigneurie bretonne* (Paris, 1983).

CHAPTER 6

1. 'Livre de raison de Léon de Trimond', Bibliothèque Méjanes, Aix-en-Provence, Ms. 1140, fols 3–4.

2. Madeleine Foisil, *Mémoires du Président Alexandre Bigot de Monville* (Paris, 1976), pp. 78–80.

3. Jacques de Parades de L'Estang, 'Mémoires', *Le Musée: Revue Arlésienne*, 2nd sér. 13–35 (1875–6), 236–8, 247–8; Louis Monmerqué, ed., *Lettres de Madame de Sévigné*, 14 vols (Paris, 1862–6), p. 143; Inès Murat, *Colbert*, tr. Robert Cook and Jeannie Van Asselt (Charlottesville, 1984), p. 89.

4. Scipion Du Roure, *Inventaire analytique de documents* (Paris, 1903), p. 143; abbé Marcelin Chailan, *L'ordre de Malte* (Bergerac, 1908), pp. 231–7; Artefeuil, *Histoire de la noblesse de Provence*, 4 vols (Avignon, 1757–9), I, 344–6; Parades de L'Estang, 'Mémoires', pp. 92, 99, 100, 152.

5. René Pillorget, *Les mouvements insurrectionnels de Provence* (Paris, 1975), pp. 528–38; Sharon Kettering, *Judicial Politics and Urban Revolt* (Princeton, 1978), pp. 128–33.

6. Roger Chartier, 'Oligarchies et absolutisme', in Georges Duby, ed., *L'histoire de la France urbaine*, vol. 3, Emmanuel Le Roy Ladurie, ed., *La ville classique de la Renaissance aux Révolutions* (Paris, 1981), pp. 158–9. Also see S. Annette Finley-Croswhite, *Henry IV and the Towns* (Cambridge, 1999), pp. 63–121.

7. Pillorget, *Les mouvements insurrectionnels*, p. 534; Parades de L'Estang, 'Mémoires', p. 100.

8. Roland Mousnier, *La plume, la faucille et le marteau* (Paris, 1970), pp. 179–368; Yves-Marie Bercé, *Histoire des croquants*, 2 vols (Paris, 1974); Yves Durand, *Les fermiers généraux* (Paris, 1971); Madeleine Foisil, *La révolte des Nu-Pieds* (Paris, 1970); Arlette Jouanna, *Le devoir de révolte* (Paris, 1989); Pillorget, *Les mouvements insurrectionnels*. See the historiographical essay on the students of Roland Mousnier.

9. Richard Bonney, *Political Change in France* (Oxford, 1978); J. Russell Major, *Representative Government* (New Haven, 1980); Peter Campbell, *Power and Politics in Old Regime France* (London, 1996).

10. Yves-Marie Bercé, *The Birth of Absolutism*, tr. Richard Rex (New York, 1996), pp. 117–92; David Parker, *The Making of French Absolutism* (London, 1983), pp. 46–93; Raymond Kierstead, ed., *State and Society in Seventeenth-Century France*

(New York, 1975); Robert Descimon and Christian Jouhaud, *La France du premier XVIIe siècle* (Paris, 1996); François-Xavier Emmanuelli, *État et pouvoirs dans la France* (Paris, 1992).

11. Peter Campbell, *Louis XIV* (London, 1993); Paul Sonnino, ed., *The Reign of Louis XIV* (Atlantic Highlands, NJ, 1990); François Bluche, *Louis XIV*, tr. Mark Greengrass (Oxford, 1990); André Corvisier, *La France de Louis XIV*, 3rd edn (Paris, 1990).

12. Roland Mousnier, *La vénalité des offices*, 2nd edn (Paris, 1971), p. 131; David Parker, *Class and State* (London, 1996), p. 158; Richard Bonney, *The King's Debts* (Oxford, 1981), pp. 272–82; James Collins, *The State in Early Modern France* (Cambridge, 1995), pp. 61–129; Jean-Paul Charmeil, *Les trésoriers de France* (Paris, 1964), pp. 13, 16, 420–1.

13. Emmanuel Le Roy Ladurie, *The Ancien Régime*, tr. Mark Greengrass (Oxford, 1996).

14. Michael Roberts, *The Military Revolution* (Belfast, 1956); Geoffrey Parker, *The Military Revolution* (Cambridge, 1988); John R. Hale, *War and Society* (Baltimore, 1985); Jeremy Black, *European Warfare* (New Haven, 1994).

15. Emmanuelli, *État et pouvoirs*, pp. 155–209; Bonney, *The King's Debts*, pp. 115–282; idem, *The Limits of Absolutism* (Aldershot, 1995), sections XI-XIII; John Lynn, *Giant of the Grand Siècle* (Cambridge, 1997), pp. 32–64.

16. Mousnier, *La vénalité des offices*; William Doyle, *Venality* (Oxford, 1996); Daniel Dessert, *Argent, pouvoir et société* (Paris, 1984); Françoise Bayard, *Le monde des financiers* (Paris, 1988); Julian Dent, *Crisis in Finance* (London, 1973).

17. Richard Bonney, *Political Change in France* (Oxford, 1978), pp. 3–158; Douglas Baxter, *Servants of the Sword* (Urbana, 1976); Vivian Gruder, *The Royal Provincial Intendants* (Ithaca, 1968); François-Xavier Emmanuelli, *Un mythe de l'absolutisme* (Aix, 1981), pp. 1–147; idem, *Pouvoir royal et vie régionale en Provence*, 2 vols (Lille, 1974); idem, *État et pouvoirs*, pp. 61–86.

18. P.J. Coveney, ed., *France in Crisis* (London, 1977), pp. 136–230; Kierstead, *State and Society*, pp. 96–197; William Beik, *Urban Protest* (Cambridge, 1997), pp. 73–172; Nora Temple, 'The Control and Exploitation of French Towns', *History* 51 (1966), 16–34; idem, 'Municipal Elections and Municipal Oligarchies', *French Government and Society*, ed. John Bosher (London, 1973), pp. 76–91; Peter Wallace, *Communities and Conflict* (Atlantic Highlands, NJ, 1994).

19. A. Lloyd Moote, *The Revolt of the Judges* (Princeton, 1971), pp. 91–219; J. Russell Major, *Representative Government in Early Modern France* (New Haven, 1980), pp. 259–672; J. Michael Hayden, *France and the Estates General of 1614* (Cambridge, 1974).

20. Robert Harding, *Anatomy of a Power Elite* (New Haven, 1978), pp. 68–107; Bonney, *Political Change*, pp. 284–317; Mark Greengrass, 'Noble Affinities', *Eur Hist Quart*, 16 (1986), 275–311; Mark Konnert, 'Provincial Governors', ibid. 25 (1994), 823–40; Ariane Boltanski, 'Le duc de Nevers', *Rev d'hist mod et cont*, 46 (1999), 117–45.

21. Sharon Kettering, *Patrons, Brokers, and Clients* (New York, 1986), pp. 141–83, 232–7; idem, 'Brokerage at the Court of Louis XIV', *Hist Journ*, 36 (1993), 69–87; idem, 'Decline of Great Noble Clientage', *Canad Journ Hist*, 24 (1989), 157–77; Arlette Jouanna, *Le devoir de révolte* (Paris, 1989), pp. 65–90; François Bluche, *Louis XIV* (Paris, 1986), pp. 448–73; J. Russell Major, *From Renaissance Monarchy*

to Absolute Monarchy (New Haven, 1994), pp. 304–10; Bonney, Political Change, pp. 90–111; 284–317.

22. Ralph Giesey, The Royal Funeral Ceremony (Geneva, 1960); Richard Jackson, A History of the French Coronation (Chapel Hill, 1984); Lawrence Bryant, The Parisian Royal Entry Ceremony (Geneva, 1986); Finley-Croswhite, Henry IV and the Towns, pp. 47–62; Jean Boutier et al., Un tour de France royal (Paris, 1984); Sarah Hanley, The Lit de Justice (Princeton, 1978); Elizabeth Brown and Richard Famiglietti, The Lit de Justice (Sigmaringen, 1994); Michèle Fogel, Les cérémonies de l'information (Paris, 1989), pp. 133–245; idem, L'État dans la France moderne (Paris, 1992), pp. 39–61; David Sturdy, Louis XIV (New York, 1998), pp. 13–21.

23. Peter Burke, The Fabrication of Louis XIV (New Haven, 1992); Robert Berger, A Royal Passion (Cambridge, 1994); Louis Marin, Portrait of the King, tr. Martha Houle (Minneapolis, 1988); Jean-Marie Apostolides, Le roi-machine (Paris, 1981); Robert Isherwood, Music in the Service of the King (Ithaca, 1973); François Bluche, L'Ancien Régime (Paris, 1993), pp. 15–52; Joel Cornette, Le roi de guerre (Paris, 1993), pp. 215–315.

24. Joseph Klaits, Printed Propaganda (Princeton, 1976); Jeffrey Sawyer, Printed Poison (Berkeley, 1990); Orest Ranum, Artisans of Glory (Chapel Hill, 1980); Christian Jouhaud, Mazarinades (Paris, 1985); Fogel, Les cérémonies, pp. 23–129; Sturdy, Louis XIV, pp. 100–122.

25. Kettering, Judicial Politics, pp. 211, 233–4, 251–97; idem, 'Causes of Judicial Frondes', Canad Journ Hist, 27 (1982), 275–306; William Beik, 'The Parlement of Toulouse', Society and Institutions, ed. Mack Holt (Athens, 1991), pp. 132–52; Richard Bonney, The Limits of Absolutism (Aldershot, 1995), sections IV–IX; Descimon, La France, pp. 151–74; Joel Cornette, Chronique de la France (Paris, 1995), pp. 349–425.

26. Pillorget, Les mouvements insurrectionnels, pp. 571, 610, 626; Kettering, Judicial Politics, pp. 233, 265.

27. Bonney, The Limits of Absolutism, section I; idem, L'absolutisme (Paris, 1989); Nicholas Henshall, The Myth of Absolutism (London, 1992); Descimon, La France, pp. 175–95; Emmanuelli, État et pouvoirs, pp. 19–34; idem, Un mythe, pp. 35–71, 102–15; Parker, Class and State, pp. 136–45; idem, The Making of Absolutism, pp. 118–51; John Rule, ed., Louis XIV and Kingship (Columbus, 1969), pp. 302–16; Ragnhild Hatton, ed., Louis XIV and Absolutism (Columbus, 1976), pp. 3–84.

28. Roger Mettam, Power and Faction (Oxford, 1988), p. 24; Beth Nachison, 'Absentee Government and Provincial Governors', Fr Hist Studies, 21 (1998), 226.

29. William Beik, Absolutism and Society in Seventeenth-Century France (Cambridge, 1985), pp. 179, 261, 303, 329–39; idem, 'A Social Interpretation of the Reign of Louis XIV', L'État ou le Roi, eds Neithard Bulst et al. (Paris, 1996), pp. 145–60.

30. David Parker, Class and State (London, 1996), pp. 107–10, 173–87, 266–8.

31. Ibid., pp. 158–67; Mettam, Power and Faction, pp. 13–54, 175–286, 309–22; Henshall, The Myth of Absolutism, pp. 52–8.

32. James Collins, Classes, Estates, and Order in Early Modern Brittany (Cambridge, 1994), pp. 26–8, 139–53, 249–70; idem, Fiscal Limits of Absolutism (Berkeley, 1988), pp. 165, 200–22.

33. Daniel Hickey, The Coming of French Absolutism (Toronto, 1986), pp. 179–91.

34. Albert Hamscher, *The Parlement of Paris after the Fronde* (Pittsburgh, 1976), pp. 119–95; idem, *The Conseil Privé and the Parlements* (Philadelphia, 1987); idem, 'Parlements and Litigants', *Society and Institutions*, pp. 190–222; J. Russell Major, *Representative Government*; idem, *From Renaissance Monarchy*.

35. Orest Ranum, *Richelieu and the Councillors of Louis XIII* (Oxford, 1963); Beik, *Absolutism*, pp. 223–44; Peter Campbell, *Power and Politics* (London, 1996), pp. 129–89; idem, *The Ancien Régime* (Oxford, 1988), pp. 46–70; Harding, *Anatomy*, pp. 21–45; Yves Durand, ed., *Hommage à Roland Mousnier* (Paris, 1981); idem, *Les fermiers généraux*, pp. 60–97; Dessert, *Argent*, pp. 310–64; Jouanna, *Le devoir de révolte*, pp. 65–90.

36. Finley-Croswhite, *Henry IV and the Towns*, pp. 23–46, 122–38; Kettering, *Patrons, Brokers, and Clients*, pp. 40–183, 233–6; Bonney, *L'absolutisme*, pp. 105–9; Henshall, *The Myth of Absolutism*, pp. 45–9; Mettam, *Power and Faction*, pp. 21–2, 58–9, 197, 271–2, 276; David Parker, 'Class, Clientage and Personal Rule', *Seventeenth Cent Fr Studies*, 9 (1987), 192–213; idem, *Class and State*, pp. 7, 25–6; Daniel Hickey, 'Tailles, Clientèle et Absolutisme', *Rev d'hist mod et cont*, 39 (1992), 263–81; Major, *From Renaissance Monarchy*, pp. 335–66; Campbell, *Louis XIV*, pp. 13–15, 29–30, 39, 106–9. Also see Jean-Marie Constant, 'La noblesse seconde', *L'État et les aristocraties*, ed. Philippe Contamine (Paris, 1989), pp. 279–301; Laurent Bourquin, *Noblesse seconde et pouvoir en Champagne* (Paris, 1994).

37. Bonney, *Political Change*, pp. 78, 205; Roland Mousnier, *The Institutions of France*, vol. 2, *The Organs of State*, tr. Arthur Goldhammer (Chicago, 1984), pp. 502–63; Nachison, 'Absentee Government and Provincial Governors', pp. 265–97; Beik, *Absolutism*, pp. 98–116; Collins, *Classes*, pp. 187–228; Sharon Kettering, 'State Control and Municipal Authority', *Edo and Paris*, ed. James McClain (Ithaca, 1994), pp. 86–101; Julian Swann, 'Parlements and Political Crisis', *Hist Journ*, 37 (1994), 810; François-Xavier Emmanuelli, *Histoire de la Provence* (Paris, 1980), pp. 190–5; idem, *Un mythe*, pp. 50–60; Julien Ricommard, 'Les subdélégués', *Provence hist*, 14 (1964), 243–71, 336–78; Michel Antoine, *Le dur métier du roi* (Paris, 1986), pp. 125–79.

38. The most recent study does not explore this relationship. See Anette Smedley-Weill, *Les intendants de Louis XIV* (Paris, 1995).

39. Ellery Schalk, *From Valor to Pedigree* (Princeton, 1986), pp. 210–11; Donna Bohanan, *Old and New Nobility in Aix* (Baton Rouge, 1992), pp. 133–4; Parker, *Class and State*, pp. 129–34; Monique Cubells, *La Provence des Lumières* (Paris, 1984), pp. 91–104; Jonathan Dewald, *The Formation of a Provincial Nobility* (Princeton, 1980), p. 309; James Wood, *The Nobility of the Election of Bayeux* (Princeton, 1980), pp. 69–86.

40. Kettering, *Judicial Politics*, pp. 233–4.

41. Bohanan, *Old and New Nobility*, p. 133; Major, *From Renaissance Monarchy*, pp. 322–3; Jean Meyer, *La noblesse bretonne*, 2 vols (Paris, 1966), I, 929; Michel Nassiet, *Noblesse et pauvreté* (Bannalec, 1993), pp. 149–98.

42. J.H.M. Salmon, 'Storm over the Noblesse', *Journ Mod Hist*, 53 (1981), 242–57; Robert Descimon, 'Chercher des nouvelles voies', *Rev d'hist mod et cont*, 46 (1999), 5–21; Roland Mousnier, *The Institutions of France*, vol. 1, *State and Society*, tr. Brian Pearce (Chicago, 1979), pp. 161, 202–10; Franklin Ford, *Robe and Sword* (Cambridge, Mass., 1953), pp. 67–76, 188–221; Major, *From Renaissance Monarchy*,

pp. 321–31; François Bluche, *Les magistrats du Parlement de Paris* (Paris, 1960), pp. 303–25; Lynn, *Giant*, pp. 87, 263; Jean-Pierre Labatut, *Les ducs et pairs* (Paris, 1972), pp. 371–430.

43. Beik, 'A Social Interpretation', p. 146; Parker, *The Making of Absolutism*, pp. 148–51; Major, *From Renaissance Monarchy*, pp. 366–75.

44. J.H.M. Salmon, 'The Audijos Revolt', *Renaissance and Revolt* (Cambridge, 1987), pp. 267–92; Jean-Marie Constant, *La vie quotidienne de la noblesse* (Paris, 1985), pp. 253–7.

45. William Church, 'France', *National Consciousness, History, and Political Culture* (Baltimore, 1975), pp. 43–66; Herbert Rowen, 'Louis XIV and Absolutism', *Louis XIV and Kingship*, pp. 303–4; Donald Kelley, *The Beginning of Ideology* (Cambridge, 1981); Julian Franklin, *Jean Bodin* (Cambridge, 1973).

46. Mousnier, *State and Society*, pp. 107–8; François Dumont, 'French Kingship', *Louis XIV and Absolutism*, pp. 56–7; Beik, *Absolutism*, p. 197; Myriam Yardeni, *La conscience nationale* (Paris, 1971), pp. 317–30; Mervyn James, *Society, Politics, and Culture* (Cambridge, 1986), pp. 308–415.

47. André Corvisier, *L'armée française*, 2 vols (Paris, 1964), I, 105; idem, *La bataille de Malplaquet* (Paris, 1997), pp. 13–30; idem, *Armies and Societies in Europe*, tr. Abigail Siddall (Bloomington, 1979), pp. 69, 133–4.

48. Lynn, *Giant*, pp. 417, 445–450; André Corvisier, *Histoire militaire de la France*, vol. 1, ed. Philippe Contamine (Paris, 1992), pp. 435–45; Fernand Braudel, *The Identity of France*, tr. Siân Reynolds (New York, 1988), p. 375; François-Xavier Emmanuelli, *État et pouvoirs*, pp. 127–207.

49. Françoise Bayard, 'Naturalization in Lyon', *Fr Hist*, 4 (1990), 277–316; Sahlins, 'The Naturalization of Foreigners', 92–5.

50. Charlotte Wells, *Law and Citizenship* (Baltimore, 1995), pp. 58–120; idem, 'The Language of Citizenship', *Sixteenth Cent Journ*, 30 (1999), 441–56; Peter Sahlins, 'The Naturalization of Foreigners', *Representations*, 47 (1994), 85–110; idem, *Boundaries* (Berkeley, 1989), p. 113; Jean-François Dubost and Peter Sahlins, *Et si on faisait payer les étrangers?* (Paris, 1999).

51. Parades de L'Estang, *Mémoires*, pp. 98–9; 26; Jonathan Dewald, *Aristocratic Experience* (Berkeley, 1993), pp. 205–8; Daniel Roche, *France in the Enlightenment*, tr. Arthur Goldhammer (Cambridge, Mass., 1998), pp. 542–7; Louis Dumont, *Essays on Individualism*, tr. Brian Pearce (Chicago, 1986).

52. Sahlins, *Boundaries*, pp. 7–9; David Bell, 'Recent Works on Early Modern French National Identity', *Journ Mod Hist*, 68 (1996), 84–113.

CHAPTER 7

1. Carolyn Lougee Chappell, 'Escape Accounts by a Huguenot Mother and Daughter', *Fr Hist Studies*, 22 (1999), 1–64.

2. Jean Marteilhe, *Mémoires d'un galérien du roi-soleil*, ed. André Zysberg (Paris, 1982), pp. 9–10; Isaac Dumont de Bostaquet, *Mémoires*, ed. Michel Richard (Paris, 1968), pp. 9–16, 112–45.

3. Samuel Mours, *Protestantisme en France* 1968), pp. 58–86; Philip Benedict, *The Huguenot Population* (Philadelphia, 1991); Myriam Yardeni, *Le refuge protestant* (Paris, 1985).

4. Mack Holt, *The French Wars of Religion* (Cambridge, 1995); J.H.M. Salmon, *Society in Crisis* (New York, 1975); Mark Greengrass, *The French Reformation* (Oxford, 1987); Barbara Diefendorf, *Beneath the Cross* (New York, 1991); Philip Benedict, *Rouen during the Wars of Religion* (Cambridge, 1981).

5. Michael Wolfe, *The Conversion of Henri IV* (Cambridge, Mass., 1993); S. Annette Finley-Croswhite, *Henry IV and the Towns* (Cambridge, 1999); Mark Greengrass, *France in the Age of Henri IV* (New York, 1984); David Buisseret, *Henri IV* (London, 1984); Jean-Pierre Babelon, *Henri IV* (Paris, 1982); Roland Mousnier, *The Assassination of Henri IV*, tr. Joan Spencer (London, 1973).

6. Greengrass, *Age of Henri IV*, pp. 102–6; Holt, *Wars of Religion*, pp. 163–72; Mousnier, *Assassination of Henry IV*, pp. 144–51, 316–63; Janine Garrisson, *L'Édit de Nantes* (Paris, 1998), pp. 186–271; Daniel Ligou, *Le Protestantisme en France* (Paris, 1968), pp. 9–25.

7. Henry Phillips, *Church and Culture* (Cambridge, 1997), pp. 104–14; Alexander Sedgwick, *Jansenism* (Charlottesville, 1978), pp. 9–13; Robert Descimon, *La France du premier XVIIe siècle* (Paris, 1996), pp. 51–8; François Lebrun, ed., *Histoire de la vie religieuse en France*, vol. 2, *Du Christianisme flamboyant* (Paris, 1988), pp. 515–37; André Latreille *et al.*, *Histoire du Catholicisme en France*, 3 vols (Paris, 1957), II, 167–78, 354–94; Pierre Pierrard, *Les papes et la France* (Paris, 1981); Aimé-Georges Martimort, *Le gallicanisme* (Paris, 1973). Also see the work of Pierre Blet.

8. René Taveneaux, *Le Catholicisme dans la France classique*, 2 vols (Paris, 1980), I, 72–8; A. Lynn Martin, *The Jesuit Mind* (Ithaca, 1988); Richard Golden, *The Godly Rebellion* (Chapel Hill, 1981), pp. 69–74, 97–122.

9. The terms, 'Catholic Reform, Reformation or Renewal', are currently preferred. Louis Châtellier, *Europe of the Devout*, tr. Jean Birrell (Cambridge, 1989), p. ix.

10. J. Michael Hayden and Malcolm Greenshields, 'The Clergy of Early Seventeenth Century France', *Fr Hist Studies*, 18 (1993), 145 and n. 2.

11. Denis Richet, 'Aspects socio-culturels des confits religieux', *Annales: ESC* 32 (1977), 764–89; also in Robert Forster and Orest Ranum, eds, *Ritual, Religion and the Sacred* (Baltimore, 1982), pp. 182–212.

12. Taveneaux, *Le Catholicisme*, pp. 70–81; François de Dainville, *L'éducation des Jésuites* (Paris, 1978); Charles Williams, *The French Oratorians* (New York, 1989); Charles Bertelot du Chesnay, *Les missions de Saint Jean Eudes* (Paris, 1985); Jean de Viguerie, *Une oeuvre d'éducation* (Paris, 1976), esp. p. 76; Bernard Dompnier, *Enquête au pays: les Capucins de Lyon* (Saint-Etienne, 1993).

13. Barbara Diefendorf, 'Give Us Back Our Children', *Journ Mod Hist*, 68 (1996), 265–307; Elizabeth Rapley, 'Women and Religious Vocation', *Fr Hist Studies*, 18 (1994), 613–31.

14. Elizabeth Rapley, *The Dévotes* (Montreal, 1990); Natalie Davis, *Women on the Margins* (Cambridge, Mass., 1995), pp. 63–139; Marie-Andrée Jégou, *Les Ursulines à Paris* (Paris, 1981); André Ravier, *Saint Jeanne de Chantal*, tr. Mary Hamilton (San Francisco, 1989); Colin Jones, *The Charitable Imperative* (London, 1989), pp. 89–205; Daniel Hickey, *Local Hospitals* (Montreal, 1997), pp. 134–74.

15. Joseph Bergin, *Cardinal de La Rochefoucauld* (New Haven, 1987), pp. 92–118, 136–247; Maarten Ultee, *The Abbey of St Germain des Prés* (New Haven, 1981), pp. 155–67; Taveneaux, *Le Catholicisme*, pp. 58–70; Gregory Hanlon, *L'univers*

des gens de bien (Bordeaux, 1989), pp. 153–88; René Pillorget, *Paris sous les premiers Bourbons* (Paris, 1988), pp. 490–509.

16. Philip Hoffman, *Church and Community in Lyon* (New Haven, 1984), p. 98.

17. Ibid., pp. 71–138; Robert Sauzet, *Les visites pastorales dans le diocèse de Chartres* (Rome, 1975), pp. 77–192; idem, *Contre-Réforme: le diocèse de Nîmes* (Louvain, 1979), pp. 325–59, 405–54; Louis Châtellier, *Tradition chrétienne et renouveau catholique: Strasbourg* (Paris, 1981), pp. 153–83; Hayden and Greenshields, 'Clergy', 145–72; Taveneaux, *Le Catholicisme*, pp. 123–64.

18. Joseph Bergin, *The Making of the French Episcopate* (New Haven, 1996), pp. 493, 542–3, 551–3, 556–7; idem, 'Richelieu and His Bishops', *Richelieu and His Age*, eds Joseph Bergin and Laurence Brockliss (Oxford, 1992), pp. 175–202; idem, 'The Counter-Reformation Church and Its Bishops', *Past and Present*, 165 (1999), 30–73; Taveneaux, *Le Catholicisme*, pp. 97–122.

19. Phillips, *Church and Culture*, pp. 76–99, 212–16; Hanlon, *L'univers des gens de bien*, pp. 307–37; Andrew Barnes, 'Transformation of Parish Clergy', *Culture and Identity*, eds Barbara Diefendorf and Carla Hesse (Ann Arbor, 1993), pp. 139–57.

20. Taveneaux, *Le Catholicisme*, pp. 165–202; Louis Châtellier, *The Religion of the Poor*, tr. Brian Pearce (Cambridge, 1997).

21. Phillips, *Church and Culture*, pp. 17–20; Emmanuel Le Roy Ladurie, *The Ancien Régime*, tr. Mark Greengrass (Oxford, 1996), pp. 37 n. 8, 42–5, 49–51 n. 33; Joseph Bergin, *The Rise of Richelieu* (New Haven, 1991), pp. 13–15; Yves-Marie Bercé, *The Birth of Absolutism*, tr. Richard Rex (New York, 1992), pp. 117–33.

22. Pillorget, *Paris*, pp. 490–509; Lebrun, *Histoire de la vie religieuse*, pp. 417–43; Victor Tapié, *France in the Age of Louis XIII and Richelieu*, tr. D. Lockie, 2nd edn (Cambridge, 1984), p. 286; Wendy Gibson, *Women in the Seventeenth Century* (New York, 1989), pp. 209–38; Denis Richet, 'La Contre-Réforme Catholique', *De la Réforme à la Révolution* (Paris, 1991), pp. 83–95; idem, 'Aspects socio-culturels des conflits religieux', ibid., pp. 15–51.

23. Châtellier, *Tradition chrétienne*, pp. 186–92; idem, *The Europe of the Devout*; Phillips, *Church and Culture*, pp. 20–9; Andrew Barnes, *Social Dimension of Piety* (New York, 1994); Robert Schneider, *Public Life in Toulouse* (Ithaca, 1989), pp. 107–20, 167–87, 192–7; idem, 'Mortification on Parade', *Ren and Ref* N.S. 10 (1986), 123–46; Robert Harding, 'Mobilization of Confraternities', *Sixteenth Cent Journ*, 11 (1980), 85–107; Pillorget, *Paris*, pp. 526–35, 561–6; Anne-Marie Gutton, *Confréries et dévotion* (Lyon, 1993); Maurice Agulhon, *Pénitents et francs-maçons* (Paris, 1984); Taveneaux, *Le Catholicisme*, pp. 224–34; Alain Tallon, *La Compagnie du Saint-Sacrement* (Paris, 1990); Marguerite Pecquet, 'Des Compagnies de Pénitents', *XVIIe siècle*, 69 (1965), 5–36; Marie-Hélène Froeschlé-Chopard, *Espace et sacré en Provence* (Paris, 1994), pp. 415–557.

24. Robert Muchembled, *Popular Culture and Elite Culture in France*, tr. Lydia Cochrane (Baton Rouge, 1985), pp. 103–5, 179–80; François Lebrun, *Médécins, saints, et sorciers* (Paris, 1983), pp. 113–27.

25. Phillips, *Church and Culture*, pp. 37–9, 262–96; Robert Mandrou, *De la culture populaire* (Paris, 1964), pp. 77–97; Roger Chartier et al., *L'éducation en France* (Paris, 1976), p. 142; idem, *Lectures et lecteurs* (Paris, 1987), pp. 214–250. Also see idem, *The Cultural Uses of Print*, tr. Lydia Cochrane (Princeton, 1987); idem, ed., *The Culture of Print*, tr. Lydia Cochrane (Princeton, 1989).

26. Louis Châtellier, *The Religion of the Poor*, tr. Brian Pearce (Cambridge, 1997), pp. 187–205.

27. Hoffman, *Church and Community*, pp. 89–97; Peter Burke, *Popular Culture in Early Modern Europe* (New York, 1978), pp. 207–43. Also see Yves-Marie Bercé, *Fêtes et révolte* (Paris, 1976).

28. Jean Delumeau, *Catholicism between Luther and Voltaire*, tr. Jeremy Moiser (New York, 1971); idem, *Sin and Fear*, tr. Eric Nicholson (New York, 1990).

29. John Bossy, *Christianity in the West, 1400–1700* (Oxford, 1985).

30. Sauzet, *Les visites pastorales*; idem, *Contre-réforme*; Louis Châtellier, *Tradition chrétienne*; idem, *Les réformes en Lorraine* (Nancy, 1986); Bernard Peyrous, *La réforme catholique à Bordeaux*, 2 vols (Bordeaux, 1995); Louis Pérouas, *Le diocèse de La Rochelle* (Paris, 1964); Jeanne Ferté, *La vie religieuse dans les campagnes parisiennes* (Paris, 1962); Pillorget, *Paris*; Marc Venard, *Réforme protestante, réforme catholique dans la province d'Avignon* (Paris, 1993).

31. Phillips, *Church and Culture*, pp. 29–42; Robin Briggs, *Communities of Belief* (Oxford, 1989), pp. 381–91, esp. 383–4; Mack Holt, 'Putting Religion Back into the Wars of Religion', *Fr Hist Studies*, 18 (1993), 524–51; idem, *et al.*, 'A Reply', ibid., 19 (1996), 853–73; 21 (1998), 611–29; Hoffman, *Church and Community*, pp. 1–6; Michel Vovelle, 'Popular Religion', *Ideologies and Mentalities*, tr. Eamon O'Flaherty (Chicago, 1990), pp. 81–113, esp. 83. Also see idem, *Piété baroque et déchristianisation* (Paris, 1978); Bernard Cousin, *Ex-voto de Provence* (Paris, 1981); Marie-Hélène Froeschlé-Chopard, *La religion populaire* (Paris, 1980); Forster and Ranum, eds, *Ritual, Religion, and the Sacred*.

32. Holt, 'Putting Religion Back', 524–51; Nigel Aston, 'The Golden Autumn of Gallicanism', *Fr Hist*, 13 (1999), 187–222; Phillips, *Church and Culture*, p. 298; Gregory Hanlon, *Confession and Community* (Philadelphia, 1993), pp. 7–10; Denis Crouzet, *Les guerriers de Dieu*, 2 vols (Seyssel, 1990); Barbara Diefendorf, *Beneath the Cross*.

33. Hoffman, *Church and Community*, pp. 168–70; Keith Luria, *Territories of Grace* (Berkeley, 1991), pp. 203–9; Hanlon, *Confession and Community*, pp. 3–6, 152–92.

34. Raymond Mentzer, *Blood and Belief* (West Lafayette, Ind., 1994), pp. 66–71.

35. Élisabeth Labrousse, *Une foi, une loi, un roi?* (Paris, 1985); Ligou, *Le Protestantisme*; Janine Garrisson, *L'Édit de Nantes et sa révocation* (Paris, 1985); Mours, *Protestantisme en France*; Holt, *Wars of Religion*, pp. 153–89; Jean Quéniart, *La révocation de l'Édit de Nantes* (Paris, 1985); Robert Sauzet, *Le notaire et son roi* (Paris, 1998), pp. 171–240.

36. Daniel Vidal, *Le malheur et son prophète* (Paris, 1983); Philippe Joutard, *Les Camisards* (Paris, 1976); André Ducasse, *La guerre des Camisards* (Paris, 1978); Liliane Crété, *Les Camisards* (Paris, 1992); Daniel Ligou and Philippe Joutard, 'Les Déserts', *Histoire des Protestants en France*, ed. Robert Mandrou (Paris, 1985), pp. 189–262; Henri Bosc, *La guerre des Cévennes*, 6 vols (Montpellier, 1985–93).

37. Emile Leonard, *Histoire générale du Protestantisme*, 2 vols (Paris, 1961), II, 331–50; tr. Joyce Reid, *A History of Protestantism*, 2 vols (New York, 1968); Jean Orcibal, *Louis XIV et les Protestants* (Paris, 1951); Benedict, *The Huguenot Population*, pp. 3–9, 101; Ligou, *Le Protestantisme en France*, pp. 120–2.

38. Benedict, *The Huguenot Population*, pp. 19, 70, 101–4; Sauzet, *Contre-Réforme*, pp. 166, 178–84, 256–8, 266–74, 279–90, 360–6, esp. 497; Hanlon, *L'univers des gens de bien*, pp. 239–41; idem, *Confession and Community*, pp. 97–116, esp. 116;

Mentzer, *Blood and Belief*, pp. 85–9; Susan Rosa, 'Turenne's Conversion', *Fr Hist Studies*, 18 (1994), 632–66; Lebrun, *Histoire de la vie religieuse*, pp. 445–513; Labrousse, *Une foi, une loi, un roi*, pp. 77–94; Bernard Dompnier, *Le venin de l'hérésie* (Paris, 1985), p. 152.

39. Phillips, *Church and Culture*, pp. 29, 208–11, 217; Ligou, *Le Protestantisme en France*, pp. 120–1, 170–7; Philip Benedict, 'Faith, Fortune and Social Structure', *Past and Present* 152 (1996), 46–78; Mentzer, *Blood and Belief*, pp. 85–9, esp. 86–7, 148–61; idem, 'Ecclesiastical Discipline', *Eur Hist Quart*, 21 (1991), 163–83; Gibson, *Women*, pp. 232–7; Myriam Yardeni, 'French Calvinist Political Thought', *International Calvinism*, ed. Menna Prestwich (Oxford, 1985), pp. 315–38; Élisabeth Labrousse, 'Calvinism in France', ibid., pp. 288–314.

40. Thomas Platter, *Journal of a Younger Brother*, tr. Seán Jennett (London, 1962), pp. 75, 81; Anne Bonzon and Marc Venard, *La religion dans la France moderne* (Paris, 1989), pp. 133–4.

41. Robert Mandrou, *La France aux XVIIe et XVIIIe siècles* (Paris, 1970), pp. 181–2; Bonzon and Venard, *La religion dans la France*, pp. 123–5; Françoise Hildesheimer, *La vie à Nice au XVIIe siècle* (Paris, 1987), pp. 179–200; Davis, *Women on the Margins*, pp. 5–62; René Molinas, *Les juifs du pape en France* (Paris, 1981); Bernhard Blumenkranz, *Juifs en France au XVIIIe siècle* (Paris, 1994); idem, *Histoire des Juifs en France* (Toulouse, 1972); Gilbert Dahan, ed., *Les juifs au regard de l'histoire* (Paris, 1985); Jean Cavaignac, *Les israélites bordelaises* (Paris, 1991); Frances Malino, *The Sephardic Jews of Bordeaux* (Tuscaloosa, Ala., 1978); Freddy Raphael and Robert Weyl, *Juifs en Alsace* (Toulouse, 1977); Esther Benbasse, *The Jews of France*, tr. M.B. DeBevoise (Princeton, 1999).

42. *Relation par la Mère Angélique*, ed. Louis Cognet (Paris, 1948), p. 65; Alexander Sedgwick, *The Travails of Conscience* (Cambridge, Mass., 1998), pp. 43–5.

43. Disputes included Simonism and Richerism. See Phillips, *Church and Culture*, pp. 115–16, 126–34, 272–5; Richard Golden, *The Godly Rebellion* (Chapel Hill, 1981), pp. 14, 72–4.

44. For the influence of Jansenism's robe origins, see Lucien Goldmann, *The Hidden God*, tr. P. Thody (New York, 1964); Schneider, *Public Life*, pp. 178–9; Marc Fumaroli, *L'âge de l'éloquence* (Geneva, 1980); Phillips, *Church and Culture*, pp. 198, 110–14, 117.

45. Sedgwick, *Jansenism*, pp. 187–92; Dale Van Kley, *Jansenists and the Expulsion of the Jesuits* (New Haven, 1975); B. Robert Kreiser, *Miracles, Convulsions, and Ecclesiastical Politics* (Princeton, 1978).

46. Phillips, *Church and Culture*, pp. 16, 103–4, 190–205; Briggs, *Communities*, pp. 339–62; Sedgwick, *Jansenism*; idem, *Travails of Conscience*; René Taveneaux, *Jansénisme et Réforme catholique* (Paris, 1992); idem, *La vie quotidienne des jansénistes* (Paris, 1985); idem, *Jansénisme et politique* (Paris, 1965); idem, *Le Jansénisme en Lorraine* (Paris, 1960). Also see the work of Antoine Adam, Louis Cognet, and Jean Orcibal.

CHAPTER 8

1. Antoine Adam, *Théophile de Viau* (Paris, 1935), pp. 355–424.
2. Ibid., pp. 9–41; F.E. Sutcliffe, *Guez de Balzac* (Paris, 1959), pp. 17–18.

3. Adam, *Viau*, pp. 161–82, 257–8, 290–1, 316–18, 344–54; Georges d'Avenel, *La noblesse française sous Richelieu* (Paris, 1901), pp. 187–8; Roland Mousnier and Jean Mesnard, eds, *L'âge d'or du mécénat* (Paris, 1985), pp. 37–57, 69–75.

4. Henry Phillips, *Church and Culture* (Cambridge, 1997), pp. 227–40; Robert Mandrou, *From Humanism to Science* (Atlantic Highlands, NJ, 1979), pp. 170–98; John Spink, *French Free Thought* (New York, 1969), pp. 3–5; Antoine Adam, *Les libertins* (Paris, 1964).

5. René Pintard, *Le libertinage érudit* (Paris, 1943), pp. 125–209; Lynn Joy, *Gassendi the Atomist* (Cambridge, 1988); Lisa Sarasohn, *Gassendi's Ethics* (Ithaca, 1996).

6. Louise Godard de Donville, *Le libertin des origines à 1665* (Paris, 1989), p. 154; Phillips, *Church and Culture*, p. 233; Arlette Lebigre, 'Le procès de Théophile de Viau', *Quelques procès criminels* (Paris, 1964), pp. 29–43; Frédéric Lachèvre, *Le procès de Théophile de Viau*, 2 vols (Paris, 1909); George Huppert, *The Style of Paris* (Bloomington, 1999), pp. 66–75, 116–20.

7. Richard Popkin, *The History of Scepticism*, 2nd edn (Berkeley, 1979), pp. 89–150; idem, *Isaac La Peyrère* (New York, 1987); Richard Popkin and Arjo Vanderjagt, eds, *Scepticism and Irreligion* (Leiden, 1993).

8. Phillips, *Church and Culture*, pp. 240–52; Michael Hunter and David Wootton, eds, *Atheism* (Oxford, 1992), pp. 1–53, 55–85; Lucien Febvre, *Problem of Unbelief*, tr. Beatrice Gottlieb (Cambridge, Mass., 1982), pp. 13–16, 461; Alan Kors, *Atheism in France* (Princeton, 1990), pp. 17–43; idem, *D'Holbach's Coterie* (Princeton, 1976), pp. 41–119; Michael Buckley, *Origins of Modern Atheism* (New Haven, 1987), pp. 37–67.

9. René Descartes, *Discourse on Method*, tr. Laurence Lafleur (Indianapolis, 1950); Stephen Gaukroger, *Descartes* (Oxford, 1995); E.A. Burtt, *Metaphysical Foundations of Modern Science* (New York, 1952), pp. 105–24; Herbert Butterfield, *Origins of Modern Science* (New York, 1962), pp. 122–8; David Maland, *Culture and Society* (London, 1970), pp. 149–53.

10. Thomas Kuhn, *The Copernican Revolution* (Cambridge, Mass., 1957); Steven Shapin, *The Scientific Revolution* (Chicago, 1996), see bibliography; L.W.B. Brockliss, 'Scientific Revolution in France', *The Scientific Revolution in National Context*, eds Roy Porter and Mikulas Teich (Cambridge, 1992), pp. 55–89; Richard Westfall, *The Construction of Modern Science* (Cambridge, 1977); A. Rupert Hall, *The Revolution in Science* (New York, 1983); James R. Jacob, *The Scientific Revolution* (Atlantic Highlands, NJ, 1998).

11. Trevor McClaughlin, 'Censorship and Defenders of the Cartesian Faith', *Journ Hist Ideas*, 40 (1979), 563–81; Mandrou, *From Humanism to Science*, pp. 183–98; Spink, *French Free Thought*, pp. 189–225; Erica Harth, *Cartesian Women* (Ithaca, 1992), pp. 78–114; Londa Schiebinger, *The Mind Has No Sex?* (Cambridge, Mass., 1989), pp. 20–36; L.W.B. Brockliss, *French Higher Education* (Oxford, 1987).

12. Phillips, *Church and Culture*, pp. 172–85; Harcourt Brown, *Scientific Organizations* (Baltimore, 1934); Peter Dear, *Mersenne* (Ithaca, 1988); Lisa Sarasohn, 'Nicolas-Claude Fabri de Peiresc', *Isis*, 84 (1993), 70–90; Howard Solomon, *Public Welfare, Science, and Propaganda* (Princeton, 1972); David Lux, *Patronage and Royal Science* (Cornell, 1989); Roger Hahn, *The Anatomy of a Scientific Institution* (Berkeley, 1971); Daniel Roche, *Le siècle des Lumières en province*, 2 vols (Paris, 1978); Katherine

Sterne Brennan, 'Culture and Dependencies' (PhD dissert., Johns Hopkins, 1981), pp. 86–189.

13. David Sturdy, *Science and Social Status* (Woodbridge, Suffolk, 1995), pp. 413–19; Alice Stroup, *A Company of Scientists* (Berkeley, 1990), pp. 180–217; Maurice Crosland, 'A Professional Career in Science', *Emergence of Science*, idem, ed. (New York, 1976), pp. 139–59.

14. Daniel Gordon, *Citizens Without Sovereignty* (Princeton, 1994), pp. 9–128, esp. 29, 33, 37; Maurice Agulhon, *Le cercle* (Paris, 1977); idem, *Pénitents et franc-maçons* (Paris, 1984), pp. i–xiii.

15. Anne Goldgar, *Impolite Learning* (New Haven, 1995), p. 7; Steven Shapin, *A Social History of Truth* (Chicago, 1995), pp. 42–125.

16. Dena Goodman, *The Republic of Letters* (Cornell, 1994), pp. 15–23; Daniel Roche, *Les républicains des lettres* (Paris, 1988); Robert Darnton and Daniel Roche, eds, *Revolution in Print* (Berkeley, 1989); Goldgar, *Impolite Learning*, pp. 1–11.

17. Daniel Roche, *France in the Enlightenment*, tr. Arthur Goldhammer (Cambridge, Mass., 1998), pp. 434–48; Keith Baker, *Inventing the French Revolution* (Cambridge, 1990); idem, *The French Revolution and Political Culture*, 4 vols (New York, 1987–94); David Bell, *Lawyers and Citizens* (New York, 1994); Arlette Farge, *Subversive Words*, tr. Rosemary Morris (University Park, 1995); Sarah Maza, *Private lives and Public Affairs* (Berkeley, 1993); Daniel Gordon, David Bell and Sarah Maza, 'The Public Sphere in the Eighteenth Century', *Fr Hist Studies*, 17 (1992), 882–956; Anthony La Volpa, 'Conceiving a Public', *Journ Mod Hist*, 64 (1992), 79–116.

18. Robin Briggs, *Witches and Neighbours* (London, 1996), p. 8; Brian Levack, *The Witch-Hunt in Early Modern Europe*, 2nd edn (New York, 1995), pp. 21–6; Richard Golden, 'The Geography of Witch Hunts', *Changing Identities*, ed. Michael Wolfe (Durham, 1997), pp. 216–47; Robert Muchembled, *Popular Culture and Elite Culture*, tr. Lydia Cochrane (Baton Rouge, 1985), pp. 237–8.

19. R. Po-Chia Hsia, *The World of Catholic Renewal* (Cambridge, 1998), pp. 150–1; Robert Rapley, *A Case of Witchcraft* (Montreal, 1998), esp. pp. 180–97; Michel de Certeau, *The Possession at Loudun*, tr. Michael Smith (Chicago, 2000); Robert Mandrou, *Magistrats et sorciers* (Paris, 1980), pp. 210–19, 264–84; Michel Carmona, *Les diables de Loudun* (Paris, 1988); Briggs, *Witches and Neighbours*, pp. 214–15; Solomon, *Public Welfare*, pp. 80–1, 190–1; Phillips, *Church and Culture*, p. 229.

20. Rapley, *A Case of Witchcraft*, pp. 3–69; Briggs, *Witches and Neighbours*, pp. 139–54, 221–56; Emmanuel Le Roy Ladurie, *Jasmin's Witch*, tr. Brian Pearce (New York, 1987), pp. 3–78.

21. Mandrou, *Magistrats*, pp. 265–9; Muchembled, *Popular Culture*, pp. 235–78; idem, *Le roi et la sorcière* (Paris, 1993); idem, *Le temps des supplices* (Paris, 1992); Joseph Klaits, *Servants of Satan* (Bloomington, 1985), pp. 128–58.

22. John Langbein, *Torture and the Law of Proof* (Chicago, 1977), pp. 16–26.

23. Brian Levack, 'State-Building and Witch-Hunting', *Witchcraft in Early Modern Europe*, eds Jonathan Barry *et al.* (Cambridge, 1992), pp. 96–115; Alfred Soman, 'Les procès de sorcellerie au Parlement de Paris', 'The Parlement of Paris and the Great Witch Hunt', 'Decriminalizing Witchcraft', selections I, II and XV in idem, *Sorcellerie et justice criminelle* (Brookfield, Vt, 1992).

24. Briggs, *Witches and Neighbours*, pp. 63–95, 289–310.

25. Ibid., pp. 259–86; idem, 'Women as Victims', *Fr Hist*, 5 (1991), 438–50; Levack, *The Witch-Hunt*, pp. 133–56; Klaits, *Servants of Satan*, pp. 48–103; Emmanuel Le Roy Ladurie, *The Peasants of Languedoc*, tr. John Day (Urbana, 1976), pp. 207–10; Robert Muchembled, *Sorcières, justice et société* (Paris, 1987); E. William Monter, *Witchcraft in France and Switzerland* (Ithaca, 1976), pp. 115–41; idem, *Enforcing Morality* (London, 1987); idem, 'The Male Witches of Normandy', *Fr Hist Studies*, 20 (1997), 563–95; André Abbiateci, 'Arsonists in Eighteenth-Century France', *Deviants and the Abandoned*, eds Robert Forster and Orest Ranum (Baltimore, 1978), pp. 157–79; Marianne Hester, 'Patriarchal Reconstruction and Witch Hunting', *Witchcraft in Early Modern Europe*, pp. 288–306; Merry Wiesner, *Women and Gender* (Cambridge, 1992), pp. 218–38; Yves Castan, *Magie et sorcellerie* (Paris, 1979), pp. 87–127.

26. Levack, *the Witch-Hunt*, pp. 27–43, 100–24; Klaits, *Servants of Satan*, pp. 59–65; H.R. Trevor-Roper, *The European Witch-Craze* (New York, 1969), pp. 130–1; John Bossy, 'Moral Arithmetic', *Conscience and Casuitry*, ed. Edmund Leites (Cambridge, 1988), pp. 215–31; idem, *Christianity in the West* (Oxford, 1988), pp. 35–8, 135, 138–9; James Farr, *Authority and Sexuality* (New York, 1995), pp. 38–40; Monter, *Witchcraft in France*, pp. 42–66; Soman, *Sorcellerie et justice criminelle, passim*; Fernando Cervantes, 'The Devil's Encounter with America', *Witchcraft in Early Modern Europe*, pp. 126–33; Briggs, *Witches and Neighbours*, pp. 9–13, 100–1, 321–2.

27. Mandrou, *Magistrats*, pp. 548–64, especially 560–4; Klaits, *Servants of Satan*, pp. 163–5; Levack, *The Witch-Hunt*, pp. 239–46.

28. Soman, 'Les procès de sorcellerie au Parlement de Paris' and 'The Parlement of Paris and the Great Witch Hunt', selections I and II in *Sorcellerie et justice criminelle*, and *passim*.

29. Muchembled, *Le roi et la sorcière*, pp. 217–38; Levack, *the Witch-Hunt*, pp. 233–50.

30. Daniel Roche, 'A Pauper Capital', *Fr Hist*, 1 (1987), 190; Thomas Adams, *Bureaucrats and Beggars* (New York, 1990), pp. 7–27.

31. James Farr, *Authority and Sexuality* (New York, 1995), pp. 142, 149, 150.

32. Roche, 'A Pauper Capital', 182–209; Olwen Hufton, *The Poor of Eighteenth-Century France* (Oxford, 1974), pp. 11–127; Cissie Fairchilds, *Poverty and Charity in Aix* (Baltimore, 1976), pp. 73–128; Jeffry Kaplow, *Names of Kings* (New York, 1972), pp. 3–92; Arlette Farge, *Fragile Lives*, tr. Carol Shelton (Cambridge, Mass., 1993), pp. 131–68; Micheline Baulant, 'Groupes mobiles', *Les marginaux*, ed. Arlette Farge (Paris, 1979), pp. 98–121.

33. Arlette Farge, *Le vol d'aliments* (Paris, 1974), pp. 116–28; idem, *Fragile Lives*, p. 144; Julius Ruff, *Crime, Justice and Public Order* (Dover, NH, 1984), pp. 68–143; Antoinette Wills, *Crime and Punishment in Revolutionary Paris* (Westport, Conn., 1981), pp. 96–140; Hufton, *The Poor*, pp. 219–351; idem, 'Women without Men', *Journ Family Hist*, 9 (1984), 355–76; Farr, *Authority and Sexuality*, pp. 124–55; Patrice Peveri, 'Les pickpockets à Paris', *Rev d'hist mod et cont*, 29 (1982), 3–35; François-Xavier Emmanuelli, 'La marginalité féminine à Marseille', *Les Marseillaises*, eds Yvonne Knibiehler *et al.* (Paris, 1993), pp. 137–47; Nicole Castan, *Les criminels de Languedoc* (Toulouse, 1980).

34. Farr, *Authority and Sexuality*, pp. 135–63; Hufton, *The Poor*, pp. 266–83; Farge, *Fragile Lives*, pp. 152–7.

35. Malcolm Greenshields, *An Economy of Violence* (University Park, 1994), pp. 14–18; Steven Reinhardt, *Justice in the Sarladais* (Baton Rouge, 1991), xiii–xiv; Iain Cameron, *Crime and Repression in the Auvergne* (Cambridge, 1981), pp. 193–211, esp. 202–3; Ruff, *Crime, Justice, and Public Order*, unpag. intro., pp. 69, 92, 97–8; Arlette Lebigre, *Les Grands Jours d'Auvergne* (Paris, 1976), pp. 99–119; Castan, *Les criminels de Languedoc*.

36. Richard Mowrey Andrews, *Law, Magistracy, and Crime* (Cambridge, 1994), pp. 307–411; André Zysberg, 'Galley Rowers', *Deviants*, pp. 83–110; Nicole Castan, 'Summary Justice', ibid., pp. 111–56; Ruff, *Crime, Justice and Public Order*, pp. 44–181; Hufton, *The Poor*, pp. 219–351; Jean Imbert, *La peine de mort* (Paris, 1967), pp. 12, 19–44, 61–3, 76–7; Farr, *Authority and Sexuality*, pp. 38–50; Reinhardt, *Justice in the Sardalais*, pp. 161–88.

37. Colin Jones, *The Charitable Imperative* (London, 1989), pp. 1–86; Robert Schwartz, *Policing the Poor* (Chapel Hill, 1988), pp. 13–49; Jean-Pierre Gutton, *La société des pauvres* (Paris, 1970), pp. 295–352; Roger Chartier, 'La ville dominante', *Histoire de la France urbaine*, ed. Georges Duby, 5 vols (Paris, 1981), III, 223–42; Roche, 'A Pauper Capital', 190; Adams, *Bureaucrats and Beggars*, pp. 28–48; Brian Strayer, *Lettres de Cachet* (New York, 1992), pp. 43–52; Isabelle Robin-Romero, 'Les établissements pour orphelins', *Hist, écon et soc*, 17 (1988), 441–52; Claude Delaselle, 'Abandoned Children', *Deviants*, pp. 47–82.

38. Farr, *Authority and Sexuality*, pp. 124–55; Hufton, *The Poor*, pp. 306–17; Erica-Marie Benabou, *La prostitution et les police* (Paris, 1987), pp. 60–108, 407–30, *passim*; Jones, *The Charitable Imperative*, pp. 241–74; Annick Riani, 'Les espaces de prostitution à Marseille', *Marseillaises*, pp. 161–73; Strayer, *Lettres de Cachet*, pp. 130–4; Jacques Rossiand, 'Prostitution', *Deviants*, pp. 1–46.

39. Schwartz, *Policing the Poor*, pp. 3–5; Adams, *Bureaucrats and Beggars*, p. 30; Alan Williams, *The Police of Paris* (Baton Rouge, 1979), pp. 5–61; Steven Kaplan, 'Réflexions sur la police', *Rev hist*, 261 (1979), 17–77; idem, 'Note sur les commissaires de police', *Rev d'hist mod et cont*, 28 (1981), 669–86; Castan, *Les criminels de Languedoc*, pp. 8–24; idem, 'Summary Justice', *Deviants*, pp. 111–56; Arlette Farge, *Vivre dans la rue* (Paris, 1979), pp. 148–62, 187–224; Arlette Lebigre, *La justice du roi* (Paris, 1988), pp. 144–76.

40. David Jacobson, 'Politics of Criminal Law Reform', (unpub. PhD dissert., Brown Univ., 1976), pp. 1–57; Andrews, *Law, Magistracy, and Crime*, pp. 417–93; Adhémar Esmein, *Histoire de la procédure criminelle* (Paris, 1882); idem, *A History of Continental Crime Procedure: France*, tr. John Simpson (Boston, 1913), pp. 211–87; André Laingui and Arlette Lebigre, *Histoire du droit pénal*, 2 vols (Paris, 1979), II, 87–109.

41. Andrews, *Law, Magistracy, and Crime*, p. 420 and note 6.

42. Michel Foucault, *Discipline and Punish*, tr. Alan Sheridan (New York, 1979), pp. 3–69; Lebigre, *La justice du roi*, pp. 211–42; Dale Van Kley, *The Damiens Affair* (Princeton, 1984); Mitchell Merback, *The Thief, the Cross, and the Wheel* (Chicago, 1998); Gordon Wright, *Between the Guillotine and Liberty* (New York, 1983), pp. 21–2, 29, 52, 201, 213.

43. Michel Foucault, *Madness and Civilization*, tr. Richard Howard (New York, 1988), pp. 38–64, 159–278; Schwartz, *Policing the Poor*, pp. 34–92; Jean-Pierre Gutton, *L'état et la mendicité* (Paris, 1973); Farge, *Le vol d'aliments*; idem, *Vivre dans la rue*; Laurence Brockliss and Colin Jones, *The Medical World of Early Modern France*

193

(Oxford, 1997), pp. 2–4; George Huppert, 'Thoughts on Foucault', *Hist and Theory*, 13 (1974), 191–207; Allan Megill, 'The Reception of Foucault', *Journ Hist Ideas*, 48 (1987), 117–41; Peter Burke, ed., *Critical Essays on Michel Foucault* (Cambridge, 1992); Colin Jones and Roy Porter, eds, *Reassessing Foucault* (London, 1994); Keith Windschuttle, *The Killing of History* (New York, 1996), pp. 121–57.

44. Gutton, *La société des pauvres*, pp. 213–417; Daniel Hickey, *Local Hospitals in Ancien Regime France* (Montreal, 1997), pp. 3–14; Fairchilds, *Poverty and Charity*, pp. 18–99; Kathryn Norberg, *Rich and Poor in Grenoble* (Berkeley, 1985), pp. 20–64, 112–56; Wilma Pugh, 'Social Welfare and the Edict of Nantes', *Fr Hist Studies*, 8 (1974), 349–76; idem, 'Testamentary Charity', ibid. 11 (1980), 479–509; Brockliss and Jones, *Medical World*, pp. 262–73; Robert Castel, 'Problemization', *Foucault on the Writing of History*, ed. Jan Goldstein (Cambridge, 1994), pp. 237–52.

45. Hickey, *Local Hospitals*, pp. 3–14, 198–207; Hufton, *The Poor*, pp. 131–76; Jones, *Charitable Imperative*, pp. 31–47, 209–74; idem, *Charity and Bienfaisance* (Cambridge, 1982); Farge, *Vivre dans la rue*, pp. 148–59; Jean Imbert, *Le droit hospitalier* (Paris, 1993), pp. 95–116; idem, *Histoire des hôpitaux* (Toulouse, 1982), pp. 137–218.

46. Hickey, *Local Hospitals*, pp. 5, 100–74; Jones, *Charitable Imperative*, pp. 8–10, 89–205; Fairchilds, *Poverty and Charity*, pp. 73–99; Norberg, *Rich and Poor*, pp. 81–112, 169–215; Norbert Finzsch and Robert Jutte, eds *Institutions of Confinement* (Cambridge, 1996).

47. Andrews, *Law, Magistracy, and Crime*, pp. 283–4, 417–21; Ruff, *Crimes, Justice, and Public Order*, pp. 44–5; Cameron, *Crimes and Repression in the Auvergne*, pp. 1–13; Reinhardt, *Justice in the Sardalais*, pp. xviii, 139–60; Schwartz, *Policing the Poor*, pp. 7–10; Langbein, *Torture*, pp. 10–11, 50–5; Lebigre, *La justice du roi*, pp. 177–210; Nicole Castan, *Justice et repression en Languedoc* (Paris, 1980), pp. 13–51, 268–305.

CONCLUSION

1. Père Henri Griffet, *Histoire du règne de Louis XIII*, 3 vols (Paris, 1758), II, 302–62; A. Lloyd Moote, *Louis XIII* (Berkeley, 1989), pp. 224–6; Pierre Chevallier, *Louis XIII* (Paris, 1979), pp. 465–8; Louis Vaunois, *Vie de Louis XIII* (Paris, 1944), pp. 407–21; Victor-Louis Tapié, *France in the Age of Louis XIII*, tr. D.McN. Lockic (Cambridge, 1984), pp. 304–10.

2. François-Timoléon, abbé de Choisy, *Mémoires*, ed. Georges Mongrédien (Paris, 1979), p. 131, cited by Jean-François Solnon, *La cour de France* (Paris, 1981), pp. 339–40; Jean-Pierre Labatut, *Les ducs et pairs de France* (Paris, 1972), pp. 121–2, 242; idem, *Louis XIV* (Paris, 1984), pp. 113, 155, 224; idem, 'Patriotisme et noblesse', *Rev d'hist mod et cont*, 29 (1982), 627; François Bluche, *Louis XIV* (Paris, 1986), pp. 370, 495, 500–1.

A HISTORIOGRAPHICAL ESSAY

1. The journal was the *Annales: Economies, Sociétés et Civilisations*, commonly abbreviated as *Annales: ESC*, hence the name Annalistes, also used in English.

2. Lucien Febvre, *The Problem of Unbelief in the Sixteenth Century*, tr. Beatrice Gottlieb (Cambridge, Mass., 1982); idem, *Life in Renaissance France*, ed., tr. Marian Rothstein

(Cambridge, Mass., 1977); Marc Bloch, *French Rural History*, tr. Janet Sondheimer (Berkeley, 1966); idem, *Feudal Society*, tr. L.A. Manyon (Chicago, 1961); Fernand Braudel, *The Mediterranean World in the Age of Philip II*, tr. Siân Reynolds, 2 vols (Berkeley, 1995).

3. Pim den Boer, *History as a Profession*, tr. Arnold Pomerans (Princeton, 1999); Jacques Le Goff, *La nouvelle histoire* (Paris, 1970); Jean-Pierre Herubel, 'The *Annales*: A Bibliography', *Fr Hist Studies*, 18 (1993), 348–55.

4. Daniel Roche, *Les républicains des lettres* (Paris, 1988), pp. 7–22.

5. There was also a strong reaction against the economic analysis of Ernest Labrousse. See idem, *Esquisse du mouvement des prix*, 2 vols (Paris, 1933).

6. Peter Burke, *The French Historical Revolution. Annales School* (Cambridge, 1992); idem, 'Strengths and Weaknesses of History of Mentalities', *Hist Eur Ideas*, 7 (1986), 439–51; Philippe Carrard, *Poetics of the New History* (Baltimore, 1992); François Furet, *In the Workshop of History*, tr. Jonathan Mandelbaum (Chicago, 1984); Traian Stoianovich, *French Historical Method: The 'Annales' Paradigm* (Ithaca, 1976); Lynn Hunt, 'The Rise and Fall of the "Annales" Paradigm', *Journ Cont Hist*, 21 (1986), 209–24; Robert Forster, 'Achievements of the Annales', *Journ Econ Hist*, 38 (1978), 58–76.

7. James McMillan, 'Social History, "New Cultural History", and the Rediscovery of Politics', *Journ Mod Hist*, 66 (1994), 755–72; Steven Hause, 'Evolution of Social History', *Soc Hist*, 20 (1995), 1191–214; Gianna Pomata, 'History, Particular and Universal', *Feminist Studies*, 19 (1993), 7–50.

8. Peter Burke, *Varieties of Cultural History* (Ithaca, NY, 1997); Lynn Hunt, ed., *New Cultural History* (Berkeley, 1989); Joyce Appleby *et al.*, *Telling the Truth about History* (New York, 1994); Roger Chartier, *The Cultural Origins of the French Revolution*, tr. Lydia Cochrane (Durham, 1991); idem, *Cultural History*, tr. Lydia Cochrane (Ithaca, 1988); idem, *The Cultural Uses of Print*, tr. Lydia Cochrane (Princeton, 1987); idem, *Forms and Meanings*, tr. Lydia Cochrane (Philadelphia, 1995); Deena Goodman, *Criticism in Action* (Ithaca, 1989); Gabrielle Spiegel, *Romancing the Past* (Berkeley, 1992).

9. Denise Riley, *'Am I that Name'* (Minneapolis, 1988); Judith Butler and Joan Wallach Scott, eds, *Feminists Theorize the Political* (New York, 1992); Joan Wallach Scott, *Only Paradoxes to Offer* (Cambridge, Mass., 1996); Elizabeth Weed, ed., *Coming to Terms: Feminism, Theory, Politics* (New York, 1989); Karen Anderson, *Chain Her by One Foot* (London, 1991); Judith Bennett, 'Feminism and History', *Gender and History*, 1 (1989), 251–72; Lise Vogel, 'Telling Tales', *Journ Women's Hist*, 2 (1991), 89–101; Louise Newman, 'Critical Theory and the History of Women', ibid., 58–68; Mary Poovey, 'Feminism and Deconstructionism', *Feminist Studies*, 14 (1988) 51–65.

10. Olwen Hufton, *The Prospect Before Her* (New York, 1996); Georges Duby and Michelle Perrot, eds, *A History of Women in the West*, 5 vols (Cambridge, Mass., 1993); Bonnie Anderson and Judith Zinsser, *A History of Their Own*, 2 vols (New York, 1988); Gerda Lerner, *The Majority Finds its Past* (New York, 1979); Renate Bridenthal *et al.*, *Becoming Visible* (Boston, 1987, 2nd edn); Sheila Rowbothan, *Hidden from History* (New York, 1974).

11. Bonnie G. Smith, *The Gender of History* (Cambridge, Mass., 1998); Joan Wallach Scott, *Gender and the Politics of History* (New York, 1988); Londa Schiebinger, *The*

Mind Has No Sex? (Cambridge, Mass., 1989); idem, *Nature's Body* (Boston, 1993); Erica Harth, *Cartesian Women* (Cornell, 1992); Elinor Accampo *et al.*, *Gender and the Politics of Social Reform* (Baltimore, 1995); Gisela Bock, 'Women's History and Gender History', *Gender and History*, 1 (1989), 7–30; Gisela Bock and Pat Thane, eds, *Maternity and Gender Politics* (London, 1991); Mary Louise Robert, *Civilization without Sexes* (Chicago, 1994).

12. For general surveys of the field, see Karen Offen *et al.*, eds, *Writing Women's History* (London, 1991); S. Jay Kleinberg, *Retrieving Women's History* (New York, 1988).

13. Lynn Hunt, *Politics, Culture, and Class* (Berkeley, 1984); idem, *Family Romance of the French Revolution* (Berkeley, 1992); Keith Baker and Colin Lucas, eds, *French Revolution and Modern Political Culture*, 4 vols (New York, 1987–94); Kristen Neuschel, *Word of Honor* (Ithaca, 1989); Jay Smith, *Culture of Merit* (Ann Arbor, 1996); Arthur Herman, 'Language of Fidelity', *Journ Mod Hist*, 67 (1995), 1–24; Brian Sandberg, 'Perceptions nobiliaires', *Hist, écon et soc* 17 (1998), 423–40.

14. Roger Chartier, *On the Edge of the Cliff*, tr. Lydia Cochrane (Baltimore, 1997); idem, *et al.*, 'Critical Pragmatism, Language, and Cultural History', *Fr Hist Studies*, 21 (1998), 213–64; Keith Windschuttle, *Killing of History* (Paddington, Australia, 1994); Richard Evans, *In Defense of History* (New York, 1999); Bryan Palmer, *Descent into Discourse* (Philadelphia, 1990); Geoffrey Elton, *Return to Essentials* (Cambridge, 1991); Christopher Lloyd, *Structures of History* (Oxford, 1993); Gertrude Himmelfarb, *The New History and the Old* (Cambridge, Mass., 1987); Eric Hobsbawm, *On History* (New York, 1997); Peter Novick, *That Noble Dream* (Cambridge, 1988); 'The Old History and the New', *Amer Hist Rev*, 94–3 (June 1989), 581–698; François Dosse, *New History: Triumph of the Annales* (Urbana, Ill., 1994); Jacques Revel, ed., *Jeux d'echelle: La microanalyse à l'experience* (Paris, 1996); Gérard Noiriel, *Sur la 'crise' de l'histoire* (Paris, 1996); Joan Scott and Lloyd Kramer, 'A Crisis in History?' *Fr Hist Studies*, 21 (1998), 383–414; Patrick Joyce, 'End of Social History', *Soc Hist*, 20 (1995), 73–91; idem, 'History and Post-Modernism, I', *Past and Present*, 130 (1991), 204–9; Lawrence Stone, ibid. II, 131 (1991), 217–18; idem, III, ibid., 135 (1992), 189–208.

15. See the letter by Jay Smith, *Amer Hist Rev*, 103 (June 1998), 1044–5, in response to a book review by the author, ibid., 103 (April 1998), 526–7.

16. J. Russell Major, *Representative Government* (New Haven, 1980), pp. 10–57.

17. Boris Porchnev, *Les soulèvements populaires* (Paris, 1963); J.H.M. Salmon, 'Venality of Office and Popular Sedition', *Past and Present*, 37 (1967), 21–43; reprinted in idem, *Renaissance and Revolt* (Cambridge, 1987), pp. 191–210.

18. Roland Mousnier, 'Recherches sur les soulèvements populaires', *Rev d'hist mod et cont*, 5 (1958), 81–113; idem, *Social Hierarchies*, tr. Peter Evans (New York, 1973).

19. Roland Mousnier, *Peasants Uprisings*, tr. Brian Pearce (New York, 1970).

20. David Parker, 'Social Foundations of Absolutism', *Past and Present*, 53 (1971), 67–89; idem, 'Class, Clientage and Personal Rule', *Seventeenth-Cent Fr Studies*, 9 (1986), 192–213; idem, *Class and State* (London, 1996); William Beik, *Absolutism and Society* (Cambridge, 1986); idem, 'Urban Factions', *Fr Hist Studies*, 15 (1987), 36–67; idem, 'Culture of Protest', *Soc Hist*, 15 (1990), 2–23.

21. James Collins, *Classes, Estates, and Order* (Cambridge, 1994), pp. 1–29; J. Michael Hayden, 'Models, Mousnier, and *Qualité*', *Fr Hist*, 10 (1996), 375–98; P.J. Coveney,

France in Crisis (London, 1977), pp. 1–63; William Beik, *Absolutism and Society*, pp. 3–33; David Parker, *Class and State*, pp. 6–27; Raymond Kierstead, ed., *State and Society* (New York, 1975), pp. 96–129; Armand Arriaza, 'Mousnier and Barber', *Past and Present*, 88 (1980), 39–57; M.O. Gately *et al.*, 'Seventeenth-Century Peasant Furies', *Past and Present* 51 (1971), 63–80.

22. Roland Mousnier, *The Institutions of France*, vol. 1, *Society and the State*, tr. Brian Pearce (Chicago, 1979), vol. 2, *Organs of State and Society*, tr. Arthur Goldhammer (Chicago, 1984).

23. Mousnier, *Institutions*, vol. 1, *Society and the State*, pp. 3–47.

24. Arlette Jouanna, *Le devoir de révolte* (Paris, 1989); idem, *L'idée de race en France*, 2 vols (Paris, 1981); idem, *Ordre social* (Paris, 1977); Jean-Marie Constant, *Nobles et paysans en Beauce* (Lille, 1981); idem, *Les Guise* (Paris, 1984); idem, *Conjurateurs* (Paris, 1987); Jean-Pierre Labatut, *Les ducs et pairs de France* (Paris, 1972); Jean Gallet, *La seigneurie bretonne* (Paris, 1983).

25. Yves-Marie Bercé, *Histoire des croquants*, 2 vols (Paris, 1974); Madeleine Foisil, *La révolte des Nu-Pieds* (Paris, 1970); René Pillorget, *Les mouvements insurrectionnels en Provence* (Paris, 1976); Elie Barnavi, *Le parti de Dieu* (Louvain, 1980); Myriam Yardeni, *Utopie et révolte sous Louis XIV* (Paris, 1980).

26. Yves Durand, *Les fermiers généraux* (Paris, 1971); Michel Antoine, *Le conseil du Roi* (Paris, 1970); Jean-Claude Dubé, *Les intendants de la Nouvelle France* (Montreal, 1984); André Corvisier, *L'armée française*, 2 vols (Paris, 1964); idem, *Louvois* (Paris, 1983); Maurice Gresset, *Gens de justice à Besançon*, 2 vols (Paris, 1978).

27. Pierre Blet, *Les assemblées du clergé, 1615 à 1666*, 2 vols (Rome, 1959); idem, *Les assemblées du clergé, 1670 à 1693* (Rome, 1972); idem, *Le clergé et ses assemblées, 1615–1715* (Paris, 1995); Myriam Yardeni, *Le refuge protestant* (Paris, 1985).

28. Yves Durand, *Vivre au pays* (Paris, 1984); René Pillorget, *La tige et le rameau* (Paris, 1979); idem, *Paris sous les premiers Bourbons* (Paris, 1988); Yves-Marie Bercé, *Fête et révolte* (Paris, 1976); Myriam Yardeni, *La conscience nationale* (Paris, 1971); idem, *Anti-Jewish Mentalities* (Haifa, 1990); Madeleine Foisil, *L'enfant Louis XIII* (Paris, 1996); André Corvisier, *La France de Louis XIV* (Paris, 1979).

29. Lenard Berlanstein, ed., *Rethinking Labor History* (Urbana, Ill., 1993); Bryan Palmer, 'Critical Theory and the End of Marxism', *Internat Rev Soc His*, 38 (1993), 133–62.

30. Philippe Ariès, *Centuries of Childhood*, tr. Robert Baldrick (New York, 1962).

31. Philippe Ariès, *The Hour of Our Death*, tr. Helen Weaver (New York, 1982); Philippe Ariès and Georges Duby, eds, *A History of Private Life*, tr. Arthur Goldhammer, 5 vols (Cambridge, Mass., 1987–91).

32. See, for instance, Maurice Agulhon, *La sociabilité méridionale* (Aix-en-Provence, 1966); idem, *La vie sociale en Provence* (Paris, 1970); Joseph Bergin, *The Making of the French Episcopate* (New Haven, 1997); Constant, *Nobles et paysans en Beauce;* Jonathan Dewald, *Pont-St-Pierre* (Berkeley, 1987); idem, *Aristocratic Experience* (Berkeley, 1987); Yves Durand, ed., *Hommage: Clientèles et fidélités* (Paris, 1981); Cissie Fairchilds, *Domestic Enemies* (Baltimore, 1984); Agnès Fine, *Parrains, marraines* (Paris, 1994); Kristin Gager, *Blood Ties and Fictive Ties* (Princeton, 1996); Jouanna, *Le devoir de révolte*; Sharon Kettering, *Patrons, Brokers, and Clients* (New York, 1986); Mark Motley, *Becoming a French Aristocrat* (Princeton, 1990); Orest Ranum, *Richelieu and the Councillors of Louis XIII* (Oxford, 1963).

33. Norbert Elias, *The Court Society*, tr. Edmund Jephcott (New York, 1983), pp. 141–5, 208–13.
34. Roger Chartier, 'A Social Figuration and Habitus', *Cultural History*, p. 78.
35. Denis Richet, 'Sociocultural Aspects of Religious Conflicts', *Ritual, Religion and the Sacred*, eds Robert Forster and Orest Ranum (Baltimore, 1982), p. 183; reprinted in idem, *De la Réforme à la Révolution* (Paris, 1991), pp. 15–51.
36. Arlette Farge, 'L'histoire sociale', in *L'histoire et le métier d'historien*, ed. François Bédarida (Paris, 1995), pp. 281–300.
37. Robert Mandrou, *Introduction to Modern France*, tr. R.E. Hallmark (London, 1975), pp. 77–138.
38. Yves Durand, *Les solidarités dans les sociétés humaines* (Paris, 1987).

INDEX